MW00338874

AVOCADOMANIA

First published in English in the United States of America in 2022 by

Rizzoli International Publications, Inc.
300 Park Avenue South
New York, NY 10010
www.rizzoliusa.com

Originally published in Spanish under the title *Aguacate* in 2022 by Trilce Ediciones, Mexico City, Mexico.

Copyright © 2022 Trilce Ediciones

For Rizzoli
Publisher: Charles Miers
Senior Editor: Klaus Kirschbaum
Assistant Editor: Meredith Johnson
Managing Editor: Lynn Scrabis

For Trilce Ediciones:
Publisher: Déborah Holtz
Design: Juan Carlos Mena

Library of Congress Catalog Control Number: 2022937673

ISBN: 978-0-8478-7142-1

Printed in China

Visit us online:
Facebook.com/RizzoliNewYork
Twitter: @Rizzoli_Books
Instagram.com/RizzoliBooks
Pinterest.com/RizzoliBooks
Youtube.com/user/RizzoliNY
Issuu.com/Rizzoli

Editors
Déborah Holtz
Juan Carlos Mena

Editorial coordination
Isabel Iglesias
Emiliano Meza Esparza

Writing
Isabel Iglesias

English translation
Debra Nagao
Michael Parker

Art direction
Juan Carlos Mena

Design
Roy Plata
Eduardo González
Lorena Galván

Cover Design
Edgar A. Reyes

Back Cover
Avocado sculptures
Daniele Barresi

Image research
Selene Nájera

Illustrations
Mariana Mena

Infographics
Mariana Mena
Roberto Anaya

Design assistance
Fernando Islas

Spanish style correction
Luis Bernardo Pérez

Coordination with chefs
Wendy Pérez

Texts coordination
Mariana Castillo

Prologue
Pedro Reyes

Introduction
Elizabeth Malkin

Texts
Fernanda Alvarado
Luza Alvarado
Margot Castañeda
Lidya Carey
Natalia de la Rosa
Alina Hernández
Ken Love
Guillermo Máynez
Alberto Peralta

Recipes
Pilar Cabrera
Juan Cabrera Barrón
Olga Cabrera Oropeza
Nelly Córdova
Óscar Cortázar Cuilty
Fabián Delgado Padilla
Regina Escalante Bush
Francesca Ferreyros
Celia Florián
Paola Garduño
Michael Katz
Lula Martín del Campo
Borja Martín-Palomino
Fernando Martínez
Nico Mejía
Eva Millán
Paco Morales
Rosalba Morales Bartolo
Jorge Muñoz
Ricardo Muñoz Zurita
Joel Ornelas
Karla Papa García
Mario Papa García
Alejandro Piñón
Javier Plascencia
Xrysw Ruelas
Roberto Ruiz
Claudia Ruiz Sántiz
Pablo San Román
Jesús Sánchez
Lesterloon Sánchez
Óscar Segundo
Hugo Soca
Maru Toledo Vargas
Raquel Torres
Mariana Valencia
Jorge Vallejo
Ángel Vázquez
Gerardo Vázquez Lugo
Juan Emilio Villaseñor
Marta Zepeda Trujillo

Trilce Ediciones expresses thanks for the participation of:
The Bannatyne Family
Ernesto Canales
Angel Bautista
GinaRose Kimball, La Habra Heights Historical Committee

AVOCADOMANIA

Everything About Avocados from Aztec Delicacy to Superfood: Recipes, Skincare, Lore, & More

RIZZOLI
NEW YORK

New York ·Paris ·London ·Milan

CONTENTS

PROLOGUE

The Seed of an Obsession

Always a staple of Mexican cuisine, avocados have become a global culinary superstar, attracting a near cult-like following.

INTRODUCTION

Starting life as a prehistoric fruit, now the avocado is a bonafide social media influencer. This unprecedented evolution developed at a lightening pace—only in the last century did the avocado finally get its spotlight.

CHAPTER 1 THE AVOCADO ORIGIN STORY

A Star Is Born

The avocado flourished in the Ice Age some sixty-six million years ago, after dinosaurs went extinct. While mammoths roamed the earth and our species had yet to appear on the scene, avocados were already making a name for themselves.

Around the World

The avocado's journey from Mexico to the world began from its cradle to the farthest reaches of the planet. This is its itinerary.

The Conquest of the Americas

From Central Mexico, it spread throughout the Americas, leaving a trail of seeds from Florida and California in the north to the Southern Cone in the south. Fearlessly crossing the Atlantic with the Spanish, it conquered the European continent.

From Palta to the Palate

Avocados took over all of South America through trade contact along the Pacific and Atlantic coasts. And it won a place of honor wherever it went, its name changing with every new home.

Crossing the Pond

The avocado astonished the Spanish, who had never seen anything like it before. Fascinated by the way the Indigenous people used this unique fruit, the Spanish loaded it onto their galleons to share it with the Old World.

The American Green Dream

In Florida and California, the avocado thrived—becoming its own distinctive variety. And so was born the Hass, eventually becoming the most popular avocado worldwide for its creamy texture and mild flavor. Now, nobody can live without it.

The Luster of the California Avocado

A Mexican farming family settled in California in the 1850s to cultivate a veritable gem.

Across the Pacific

The discovery of the Pacific Ocean changed all notions of the known world. The earliest ships sailing from Mexico to Asia were carrying avocados in the hold.

Hawaii's Avocado

With forty years of experience in the Asian market, this American expert shares first-hand knowledge on growing this fruit on his farm in Hawaii.

A World of Avocados

Everyone wants an avocado on their plate and now, you can get them almost everywhere, from Berlin streets to Kyoto markets. However, prices vary, depending on the time of year and seasonal events.

Michoacán, World Avocado Capital

Michoacán is considered the avocado capital of the world as the leading producer in Mexico. Two towns are in the running for this title: Tancítaro and Uruapan.

Green Agenda For Michoacán

The APEAM has developed an ambitious "green agenda" to achieve a higher level of sustainability in the avocado industry and in communities in Michoacán.

A World of Avocados

To say avocado is to say Mexico. Mariachis, piñatas, and Day of the Dead are less ubiquitous than this ancient fruit, now found everywhere you look, from popular songs, to tequilas, to thousands of dishes.

CHAPTER 2 GREEN TRENDS

Vegetable, with Skin and Seed?

The avocado is one of the most versatile foods in the world, but is it a fruit or vegetable? Let's take a closer look and decide once and for all.

The Taste Is in the Variety

There are countless avocado varieties, from the king, the Hass, to the South African Maluma, the Mexican and the recent Gem, besides the three pioneers: Mexican, Guatemalan, and Antillean varieties.

Nutrition's Cure-All

The avocado is considered a superfood because of its nutritional value, and coveted by those in the pursuit of good health. This chapter unpacks all of the health benefits: from good fats to antioxidants.

Green Beauty

Homemade avocado masks have have become a beloved DIY beauty secret. This chapter explores the cosmetic uses of avocado oil in hydrating skin and hair, among other beauty beauty products.

Keep Them Green!

The unctuous green of the avocado's pulp can quickly lose its color due to oxidation. In this chapter, we investigate the avocado's chemistry and what can be done to keep them ripe for longer.

Genuine or Imitation?

Global demand for avocados has filled the market with fakes. From taco stands with dubious guac to avocado shampoo . . . without an ounce of avocado.

Much More than Pulp

The enormous consumption of avocado has led to creative new ways of recycling food waste to give new life to cultivate a more sustainable usage.

An Internet Idol

Don't look for the best-looking avocados in the market: search for them on Instagram. There you'll find them the subjects of adoring fans turning them into works of art.

Sow Your Own Avocado Seeds

Even though tons of tutorials are on the Internet, the seed you planted at home might not thrive. Here's a basic guide to successfully prepare your home avocado plant.

CHAPTER 3 A CENTURY OF FEVER

The Star of the Decade

In recent decades the avocado has become the symbol of a lifestyle all over the world. How did this charismatic food make it onto everyone's plate?

Alligator Pear Lovers

Early in the twentieth century, the avocado became known by the unappealing name "alligator pear." After an intense marketing campaign, it managed to rebrand and reach global fame.

Careful with that Knife!

You can be seriously injured if you don't know how to cut this fruit properly. To eliminate this danger once and for all, farmers have created a seedless variety in order to eradicate the problem altogether.

How to Safely Cut an Avocado?

Never fear, the internet is full of helpful how-tos on cutting avocado and not die in the process. We offer our favorite method.

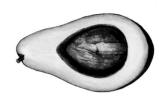

Avocados Everywhere

Pajamas, T-shirts, beach hats, pets dressed up as avocados. Anything you can possibly imagine can look like an avocado!

¡Santo guacamole!

The number one salsa has become Mexico's ambassador to the world, even converting the biggest avocado-haters. Let's look at the secret behind the peel.

Guacamole touchdown

How did guacamole turn into the Super Bowl star that it is today? Let's investigate the meteoric rise of its consumption in the US, spotlighting celebrities and brands.

Eat Diferent

CHAPTER 4
RECIPES 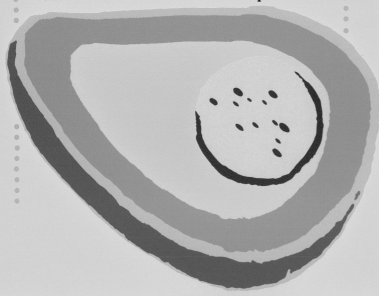 194

Starters

Sauces

Main Dishes

Desserts And Beverages

Next-Level

Other Recipes

"With all due respect, Miss: I'll take you for avocado, like any guacamole."

Phrase from the film
Los Caifanes (1967)

PROLOGUE
The Seed of an Obsession

Avocado is trending. Among Pre-Columbian civilizations, it was like money, used in barter and imperial tribute. Its use as valued currency has continued metaphorically to this day in: "We have avocados" or "Put in your avocados," avocados refer to greenbacks. Although it was one of the favorite Mesoamerican fruits, for many years the avocado was seen by the Spanish colonizers as a garden fruit, of no special worth, only for domestic consumption. But in the last century and a half, it's increased in value along with Mexico as the leader in its cultivation, production, and consumption. Today, more than ninety species of the *Persea* genus are known spanning the southern United States to Chile. And at least twenty of them are Mexican.

From Molcajete to the World

Industry couldn't exist without consumers. And it's always been easy for the avocado to seduce us in ceviches, tostadas, quesadillas, soups, fried fish, eggs, tacos, tortas . . . The silky green of this fruit looks good, garnishing any Mexican dish. We eat tacos with avocado, tortas with avocado . . . and we eat an avocado taco and torta. We don't need anything else; it's a dish on its own.

It's the same everywhere in Latin America, where the avocado has been used in local cuisines for generations. It might need a sprinkle of salt to eat it by the spoonful; or a pinch of sugar, like in Brazil. It can be served as the base for a tuna

↑ *Tlayuda Stall*, work by Elena Climet, 2016.

↖ Street market: traditional street vendor.

11

In Mexico, avocado is also known as *cucata* (totonaca), *cupanda* (purépecha), *yashu* (zapoteco), *tzitzito* (some regions in Chiapas).

↑ Avocado vendors in the street, early twentieth century.

salad with mayonnaise, as the creamy soul of a green sauce, or the star of haute cuisine. Examples of the latter are the avocado pizza served by chef Maycoll Calderón at the Hotel St. Regis in Mexico City, or grilled *palta*, the signature dish of chef Virgilio Martínez at Central, an exclusive restaurant in Lima, selected as the best restaurant in Latin America on numerous occasions.

Could Not Be More Mexican

Perhaps the first avocado dish on the tables of other countries was the Mexican classic: guacamole, the avocado dish par excellence. Originally it was simply a mixture of avocado mashed in a grinding bowl, with a touch of chili and salt. From there, the recipe has morphed into hundreds of variations, with one version completely liquified in a blender, used as a dip or as avocado puree in the most sophisticated dishes.

As a symbol, guacamole has been a Mexican banner in foreign kitchens. No matter how mediocre Mexican restaurants might be in Germany, Turkey, Chile, or even the United States, guacamole always stands up for itself. Trying to replicate good Mexican food, the US has established a close relationship with guacamole. With the fusion of Tex-Mex, guacamole is used as a side for hard-shell tacos, chimichangas, and of course, spooned over nachos. Yes indeed, gringos are crazy about their guacamole.

The Pop Phenomenon

No, we'll never tire of repeating: avocado is trending. And the world went nuts over avocado toast. If we think about it, it makes sense: avocado is almost a butter. Its relationship with bread is so natural that it doesn't matter what you put on top of it. It works with everything, even on its own. In 2017, *Time* magazine reported that gringos spent almost nine hundred thousand dollars a month just on avocado toast. At that time, any new restaurant had to have one or more versions of it. Monothematic restaurants with everything avocado on the menu appeared: Avocadería in Brooklyn, Guac & Go in Singapore, Good Fat in Sydney, Avocado Appetit in Manhattan's Chinatown, The Avocado Show in Amsterdam . . . At the same time, more industrialized versions came onto the market, like Starbucks' avocado dip to smear on bread, Dunkin' Donuts' avocado toast, and other oddities like avolatte, a café latte served in a half avocado skin like a cup at Truman Café in Albert Park, Melbourne.

This euphoria meant that avocados went from being a basic Mesoamerican staple to becoming a transnational gastronomic obsession. Today it's become a pop phenomenon that transcends time, space, and culture. Neckties, toys, socks, plush toys, blankets, cellphone covers, backpacks . . . avocados have become the Pokémon of twenty-first century foodie culture.

This obsession with being served trendy food on social media has caused a scarcity of the product, because of higher prices, over-exploitation of soils, deforestation, and an indelible carbon footprint. With luck, we will remember that avocados are an exotic product that doesn't need to be exclusive, nor does it have to—nor can it—be over-exploited for unsustainable, mass consumption purposes. Most importantly, they need to be more accessible for the people who have always had them, worked them, and taken care of them for generations.

Today, avocados are a Mexican symbol worldwide. And that should be consciously celebrated. This book takes stock of all the preparations that remind us of the many ways that the avocado has played a starring role on our tables and those of the world, leaving behind the perception of "trendy food" and seeking the reasons for its resiliency. Because the avocado belongs to everyone and is for everyone. For all time.

↑ Avocado packing plant, 1915.

INTRODUCTION

The image could not have been more tender. While Catherine, Duchess of Cambridge, was suffering from severe morning sickness, a little boy offered up a cure. During a visit to northwest England, Prince William was greeted by a group of excited schoolchildren. That's when four-year-old Archie handed the future King of England an avocado wrapped in a yellow bow—an antidote for morning sickness symptoms that he learned about from his mother, who suffered from a similar illness. "I've never been given an avocado before," William said. "Catherine will love the avocado. That's very sweet."

And just like that, the humble avocado received its royal blessing.

Prince William and Catherine may have come a little late to avocadomania but they have plenty of millennial company. If you were looking for one food to define millennial taste, go no further than the avocado. Millennials have turned it into an object of cult worship, endowing it with infinite powers and treating it with the reverence that was previously reserved for caviar and champagne. They slice, swirl, chop, and dice their avocados every which way and then pose with their artistry for a post—almost thirteen million of them on Instagram and counting.

At times, the passion for avocados breaks all bounds of culinary reason. Take, for example, the Avocado Royal, a dish dreamed up by a Beirut eatery, which combines avocado with Nutella. Or breaded and deep-fried avocados, or avocado brownies. The Avocado Show, a chain with restaurants in Amsterdam, Brussels, London, and Madrid, offers vegan Peanut Butter Avo Ice Cream.

The list is endless, putting the fruit's generous versatility to the test.

But perhaps we should stick to the basics: avocado toast and guacamole, the two dishes that have come to embody the avocado craze in the United States—and increasingly the rest of the world. They are so ubiquitous that it's quite easy to forget that avocados are relatively new to the American table. And their popularity is not an accident.

In fact, like so much of contemporary American culture, there is marketing behind the mania. It began about a century ago when growers in California decided they had to change the unappetizing name for the "alligator pear"—named for its lumpy green skin. According to the food historian, Emelyn Rude, writing in *Time*, in 1915, the growers met in a California hotel and decided on a new name: the avocado. "They informed the nation's dictionaries of their decision, and organized themselves into the California Avocado Association to champion their cause," Rude writes.

They promoted a premium avocado, the Calavo, and because avocados were rare and expensive, the growers' marketing in the 1920s was pitched to the wealthy readers of *Vogue* and *The New Yorker*. "The aristocrat of salad fruit," one advertisement read. "Now acclaimed by hostesses as the food delicacy supreme for smart occasions."

With Mexican produce shut out of the American market, prices remained high and avocados remained a luxury for decades. By the 1980s, avocado marketing ran into another roadblock: a campaign against fat that put avocados on the list of "bad" foods.

As Olga Khazan recounts in *The Atlantic*, the California Avocado Commission fought back, producing research to promote the health benefits of the fruit. And who better to promote that message than the legendary *Ocean's 11* (1960) actress Angie Dickinson? "This body needs good nutrition," she said in a 1982 television ad. As the camera pans over her silver stilettos and white leotard,

⌃ Young "Fuerte" avocado trees.　　⌃ Trapp avocado packed in crates.　　⌃ The original McDonald avocado tree.

Dickinson rattles off a list of vitamins and minerals. "And this body gets them all—in California avocados," she concludes as the music swells.

But it was not enough to convince Americans that avocados were healthy. There was one additional hurdle to cross. Americans didn't understand that a ripe avocado isn't green, it should be between eggplant purple and brown. So the growers hired the public relations company, Hill & Knowlton, which came up with a mascot: Mr. Ripe Guy. Dressed in an avocado-shaped costume driving a soft green car, Mr. Ripe Guy would turn up everywhere with a basket of ripe avocados.

To keep interest up, Hill & Knowlton decided that Mr. Ripe Guy needed a mate and launched a competition for Ms. Ripe. She was chosen from contestants across the U.S. to reflect "the California lifestyle of good health and healthy eating." Fortunately, she didn't have to dress up in a stuffy avocado suit.

But the marketing people needed more to make avocados a mass-market product. And in the United States, that means sports. Guacamole was beginning to be make its appearance as a snack—but the trick was to associate it with a big event.

Hill & Knowlton turned to the Super Bowl. Not only was it the biggest television event of the year, but it was becoming a snack food showcase. And there was another advantage: the American football championship is played in late winter when many avocado crops are ripening.

As Khazan describes in her article, Hill & Knowlton came up with the idea of involving the players, soliciting recipes from them for guacamole and then asking the public to vote for a winner. And in the press box, sports writers were treated to free samples of guacamole.

The ploy worked. For the past twenty years, guacamole and the Super Bowl have been inextricably linked.

Now with avocados firmly fixed in the American mind, along came the shipments from Mexico. Under NAFTA, the free trade agreement among the

↑ Leucadia sold supplies for avocado cultivation in California.

United States, Mexico and Canada, the protected American market was gradually opened to Mexican avocados. Finally American consumers could eat avocados all year round. According to *The Washington Post*, the percentage of imported avocados eaten in the United States grew from 40 percent in 2000 to 85 percent in 2014.

Mexican producers and importers followed the marketing example set by their California competitors years earlier. They ran an ad during the Superbowl and began to churn out recipes— almost three hundred just for guacamole and avocado dips alone—on their website, Avocados from Mexico. Strawberry margarita guac, anyone?

Then came avocado toast. Many food writers date its origins to 1993, to a café in Sydney, Australia. But it took a member of Hollywood royalty, the queen of the wellness movement, to turn avocado toast into a global phenomenon. In 2013, Oscar-winning actress Gwyneth Paltrow included a recipe for avocado toast in her cookbook *It's All Good*.

"It's the holy trinity of Vegenaise, avocado and salt that makes this like a favorite pair of jeans— so reliable and easy and always just what you want," she wrote, according to *The Washington Post*.

After that, avocado toast was ready for its close-up. Now, the popular snack has almost 2 million starring roles on Instagram. Since then,

avocado toast has become so popular that it has become a caricature of itself.

The actress Meryl Streep was photoshopped onto avocado toast by content creator @tasteofstreep. Saucony was moved to design an avocado toast sneaker; light brown leather on the sole, with extensive detailing on the textured green suede "avocado." According to *Esquire* magazine, it quickly sold out.

Nothing it seemed, could dampen millennials' love for avocado toast. Not even criticism from an Australian millionaire who asked how they could afford to eat so much of it. "When I was trying to buy my first home, I wasn't buying smashed avocado for $19 [15 USD]," Tim Gurner told Australian television.

Celebrities were quick to flaunt their love for avocados. The singer Miley Cyrus got a small avocado tattoo on her arm in 2015 and handed out avocados to the press after a music awards concert. Kourtney Kardashian touted her avocado pudding as a daily pre-workout snack. Model Miranda Kerr has said that one of her favorite snacks is half an avocado with sea salt. Singer Jason Mraz grows avocados on his California farm.

Meghan Markle posted her own recipe for avocado toast (add a sprinkle of feta cheese and a dash of red chile flakes) when she was still a working actress. Then she married Prince Harry and served avocado toast at Kensington Palace. We can assume that after returning to her native California, she is eating more avocados than ever.

The passion extended beyond millennials. A 2017 poll by *HuffPost* found that millennials like avocados—but they are even more popular with older generations.

Long reigning queen of American entertainment, Oprah Winfrey said in an interview on *The Daily Show* that she always travels with avocados—grown in her very own orchard.

And why did she buy her own orchard? The queen had a simple answer: "I think it's ridiculous to pay for avocados."

Il y a aussy ung fruict qui sappelle acoiatea de la grosseur
de grosses poires d'hiuer fort verd par dessus et comme
l'oy a leue la peau l'oy trous de la chair fort espaisse qui
l'oy mange auec du sel et a le goust de cheruaux ou noise
vertes Il y a ung noyau de dans de la grosseur d'une noix
dont le de dans est amer l'abre ou croit le s fruict est
Is figures ensemble de dict fruict

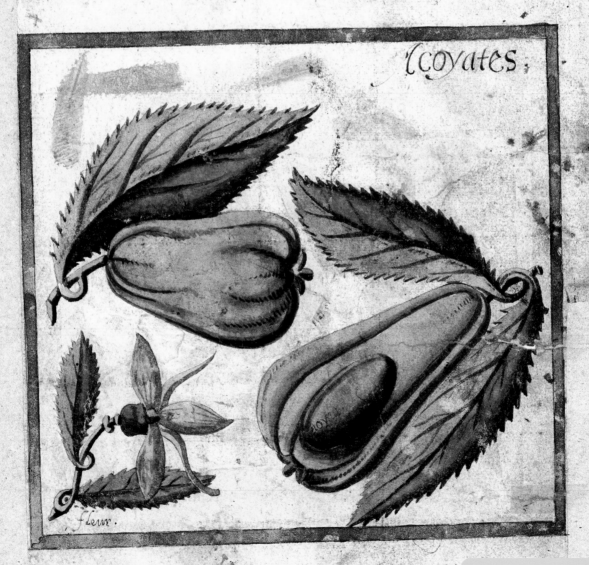

lcoyates.

fleur.

↗ Ancient botanical record vs.
modern botanical record.

PLANTAE GUINEÆ ÆQUATORIALIS
AB HORTO REGIO MATRITENSI DISTRIBUTÆ

LAURACEÆ

Persea americana Miller

BIOCO: Malabo - Cupapa, km 11-12, 32NMK8311,
350 m, plantaciones de cacao, *Carvalho 3613*, 10-IX-
1988. Árbol, 6-8 m. Flores verdes.

Det. J. Fernández Casas, 1991

HERB. HORTI BOT. NAT. BELG.

A. Guabas ó Pacaes = B. Aguacate = C. Chixi
F. Llama = G. Muca muca = H. Danta ó óxan Ue
M. I

THE AVOCADO ORIGIN STORY

Sixty-six million years ago, the dinosaurs had gone extinct and only enormous mammals roamed the planet. Modern *Homo sapiens* had not yet appeared on the scene, but avocados were already here.

oyo = D. Granadilla = E. Frutilla ó fresa de Quito
tía = I. Quinual = K. Achupalla = L. Palo de luz
c-huchu =

A STAR IS BORN

Temptingly hanging amidst the foliage, avocados were the preferred delicacy of the large herbivores who devoured them whole, leaving a trail of seeds in their excrement. Imagining how a creamy avocado becomes mammoth waste might take away your appetite for guacamole.

But this theory is being discussed by many scientists. Regarded as an "evolutionary anachronism," the avocado managed to survive, even when most species of its time have become extinct. With its reptilian skin, delectable pulp, and seed that suggests the apple of Adam, it's one of the few surviving witnesses of the prehistoric world.

↑ Hand-colored lithograph by J. F. Schreiber, 1873.

23

A Controversial Origin: Mexico or California

Avocados are believed to have originated in the central zone between Mexico and Costa Rica, according to the most widely known research. In the Sierra Nevada of California, however, archaeological remains of the avocado's ancestors have been found dating back fifty million years! Those early avocados went extinct, along with many other living beings, during the last Ice Age and disappeared from California because of climate change.

↑ Avocado fossils from California.

↗ In prehistoric times, the avocado was the favorite fruit of the earliest peoples.

The Untiring Traveler

The avocado is a traveler by nature. When the climate became colder in California at the end of the Pleistocene, the avocado seed migrated with a first-class ticket inside one of its herbivore carriers and settled in the warmer climate zones of northern Mexico: the Sierra Madre Occidental, Durango, and Sonora. From there, Central Mexico was only steps away . . . in mastodon steps.

That's what the avocado was doing when the earliest human beings reached Central America. They were now *Homo sapiens sapiens*, who survived by hunting and gathering the fruit they found.

From that love at first sight between humans and avocados arose a fruitful relationship of cultivation and consumption that has continued for millennia.

↑ Rock paintings found in caves in Tehuacán, Puebla.

The discovery of the Coxcatlán cave (Puebla) is the most ancient evidence of avocado consumption by humans.

The First Avocado Was from Puebla

Agriculture began in Mesoamerica between 8000 and 5000 BCE with the domestication of animals, trees, and plants.

In 1964, American archaeologist Richard Mac-Neish discovered a cave at Coxcatlán in the Tehuacán Valley (Puebla, Mexico) containing the remains of three plants domesticated during the Archaic period, approximately 8000-2000 BCE. It's believed this cave was used by gatherer groups as a shelter, meeting place, and a storage space for their harvests. These early sedentary tribes began to plant seeds from the most fruitful trees near their homes. This is how they protected the avocado from the elements.

It's hard to know which fruit species was the earliest selected for human consumption, but the size increase of fossilized seeds found in Coxcatlán indicates that fruit was selected based on size or the tree's characteristics. In the case of the Mexican avocado, the pleasant anise scent of its leaves might have been a factor in its selection.

↗ Mexico.

↗ Fossilized avocados from the Tehuacán Valley.

→ Puebla, Mexico.

↑ Coxcatlán, Tehuacan Valley, Puebla.

Ahuacatl, the Tree's Testicle

As it is known in Spanish, *aguacate* comes from the Nahuatl for "container of moisture" or "testicle" for its long, oval pear shape, hanging from trees in such a "manly" way. This etymological hypothesis doesn't sound so farfetched. After all, Nahuatl is a metaphorical language spoken for centuries by the inhabitants of the precise areas where the avocado is found: Puebla, Oaxaca, Jalisco, Nayarit, Michoacán, Morelos, and the State of Mexico.

Cuates, mis tompiates.

The Lands of Our Ancestors

In addition to the evidence found in the Tehuacán Valley, the avocado tree was present and highly important for other prehistoric cultures. Among Nahua tribes in the Sierra de Zongolica and Maltrata (Veracruz), avocado leaves have been used as a condiment since ancient times. Similarly, Zapotec groups in the state of Oaxaca used an avocado leaf condiment in stock, tamales, and *barbacoa* (meat pit-roasted in agave leaves).

The presence of the prehistoric avocado is even greater in the Chiapas and Guatemala highlands. It's believed that the avocado arrived in this region through trade with tribes from Tehuacán, where it was successfully cultivated. Avocados perfectly adapted to this mountainous region, with altitudes between 3,280 and 6,560 ft (1,000 and 2,000 m) above sea level. Other studies claim avocados naturally grew here since earlier times.

Whether from deliberate domestication or a fate of nature, the avocado became an integral part of Mesoamerican culture.

Primitive avocado trees went extinct 15,000 years ago in California. Today's avocados are descendants from those in the Tehuacán Valley 10,000 years ago.

The Avocado Grasshopper

In the *Diccionario de mitología nahuatl* (1908), Mexican philologist and writer Cecilio Robelo recounted a curious Nahua legend about Yaotl, a cruel and bloodthirsty demigod, who was turned into the avocado grasshopper (*ahuacachapulin*) in divine retribution.

As the legend has it, a man named Yappan left his wife to withdraw to a remote rocky crag to live a life of abstinence and asceticism. To confirm whether he was truly leading a life of purity, the gods sent a spy, the cruel Yaotl, to watch him day and night. Yaotl grew increasingly angry that Yappan observed all privations, despite many temptations. Eventually, the Yappan was seduced by Tlazolteotl, goddess of passion and lust, and he broke his abstinence. This pleased Yaotl, who decided to punish Yappan on his own, without consulting the gods. He decided to decapitate him and turn him into a scorpion.

The gods, infuriated with Yaotl because he dared to administer justice without their consent, turned him into the ahuacachapulin or "avocado insect."

↑ Codex Borgia.

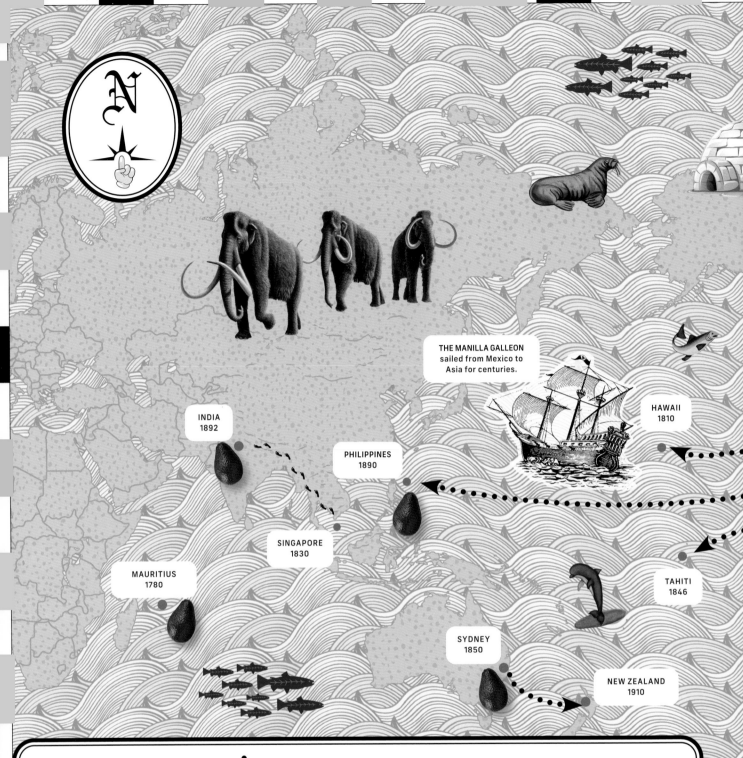

THE MANILLA GALLEON sailed from Mexico to Asia for centuries.

INDIA
1892

PHILIPPINES
1890

HAWAII
1810

SINGAPORE
1830

MAURITIUS
1780

TAHITI
1846

SYDNEY
1850

NEW ZEALAND
1910

AROUND THE WORLD

🐾🐾🐾🐾 LAND ROUTE

•••••► SEA ROUTE

This adventurous fruit didn't just stay in the Puebla Valley where it was born. Soon, it conquered all Mesoamerica and served as currency in trade with communities in South America. When the Spanish arrived, avocados were shipped to Europe where they influenced local cuisines, even reaching Russia. Not satisfied with its expansion throughout the Mediterranean and Asia Minor, the intrepid avocado crossed the Pacific to the Philippines, where it spread to Southeast Asia and Africa. Now quite the conqueror, it returned to its homeland as king of the world.

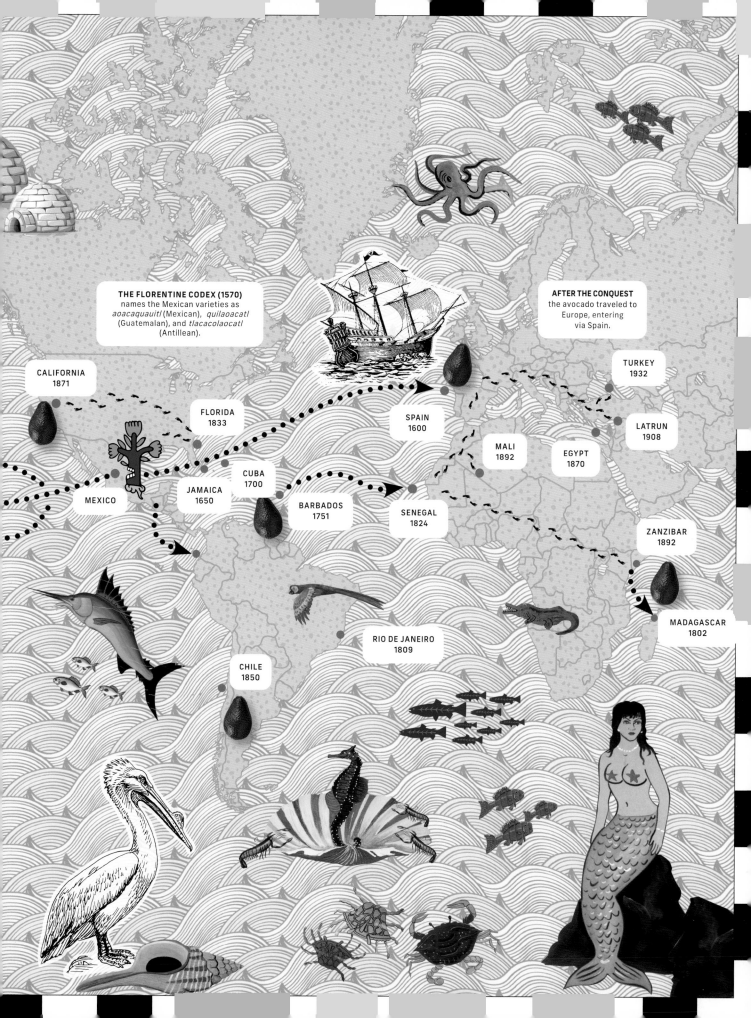

THE FLORENTINE CODEX (1570)
names the Mexican varieties as
aoacaquauitl (Mexican), *quilaoacatl*
(Guatemalan), and *tlacacolaocatl*
(Antillean).

AFTER THE CONQUEST
the avocado traveled to
Europe, entering
via Spain.

CALIFORNIA
1871

FLORIDA
1833

SPAIN
1600

TURKEY
1932

LATRUN
1908

MALI
1892

EGYPT
1870

CUBA
1700

JAMAICA
1650

MEXICO

BARBADOS
1751

SENEGAL
1824

ZANZIBAR
1892

MADAGASCAR
1802

RIO DE JANEIRO
1809

CHILE
1850

THE CONQUEST OF THE AMERICAS

Mesoamerica and the Earliest Cultures

• •

Avocados are known to have grown in the Maya lands of Yucatán, Belize, and Guatemala since at least 3,400 years ago. The Maya were integral to the domestication of the avocado, who grew them in their backyard gardens. In fact, the Maya were among the earliest to give a name to the fruit: *oon*.

↖ Young woman with Guatemalan avocado variety.

← Stela from the ruins at Copán, Honduras.

Avocado Worshippers

Maya veneration of the avocado is reflected in its solar calendar, the *Haab*. The glyph for the fourteenth month (between April 12 and May 1) is represented as a barren tree with round black fruit like the avocados of the Chiapas highlands. This culture called the month *kankin*, which in the ancient Chol language meant "to receive the light of wisdom from the master." Perhaps for the Maya, the mythical tree of enlightenment was an avocado tree.

At the site of Palenque (Chiapas, Mexico), a Maya urban complex discovered in 1952 by the French-naturalized-Mexican archaeologist, Alberto Ruz Lhuillier, there is a temple housing the tomb of Pakal (683 CE), the king and demi-god of agriculture. The side of his sarcophagus bears a relief representing this deified ruler's great-grandmother being reborn from a leafy avocado tree amidst an exuberant garden. It's believed to represent a new paradise where Pakal would reign again surrounded by his ancestral protectors, symbolized by an array of exotic and fantastic trees.

Curiously, the plant symbols are fruit trees and not maize, the traditional staple and focus of the region's agriculture. This detail highlights the importance of family gardens for domestic subsistence in Maya culture. Indeed, we can still find centuries-old avocado trees at almost all Maya archaeological sites, as if they were essential life-sustaining elements ornamenting ancient cities.

↑ The tenth month of the Maya solar calendar, the *Haab*, is represented with the avocado glyph: *Kankin* in Cholan Maya.

↑ Location of Palenque, Chiapas.

→ The Maya king, Pakal, was buried in an elaborate tomb in the pyramid.

↗ Temple of the Inscriptions at the ancient city of Palenque (Chiapas, Mexico).

→ Pakal's ancestors are represented waist up, rising from the earth with fruit trees: cacao, sapote, guava, and avocado.

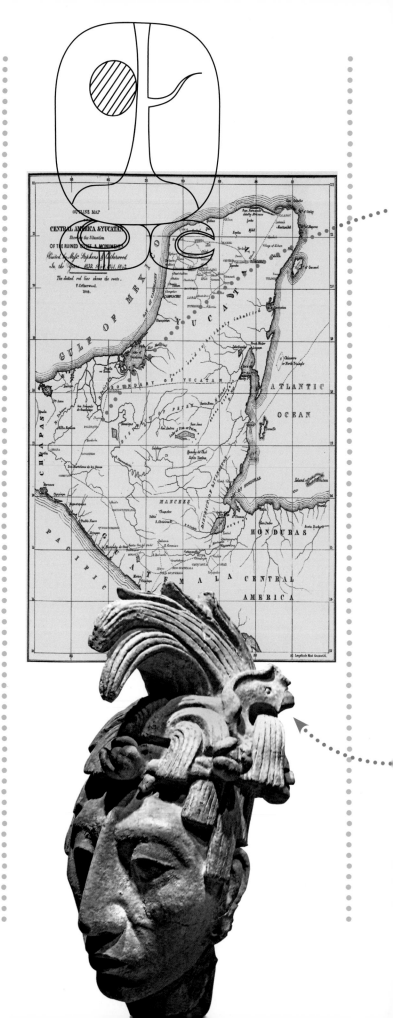

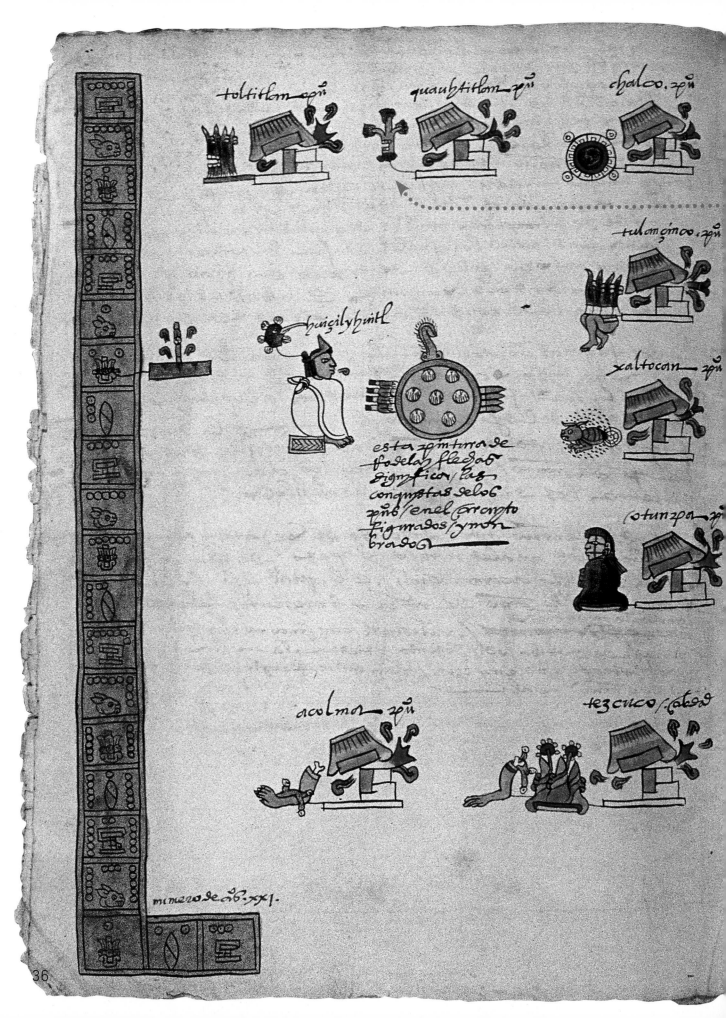

toltitlan. 2pñ

quauhtitlan. 2pñ

chalco. 2pñ

tulançinco. 2pñ

xaltocan. 2pñ

huiçilyhuitl

otunpa. 2pñ

esta 2pñ tierra de
todelas fledas
significa las
conquistas delos
2pñ/ enel arronto
figurados/ y mon
brados

acolman. 2pñ

tezcuco/ cabeça

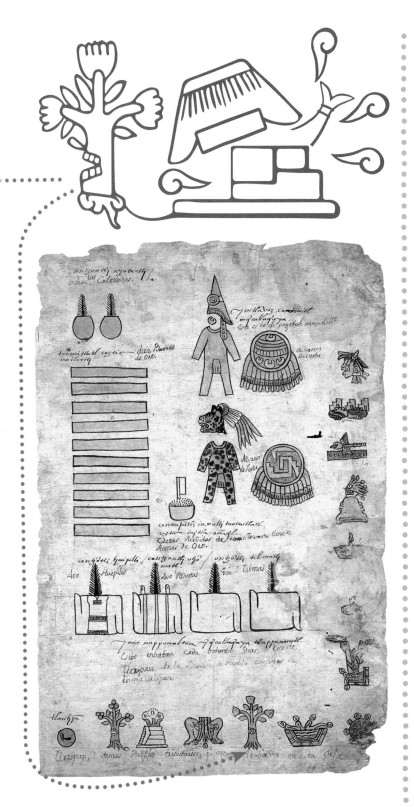

Ahuacatlán, The Avocado Kingdom

An example of the avocado's importance to Pre-Columbian cultures was the kingdom of Ahuacatlán, which in Nahuatl literally means "place where avocados are plentiful." Interestingly, there were two sites with the same name: one in Puebla and the other in Nayarit. The latter became a key hub for trade after it was founded by migrating groups on their way to central Mexico, before the arrival of the Spanish. The Ahuacatlán people paid tribute to the rising Mexica Empire with avocados, suggesting they were valued not only for their taste, but also because they symbolized wealth.

The Mexica were eager for more avocados in their treasure chests. Francisco del Paso y Troncoso (1548) cites evidence of their continued consumption in the viceregal period in *La Suma de visitas de los pueblos*, detailing tribute from the town of Aculma (now Acolman) in the Texcoco area of Mexico:

It pays tribute every eighty days [of] 154 pesos, two bed cloths; each day they give two bushels of maize, 4 hens and 4 loads of firewood and a handful of ocote pine and a piece of charcoal and a cake of salt and 160 chilies and 10 avocados and 10 tomatoes and 20 prickly pear cactus fruit and a basket of green tomatoes and a cupped handful of squash seeds and 100 tortillas and with them a bag of chili and salt and 10 loads of grass and 20 Indians for the service of the encomienda holder.

↑ Detail of the avocado tree in the Codex Mendoza.

↗ Avocado tree in the Matrícula de los tributos.

← Codex Mendoza.

The Mexica and Maya received the avocado as a means of tribute payment from roughly 1200 CE to the arrival of the Spanish early in the sixteenth century.

37

FROM PALTA TO THE PALATE

From Mexico and Mesoamerica, the avocado sailed south looking for warmer winds and stayed in the region now occupied by Ecuador, Colombia and Peru. Although it is not known how it got there, it is believed that it spread throughout the continent through commercial exchanges between agrarian populations on the Atlantic and Pacific coasts.

↖ Monument to the palta (avocado) in Catacocha, Ecuador, in the Paltas canton, Loja province.

← Avocado vestiges were found in the Supe Valley, Peru.

← Avocado sculpture in Catacocha, Ecuador.

These days, tourists who visit Catacocha, a small town in the Loja province of Ecuador, are surprised to find a monument to the avocado. This enormous piece of stone covered with small mosaic tiles rises from a traffic circle illuminated at night with a series of colored lights that make the huge avocado gleam blue and green.

The monument dates to 2013 and attests to the appreciation the townspeople have for this fruit, locally known as "palta." This word, which comes from the Quechua language, also was the name for an Indigenous ethnic group that had settled precisely in this Ecuadorian province north of Peru.

The Itinerant Avocado

How did this fruit manage to travel thousands of miles to reach Ecuador, Colombia, Peru, and even Brazil, countries where it is equally beloved as in Mexico and known by other names.

According to María Elena Galindo-Tovar, of the Faculty of Biological and Farming Sciences of the Universidad Veracruzana, "Human migration and commercial and cultural exchange carried out from ancient times among different groups that lived in Mesoamerica to upper South America led to its dissemination and different domesticated varieties." A traveler by nature, the avocado was part of the cultural heritage of the peoples who moved from Mexican territory southward. The fruit continued to be the food for these migrants, as well as a product traded and planted in other lands.

Evidence of this trade is the discovery of Moche culture (100–700 CE) by Max Uhle, regarded as the father of Peruvian archaeology. It was a civilization highly advanced in metallurgy, ceramics, and commercial navigation. The latter activity was carried out on board "totora boats," handcrafted from the totora reed and known to have been used for at least 3000 years. These sailing vessels can hold up to 440 lbs (200 kg) of cargo . . . Avocados must have traveled by such crafts between Peru and Mexico!

This discovery led to Max Uhle's "Immigrationist Theory." He proposed that ancient Peruvian cultures thrived as a result of contact with Mesoamerican peoples—by land and by sea—primarily with the Mayas. This hypothesis isn't so farfetched, because the avocado has been an important food in South America for 5,000 years, although it spread the most under the Inca Empire in the fifteenth and sixteenth centuries.

Also in Peru, the Caral culture was discovered in the Supe Valley, north of Lima. It is one of the oldest Pre-Columbian civilizations on the continent. Archaeologists found traces dating back to 3100 BCE of the avocado and other plant species, preserved thanks to the extremely dry local conditions and sparse annual rainfall. However, these conditions are uncommon in South America, so perishable materials from most archaeological cultures on the Ecuadorian and Colombian coasts, the Amazon rainforest, and the Andes have long since disappeared.

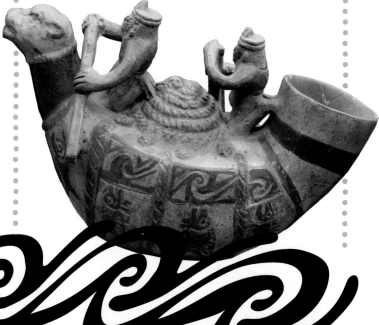

↗ Pottery vessel of a totora reed aft.

DIFFERENT NAMES FOR THE AVOCADO IN AMERICA.

Avocado

Avocat

Aguacate

Abacate

Palta

↑ Mural *Migration and Identity: Presence of Tlaxcala in the Americas*, by the visual artist Abel Benítez, in the administration building of the Universidad Autónoma de Tlaxcala (UATx).

And the Paltas Arrived

The territory inhabited by Neolithic cultures was later occupied in pre-Inca times by the Paltas, a Jibaro-language group (today called the Shuar) from Amazonia that settled in southern Ecuador. They were a sedentary agricultural group, whose diet depended on maize, which was successfully cultivated alongside native species in these new lands. Palta territory is believed to have housed the major domestication centers for the avocado in South America prior to the arrival of the Spanish. In the fifteenth century, the Palta peoples were forced to disband and disperse when the Incas invaded the region, found the *palta* tree, and began to expand its cultivation throughout its vast empire, spanning modern-day Colombia, Peru, Ecuador, Bolivia, Chile, and Argentina. Peruvian chronicler Inca Garcilaso de la Vega—considered the "first biological and spiritual mestizo of the Americas"—describes how Tupac Inca Yupanqui (the tenth Inca emperor), conquered southern Ecuador and took "that delicious fruit called *palta*" to his capital, Cuzco. That the avocado—so Mexican in origin—became the palta and took the name given in the Jibaro language by the Palta people, who cultivated it so successfully, is a beautiful and sad metonym, for the fruit outlived the civilization that gave it life. In fact, today, only the remnants of the Jibaro (Shuar) peoples remain in the Amazonian region, while the avocado has spread worldwide.

Abacate, the Brazilian Version

The fruit that samba-singer and actress Carmen Miranda carried in her fruit-laden hat probably included the avocado. However, in Brazil the avocado is not called "aguacate" or "palta," but rather "abacate."

This fruit did not reach Brazil through trade with Pre-Columbian cultures. Amazonia might have been a barrier that prevented the fruit from reaching markets in Rio de Janeiro. In fact, it came to that country relatively late. There are reports of avocado cultivation in the region from 1787, but the earliest official introduction dates to 1893, when four Antillean trees from French Guyana provided the first seeds of the species taken to Brazil.

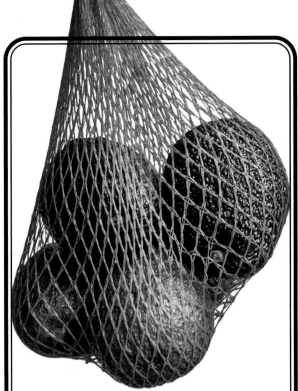

In Brazil, avocado is called abacate and not palta, the name used from Peru to Uruguay.

The Palta that Rises

Palta is a word in the Quechua language, native to the coasts of Ecuador and Peru. It is derived from the root "pall", the verb meaning "to raise" and the suffix "ta", which means "help." So palta came to mean "something for raising." Among Quechua-speaking cultures, palta is also used to refer to a "carrying bundle that hangs." The image brings to mind the term *ahuacatl* as testicle, which is essentially a hanging bag of sorts. In this regard, linguist Rodolfo Lenz suggests the term palta was also used by pre-Inca cultures to describe the erectile virtues of the fruit, which, apparently, was able to raise something more than the spirits. You get the idea.

← Carmen Miranda, Portuguese singer and actress.

↗ Mexican flavor on the Colombian Mountains.

↑ Just like coffee, avocado is grown at a high altitude.

From Cantina to Cantina, It Reaches Medellín

Ernesto Canales, pioneer in avocado cultivation in Colombia, tells us about his experiences as a producer in South America.

My mom's family had avocados in their town, Bustamante (between Monterrey and Laredo), in a 148-acre (60-ha) piece of land. Not the Hass avocado, but the Criollo, with that very thin peel that gets battered in transport, but that gives it a delicious buttery flavor.

When I got interested in growing it, I went to the cantinas in Michoacán and found the price of 2.5 acres (1 ha) in production was between about $80,000 and $120,000, which was a fortune to me. Also, in Michoacán, they weren't interested in producing abroad. So, I investigated in Medellín (Colombia), where the same acreage was going for $15,000 for land with an hour and a half more sunlight, an altitude not conducive to pests, and a climate where wells aren't necessary. One of my partners discovered a zone apt for avocados and bought the first 200–300 ha, and I got myself another 1,200 ha already cleared. They are very mountainous areas where families had small lots with grassy pastures for sheep and cows. By the time we got there, they had already been deforested, which was an incredible stroke of luck. So, I saw a business opportunity. We choose Hass seeds crossed with Méndez (a Michoacán variety) and we planted. We had our first harvest on lands with six-year-old trees, and we sold it to Colombia's biggest exporter that was selling to Europe and Asia. Now, we're exporting 120,000 tons a year, but my partners want to reach 300,000 a year. The best thing is that we hit the mark by planting this Hass variety: it's bigger and has a smaller seed, so it has lots of pulp, the skin is a bit thicker, which gives it a three-week shelf life from the time it's cut from the tree, cleaned, and packed.

However, we're facing a serious problem that we didn't anticipate. Since avocado orchards hadn't been planted in Colombia, we didn't know how long these trees could live here: those in Michoacán live sixty to seventy years but given the amount of water in this zone and the soil type, we think that ours won't last more than twenty years. We have some four-year-old trees that are very tall, but very fragile. This is a tragedy because we'll have to replant them all. We were pioneers and this is the price that we have to pay.

Now lands are being bought and habilitated for cultivation all over, especially in the mountains, because the avocado, like coffee, is a highland fruit. Also, more investors are arriving from Peru, Chile, and the United States. We just sold 10 percent to a group from California that wanted to invest in the zone. And it doesn't surprise me because our place is a Cauca River canyon. The slopes are planted like terraces and the sun shining on the river produces water vapor that irrigates the trees. A miracle of nature for the avocado's benefit.

q Ay otros arboles que se
llaman Pochotl: son lisos,
son muy altos, y hazen gra
rueda, y gran sombra, tie
nen siempre hoia: la hoia
es anchuela, dellos se coge
el maña que es medicinal,
y dulce, y blanco.

q Ay tambien en esta tie
rra robles, que se llaman,
Avaquavitl.

q Pochotl: xipetztic, xixipetz
tic, tlatztic, veltevilacachtic
veliaoaltic, veliaoalivhqui, ce
vallo, hecauhio, ceoalloa, mo
ceoallotia, moiacauhiotia, te
ceoalhuja, itlan neceoalhuijlo:
ic ipapanjtva in tepachoanj.
Capochotl, avevetl mochiuh
ticac: xocoioa, tlaaqujlloa,
acan moneguj injtlaaqujtic
mo ontlatzieih, valmotepeoa:
ic impa mjtva in mopoanj,
in ça tepa cenca icnoiotl ite
chiauh. val xoxocotioa tlal
ticpac, onjcucic, o, ieval tha
pantiveti. —

q Avaquavitl: avatl, teuqua
vitl tepitztic, tlaquaoat, ol
tic, picquj, tlaqualtic, quauh
iaoaliuhquj, iaoaltic, ma
mae, mamaxaltic, mamatzo
coltic, mamatzocollo, avaz
vaio, pachio, quauhtzotzocol
tic, quauhtzotzocolli; atlaca
cemelle, acemelle, teteceujtz
tic, teteceujztic moquauhte
malacachioa, moquauh tema

CROSSING THE POND

In 1492, Columbus sailed from Spain in search of a new way to reach the Far East, but on the way, he came across an entire continent. This discovery had such enormous repercussions for humanity that some scholars regard it as "the most important biological event since the end of the Ice Age."

The Importance of Records: Chronicles and Codices

The first lands in the Americas where the Europeans set foot were the Antilles, where they got to know local foods and carried them onto the mainland. Those that stood out among these fruit trees were guavas, pineapples, cacao, and avocados. The Spaniards were initially disconcerted when they saw this fruit, but by observing how the native peoples used it, they began to discover its many benefits.

Many Spanish chroniclers offer descriptions of the avocado fruit, which seems to have fascinated them. And so, Francisco Hernández, court physician and historian to King Philip II, described the *ahoacaquahuitl* as "a tree like the oak from which hangs a fruit, somewhat larger than a dove's egg."

Of all these codices, chronicles, and studies, one of special importance is the *Medicinalibus Indorum Herbis*: a pre-Hispanic medicinal and botanical treatise written in Nahuatl by the indigenous physician Martín de la Cruz and translated into Latin by the monk Juan Badiano. It's important for the description of 263 native plants—especially from the Valley of Mexico—accompanied by lavish color illustrations. The avocado stands out from these images.

Europe Is Eager for Its Seeds

From the final decades of the sixteenth century, some plant species originating in the Americas were incorporated into the Old-World diet, specifically the Spanish diet. New World species began to blend in harmony with the Mediterranean triad: wheat, olives, and grapevines, the staples in northern Europe. In fact, it was in Mediterranean countries (eastern Spain, southern France, Italy, Greece, Turkey, Israel, Syria, Palestine, and northern Africa) where plants from the Americas were most widely accepted and established, thanks to this zone's favorable climate and soil. Later, some species—such as the potato, tomato, cacao, and maize—were incorporated into the everyday diet of most people in Europe.

Avocado and Olé

The oldest reference to an avocado tree planted in Spain comes from the foundation of the Valencia Botanical Garden, which was created as an orchard of botanical samples. In 1567,

← This is how Fray Bernardino de Sahagún drew the avocado tree.

↖ Christopher Columbus reached the American continent on October 12, 1492.

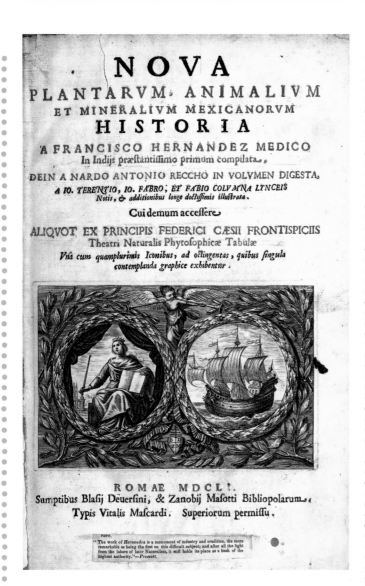

De *AHVACA QVAVHITL*, feu Arbore Querciformi butiraceo fructu. *Cap. LVIII.*

AHVACAQVAHVITL, feu arbor Quercui fimilis, cui fructus appendet, arbor eft procera, mali Medicæ folijs, virentioribus, amplioribus, & afperioribus. flore paruo, ex albo pallefcenti. fructu oui forma, fed interdum maiore, aut, fi mauis, ficuum præcocium forma, & magnitudine, extra nigro, intra virefcenti. pinguis qua butyrum æmulatur naturæ, & fapore viridium nucum, folia funt odorata, calidaq. & ficca ordine fecundo temperiei, quamobrem commodè lotionibus adhibentur; poma quoque calefaciunt, guftui funt grata, & non omnino malæ alimoniæ, fed pinguis, humentifque, & venerem mirum in modum excitantis, augentifq femen. Hæc nucleos continent è candido in rubrum vergentes, folidos, duros, nitidos, atque in duas fiffos, veluti amygdala, partes, quamuis oblongi fint, & columbinis ouis paulò ampliores; ij fapore amygdalarum amararum conftant, funduntq. fi prælo comprimantur, oleum amygdalino haud abfimile, non odore modo fed fapore quoque, & facultate; medetur enim impetigini, ftigmatifque. Adftrictione quadam opitulatur dyfentericis, ac findi capillos prohibet. Arbos toto anno viret, & quibufuis regionibus, fponte, aut culta adolefcit, ac gaudet; calidioribus tamen, planifque locis lætior prouenit, & in maiorem affurgit magnitudinem.

↑ Francisco Hernández's history of plants, animals and minerals of Mexico, 1560.

↑ Description of avocados in *Historia de las plantas*.

Joan Plaça, the botanist in charge, showed a Flemish colleague, Charles de L'Escluse, an avocado planted and acclimatized to Mediterranean Europe. But this tree was an exception, for it's believed the avocado was taken to Spain regularly until 1600. Perhaps early on, it was only used as a medicinal remedy, for they rubbed the seed on their feet, to cure swollen insteps, heal blood chambers, and to prevent split ends in hair.

We should bear in mind that in the seventeenth century medicine was closer to superstition and folk medicine than to science. Instead, it was more like protoscience mediated by Catholicism, which continued seeing the indigenous peoples in the Americas as children of a devil difficult to define.

From that Eurocentric and ultra-Catholic perspective, Spanish missionary Pablo José de Arriaga wrote in his controversial work *La extirpación de la idolatría en el Perú* (1621) of a propitiatory celebration to promote the ripening of avocado fruit:

In the month of December, when the paltas begin to ripen, they held a celebration that they call Acataymita, which lasted six days and nights, so that the fruit ripen (sic). Men and boys gathered in a small plaza between gardens, buck naked, and from there they ran to a very tall Hill, and with the woman whom they reached in the race they abused them. This celebration was preceded by abstinence, five days of fasting not eating salt, or chili, or being with women.

Meanwhile, in northern Europe the earliest record of the "avocado" in English dates to 1696 and was made by Hans Sloane, an Irish naturalist who served as physician of the governor of Jamaica.

The interest in the natural and botanical world spread like wildfire in Europe in the early eighteenth century, in response to a current of thought known as "physiocratism," which regarded agriculture as the most noble of human activities. In tune with this glorification of nature, Francisco Javier Clavijero, a Jesuit priest—born in Veracruz and considered one of the precursors of Mexican indigenism—refers to the avocado as a noble native fruit in his *Historia antigua de México*. In the mid-eighteenth century, at the time of the first Industrial Revolution, people in Europe began to grow native species from the Old and New World more intensively.

Throughout the viceroyalty with well-to-do Spaniards and Creoles flocking to Mexico City, the numbers of mestizos and native peoples working in kitchens increased. As a result, they added pre-Hispanic touches that transformed traditional cuisine,

Censorship Avoided

Through a royal decree on April 23, 1577, the king in Madrid ordered Martín Enríquez, the viceroy of New Spain, "not to in any way allow anyone to write things about the superstitions and way of life these Indians had." This edict triggered a campaign of repression targeting Pre-Columbian culture in order to erase any trace of its legacy in the territories of the Spanish Empire in the Americas.

As a result, many chroniclers were censored and prohibited from publishing their works. This was the case of fray Bernardino de Sahagún who was accused of "having composed a Universal History of the most noteworthy things in that New Spain, which is a highly copious compilation of twelve books in the Mexican [Nahuatl] language on all the rites, ceremonies, and idolatries that the Indians used as infidels. It seems it is inexpedient to print that book and for it to circulate there. Be careful to keep those books, so that no original or copy of them remain."

Fortunately, many Spanish and mestizo writers did not obey this decree; an act of rebellion that world history has not yet thanked them for sufficiently.

↑ Acataymita, ritual celebration to promote avocado ripening, Peru, 1621.

Aqui se Juntan las comidas para los Españoles.

Este es el General Nanuma.

Aqui se demuestra donde se hizieron los banquetes, y se Juntaron las comidas que para esto dieron los naturales, à que assistió el Valiente Nanuma General de las armas del gran Caltzontzi, y concurrieron los demas Cabos militares —

giving rise to a culinary *mestizaje*. This phenomenon prompted the avocado's popularization on the tables of wealthy Spanish landowners who probably took it to Spain, in a new migration for a fruit that never tired of traveling.

The French also joined this craze for nature's riches and began to experiment with avocado plantations in one of its colonies: Algeria, specifically in the Hamman Botanical Garden. By the twentieth century, at the easternmost end of Europe, Russia experimented with avocado plantations on the shores of the Black Sea. The last country in Mediterranean Europe to join the avocado euphoria in the twenty-first century was Turkey, triumphant in its cultivation and export.

↑ Natives paid tribute in food to Spanish soldiers.

↖ Saint Paschal Baylón's fruit bowl included avocados.

Moctezuma's Table

According to oral accounts of myths, Hernán Cortés would have been familiar with the avocado and guacamole from Moctezuma's famed table, where the tlatoani (emperor) held his magnificent banquets and rituals. Bernal Díaz del Castillo, in his *True History of the Conquest of New Spain* (1568), mentions these sumptuous feasts that consisted of a menu of more than 300 different dishes. He also described the protocols and rules of etiquette of a Mexica royal table: the fine tablecloth, cloth napkins, and almost idolatrous reverence for the figure of Moctezuma. Hernán Cortés, as well, in his second Letter to the King (1520) wrote: "The meals were served by three or four hundred youths, who brought an infinite variety of dishes . . . every kind of meat, fish, fruits, and vegetables that the land produced. And as the climate is cold, they put a dish with live coals under each plate to keep them warm."

↑ Evocation of Moctezuma's table.

ONCE UPON A TIME IN THE EAST

Sunny Florida was the first to cultivate the avocado in the United States in the early twentieth century. The subspecies most widely produced in this country is a Mexican hybrid that gained popularity in California. From there, it swept and still dominates the world. The Hass avocado is the indisputable king on the international market.

Florida: Sun, Beach, and Avocado Seeds

The first time that Florida imported avocados was in 1833. In addition to importing species from Mexico, in the mid-nineteenth century settlers from Miami found naturalized Antillean avocados in the hammock area of this county and began to propagate them by grafting. Between 1904 and 1906, the earliest hybrids arose by crossing Antillean and Guatemalan avocados, introduced by the United States Agriculture Department (USAD). In the first decades of the twentieth century, most commercial orchards produced the Antillean variety of this fruit. However, this panorama changed when an avocado visionary settled in Florida.

← Krome family at Avocado Drive, Homestead Town (Miami-Dade).

↖ Crocodile pears hanging from a branch over 607 Ashe Street in Key West, Florida.

Mr. Avocado Krome

The history of the avocado in Florida and the United States in general can't be understood without the work of railway engineer William J. Krome and his wife, Isabel Burns. Around 1918, he and his wife established orchards of pomelos, lemons, limes, oranges, tangerines, mangos, and of course, avocados, in Redland (Miami-Dade County). Unlike other families involved in large-scale production, the Kromes' passion was research and experimentation, the focus of much of their efforts. In 1928, they found some thirty plant species from Java, West Africa, China, and other semitropical countries that could be adapted to the Florida climate. To study these species more closely—especially the Antillean and Guatemalan avocado varieties—Krome set up an experimental plantation in the small community of Homestead Town. Since that time, the street where he built his farm was named Avocado Drive in his honor.

The Krome family primarily cultivated the Antillean-Guatemalan avocado hybrid, and the grafts best adapted to Florida's hot coastal climate were the Pollock, Trapp, and Taylor subvarieties. Although the Krone orchards have since disappeared, the United States avocado—and the California avocado in particular—owe everything to this horticultural visionary. The scope of his work was truly remarkable for the time. After his death, the Florida State Horticultural Society (FSHS) recognized him as a distinguished honorary member and established the Krome Memorial Institute in 1933. His legacy continued with his wife and above all, his son, William H. Krome, who championed major economic and legal improvements for the United States farming community.

↑ Engineer Willian J. Krome.

ONCE UPON A TIME IN THE WEST

· ·

It's believed that in modern California the first avocado tree was planted in 1848, although the first importation record dates to 1856. In 1900 new Mesoamerican avocado variants arose, such as the Fuerte and Zutano, which dominated the market and consumption in the early decades of the twentieth century on the West Coast of the United States. However, the history of the avocado in California has its own name: Hass.

Our Daily Hass

Born in Milwaukee (Wisconsin) of German descent, Rudolf Hass was a door-to-door salesman who decided to devote his life to growing avocados after seeing a picture in a magazine of this fruit tree sprouting dollar bills. In 1925, Hass invested all the money he had, plus a loan from his sister, to buy an acre and a half of avocado trees in La Habra, California. The old avocado trees were of the Fuerte variety, along with some Mexican and Guatemalan species. Because Hass wasn't a botanist, he bought seeds from a nursery run by

← Rudolf Hass makes the first avocado shipment by air.

Mommy, What Does the Hass Avocado Want?

The most widely consumed avocado in 2020 was the Hass variety. From California to Australia and New Zealand, passing through Israel and returning to Mexico, the Hass's worldwide trip has been unstoppable.

In the 1960s, the earliest commercial tree nurseries of this variety were established, but its massive production skyrocketed in the late 1990s, when the United States industry shifted cultivation to Mexico with the intention of producing and exporting it to the United States. Given its success, the Mexican Criollo was the most widely consumed and known variety in Europe in the early 1980s. However, as soon as the Hass appeared on the European market, it had no rival. The same happened in Asia starting in the 1990s.

The secret of its success is in plain sight: it can be harvested before it's ripe and thanks to its thick, firm skin, it stays fresh during transport. This means it can reach the point of sale in ideal conditions for its consumption. Therefore, it is the optimal product to cross continents and become the international star of all tables.

↖ Rudolph Hass and wife Elizabeth Hass in front of the Mother Hass Tree. Courtesy of the La Habra Heights Historical Committee.

the Rideout Family to graft with the Fuerte variety he already had in his orchard. In July 1932, one of his hybrid seedlings grew quickly and produced more fruit than the Fuerte variety grafts, which made it possible to plant more trees of this new variety. The first trees of this new, never-before-seen Fuerte and Guatemalan hybrid soon grew. This was the birth of the future Hass avocado.

When the fruit grew enough and was ripe, he picked it and gave it to his children to try. The family agreed that this avocado tasted as good or better than the Fuerte variety. As the tree grew, it produced more fruit that the family could eat, and so Hass sold avocados to his Pasadena post office coworkers, who began to regularly buy a bag of four or five avocados for a dollar. Encouraged by this small success, the family began to sell avocados at a stand on the highway beside the grove near their house in La Habra. Soon they began to distribute their avocados to grocery stores in Pasadena, and they discovered that the chefs of the wealthy who had tasted their variety didn't mind paying a dollar for each piece of fruit.

The business was growing and in August 1935, Hass patented his avocado tree and signed an agreement with a Whittier tree nursery to cultivate and sell the variety. Hass was to receive 25 percent of the

↑ Hass Mother Tree Commemoration. Photo Credit: La Habra Review.

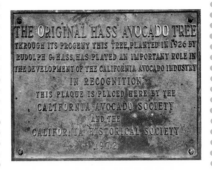

↑ Historical Marker of the Mother Hass Tree permanently mounted bronze plaque supplied by the California Avocado Society and California Historical Society.

The Tree that Changed the World

The Tree that Changed the World To remember the significance of the Hass variety, a commemorative plaque was placed on the spot where the original tree once stood. However, the tree had to be cut down on November 9, 2002, after dying at the age of 76 when its roots rotted. Not bad for a tree, Dear Old Hass Tree.

profits. However, the patent was violated, for Whittier gave producers the right to graft the seed onto their own trees *for free!*

Hass earned less than $5,000 in royalties during the seventeen years this patent was in force. Although he was never able to make a fortune with his business, he was the first to have a Hass avocado-producing orchard, which expanded in 1948 to Fallbrook with its first major harvest in 1952. He died at the age of sixty, one month after his controversial patent expired.

Almost all Hass avocado grafts known in the world come from his plantation. This avocado has become the favorite of consumers for its flavor and of markets for its durability and long shelf life.

You're the Cream in My Coffee, You're the Avocado on My Toast

The Hass variety is native to California, but it comes from Guatemalan (90 percent of the genes) and Mexican (10 percent of the genes) varieties.

It is oval-shaped and weighs between 125 and 350 grams. Its seed is medium-sized, so it has lots of soft, creamy pulp with an intense flavor, like that of dried fruit. Its rough skin ranges from green to purple when it's very ripe, but it peels off easily.

That's why more than 90% of the avocados grown in California are of this variety. Israel is also one of the major Hass producers that exports all over Europe.

For many experts it's the best avocado variety produced to this day . . . but competitors are already emerging, and they're coming on strong.

THE LUSTER OF THE CALIFORNIA AVOCADO

From a family of Mexican farmers who settled in California in the 1850s to cultivate a true *gem*.

My father's family is of Welsh and Scotch ancestry, who settled in San Francisco, although my father was born near Napa. His grandfather had a ranch that they sold when he was an adolescent. My maternal great-grandfather emigrated from Mexico to California, my grandmother was born in East LA, and my mother is second generation Mexican American. My father's history is typical of Mexican immigrants whose aim in life is success. That's my heritage: we're a bilingual family and recognition of Mexico and Mexicans is our business, and our community is very active.

My father was an art dealer and my mother was a teacher, but they always wanted to move to Southern California, because my mother wanted a weekend home. Looking around, they found a piece of property in Fillmore where they grew oranges, grapefruit, lemons, and of course, avocados. And what started out as a vacation home, my father turned into a 375 acres (1.5 square km) business in Ventura County. Even though last year we sold two of our ranches, today we have a cultivated area slightly smaller than 200 acres (1 sq km).

GEM, the Gem of Rancho Resplandor

Like good Californians, we grow Hass. We also produce Bacon, Fuerte, and Zutano. And even though we don't have many miles (kms) of GEM (just 10 percent of the fields), we're fervent defenders of this new variety: a Hass hybrid that we consider superior for its qualities. It is a larger, more oval fruit. Its peel has an appealing pattern of golden specks; and in my opinion, the pulp is creamier and meatier than that of the Hass. Also, the GEM tree is more tolerant to heat and cold. It is a true *gem*.

← Rancho Resplandor.

↖ Margarito Veyna 1954, Alexa's great-grandfather, taken at Orange County Nursery.

↖ "My grandmother, Esther Veyna. My mother, Elaine Bannatyne, My uncles; Richard and Robert Veyna," at Orange County Nursery around.

Even though the massive phenomenon of global avocado demand is fabulous, the question is whether it can be maintained and satisfied. The danger is that the flood of fruit from other parts of the world diminishes the value of the avocado and devalues the producer. And it's true that the fruit of greater quality and size comes from California. It is larger than what is imported from Mexico, Chile, and Peru, which are much smaller and watery. We call them "black" because they turn dark quickly.

In the case of Rancho Resplandor, we stand out for offering maximum quality. We have Good Agricultural Practices (GAP) certification. Therefore, our fruit can pass directly from the field to the packers for sale and export. The distributors have told us that much of our produce remains in Califonia.

> We believe that by increasing quality, we'll be a more profitable business. That is our philosophy of success.

The Industry in California

Producers—and in general the entire industry—must keep interest in avocado consumption alive year-round so that the business is always active. The production season is very short: from late spring to the first part of fall, and the harvest is in January, coinciding with the Super Bowl. So, imports are very valuable for the business, because they allow the market to function all year.

My parents have participated in organizations like the Hass Avocado Board of California: an international organization that reports directly to the US Secretary of Agriculture and global avocado production representatives. Historically, agriculture is a world of men, so that opening the way and finding a place as a woman

← Gonzalo Veyna, Bryce's father and Alexa's grandfather, 1954.

> **All segments in the production chain must be connected. If it isn't cultivated properly, no one benefits.**

is a great challenge. My mother campaigned to be on the Hass Avocado Board, and my father has been in associations like the CAC (California Avocado Commission) and the CAIC (California Avocado Inspection Committee), where he was director, because he is very involved in improving the market.

We have to cope with lots of problems: water scarcity, imbalance in the import market, bad practices in cultivation and production systems. . . All of this affects the producer, and that's why transparency and a flow of continuous information among all those involved in this business is so important. For instance, Los Angeles stands out for its mindful gastronomic scene that tends to give credit to the producer, naming the farm on their menus. In this respect, Rancho Resplandor is a registered trademark, and we would be delighted if our avocados reached the hands of world-famous chefs. The quality of our products deserves it.

Interview with Alexa and her father, Bryce Bannatyne

Pasta with Avocado Pesto

Although Alexa Bannatyne claims you can't beat avocado toast, she has experimented with avocados as a cream base for sauces. She offers us this delicious and easy recipe.

Ingredients
4 servings

- 1 package of pasta of your choice (rigatoni or penne, recommended)
- 2 medium or large ripe avocados
- Juice of 1 large lemon (3 tablespoons)
- ½ cup of starchy pasta water
- ½ teaspoon of lemon zest
- 1 clove garlic
- ⅓ teaspoon salt (or more, to taste)
- 1 pinch of salt to season the water
- Pepper to taste
- 1 cup fresh basil (for garnish)

For garnish and decoration
- 1 sprig of cherry tomatoes
- 2 tablespoons olive oil
- 1 pinch salt
- 1 pinch pepper
- 2 tablespoons of minced basil
- Parmigiano Reggiano, grated

Preparation
1. Preheat oven to 350 °F (180 °C).
2. Daub the sprig of tomatoes with olive oil using the brush and sprinkle them with salt and pepper to taste.
3. Place them on a baking tray and roast them for 10 to 15 minutes.
4. Set them aside.
5. Boil the whole package of pasta in a large pot of water, for the time recommended on the package, seasoning it with a generous handful of salt.
6. Drain the pasta, but reserve slightly more than half a cup of the pasta water.
7. Immediately mix the drained pasta with one or two tablespoons of oil to prevent it from sticking together.
8. Set the pasta aside.

Making the pesto
1. In a food processor or high-power blender, mix the avocados, basil, garlic, lemon juice, lemon zest, pasta water, salt, and pepper.
2. Adjust the pesto to your taste: if it's too thick, add more pasta water; if it's too bitter, add olive oil.

Plating
1. In a large bowl or serving dish, mix the pasta and pesto. Garnish with minced basil and grated Parmigiano Reggiano.
2. Decorate with roasted tomatoes.

A Superb Ingredient for Kosher Cuisine

Just like the rest of the world, the avocado has become popular in Israel. In fact, now it's one of the best producers. Chef Michael Katz confirms it: "Since I was a kid, avocado has been part of my diet: the most popular breakfast was toast smeared with avocado, a few drops of lemon juice, salt and pepper." When chefs in Israel discovered the avocado's gifts, they started incorporating it into cuisine because of it's creamy texture and adaptability.

For instance, meat and dairy products can't be mixed in kosher restaurants. So chefs use avocados to emulsify sauces and enrich dishes. This is why at Jewish celebrations, the avocado is ideal for making dips. For its varied uses, vibrant color, and Mediterranean flavor, the avocado became the star ingredient in many dishes, especially in salads. The most famous is *Fattoush*, traditionally made with cucumber and tomato, but now avocado is added. Avocado *carpaccio* and fried avocado (prepared like a cutlet with flour, eggs, and breadcrumbs) are popular appetizers. It can also be combined with *queso fresco* (a fresh cheese) and olives. In sandwich shops, avocado can replace mayonnaise and be mixed with tahini.

Ceviche—a Peruvian dish par excellence—was introduced to Israel by young Israeli chefs who traveled to South America to "clear their head," after being discharged from the army.

Michael Katz is a chef with international experience, born in Israel to a Belgian father and Israeli mother. He is a connoisseur of Israeli cuisine and cooking with avocado, especially the Hass, the most widely produced and consumed variety in his country.

ACROSS THE PACIFIC

. . . .

Although the Portuguese were the earliest European explorers to reach Asia in the early sixteenth century, Spaniard Vasco Núñez de Balboa made a fortuitous discovery in 1513 that changed the course of history, geography, and the known world at that time. From Panama, he sighted what he thought was a new sea, but it turned out to be the Pacific Ocean. From there, the avocado would soon be introduced to a whole new continent.

HAWAII

SYDNEY

SINGAPORE

MANILA

The Manila Galleon Sails Back and Forth

Forty years later, several Spanish expeditions crossed the Pacific from Mexico to the Philippines on a round trip known as the *tornaviaje* (return voyage): the longest trade route in history, which some scholars cite as the origin of today's commercial globalization. This four-month crossing linked the port of Manila, Philippines, to Acapulco, Mexico, from there to Veracruz, Mexico, then to Cádiz and Seville, Spain. This created a new maritime route that joined opposite ends of the globe, spreading Spanish culture throughout the world.

The most famous ship that navigated this route was known as the Manila (or China) Galleon, Acapulco Galleon, or Nao de China. It wasn't just one ship, but a fleet of 110 vessels that traveled continuously from 1565 to 1815, when the Wars of Independence brought the voyages to a halt.

The ships transported spices, ivory, lacquer, and luxury goods: cloth (taffeta, silk, velvet, satin), fans, folding screens, Chinese porcelain, Japanese swords, and Persian rugs to the Americas. On the return journey to Asia, ships carried Mexican silver—highly prized on Chinese and Japanese markets—as well as plants and animals from the Americas and Europe.

The Abukado's Adventures

The avocado's journey on the Indian and Pacific oceans between the eighteenth and nineteenth centuries makes a gripping adventure story.

The Mexican avocado crossed the Pacific to the Philippines on the Manila Galleon in the sixteenth century, attracting new devotees with its texture and flavor.

Since the sixteenth century, the avocado has been known in the Philippines, where it's called "abukado," referring to its Nahuatl origin.

On the rest of the continent, it was documented for the first time on Mauritius in 1780. It remained unknown until it reappeared twenty years later in Madagascar, another commercial hub with European countries. It's possible that in 1810, the English brought avocados from Madagascar to the Sandwich Islands, a small cluster of islands in the Pacific that now make up Hawaii.

From there, the avocado showed up in Singapore, a thriving English port in Southeast Asia, around 1830. In 1850, the avocado jumped to southern China. The Sangleys—Chinese merchants based in Manila—had been trading this fruit for some time, along with other products that passed through the Philippines on the way to Asia and the Americas. In 1850, the avocado was documented in Australia. It reached India in 1892 and took root around Madras and Bangalore, where it multiplied, although it was not popular among the locals, who considered its taste very bitter.

In the twentieth century, it spread throughout Asia and Oceania. It was taken to Thailand in 1909 by Catholic missionaries who began planting it in Nan province. In 1920, it appeared in New Zealand, where it became extremely popular. It was cultivated in 1939 in Burma (now Myanmar), where its highly favorable climate helped it flourish. During World War II, the avocado appeared in Vietnam when the French successfully produced it in Lam Dong province. Today, it is known, adored, and consumed in all Asian countries.

Now the avocado can indeed boast of having conquered the world.

↗ Chinese merchant selling porcelain.

→ Re-creation of the port of Manila in the 19th century.

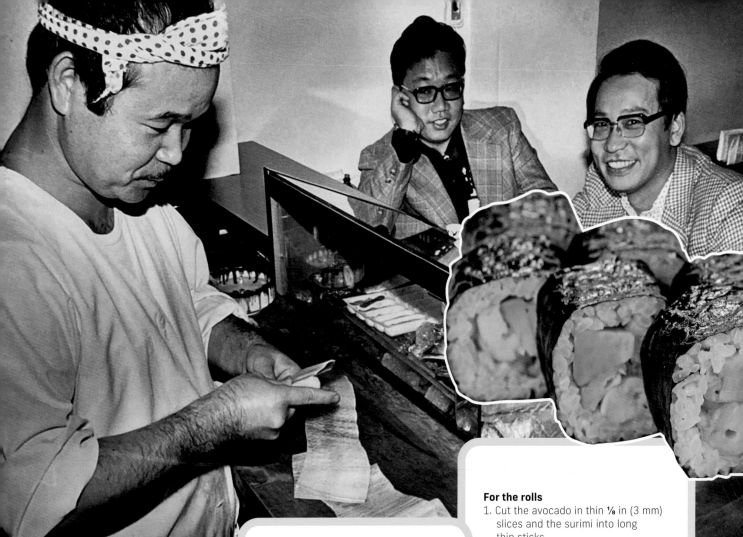

California Roll

Ingredients
2 servings

Sushi rice
- 6 cups (1.2 kg) short-grain sushi rice
- 2 teaspoons salt
- 6½ cups (1.5 l) water
- 6 tablespoons sugar
- 6 tablespoons rice vinegar

To make the rolls
- 1 avocado
- 10.5 oz (300 g) surimi
- 1 cucumber
- 4 sheets of nori (dried seaweed)
- Toasted sesame seeds
- 4 slices of pickled ginger
- 1 teaspoon prepared wasabi
- Soy sauce

Preparation
For the sushi rice
1. Put the rice in a bowl. Add cold water to cover it.
2. Swish the rice around in the water, strain it, and repeat until the water is clear.
3. Put the rice and water in a pot over high heat and bring to a boil, without covering it.
4. Lower the heat to a simmer, put on the lid, and leave for 5 minutes.
5. Remove it from the heat and let it sit for 10 minutes (don't open the lid).
6. Mix the rice vinegar with the sugar and salt in a bowl and heat the mixture in a microwave for 30 seconds.
7. Put the rice in a large wood or glass bowl and add the vinegar mixture.
8. Gently stir it with a wood or plastic spoon to cover all the rice.
9. Let it cool at room temperature. (Do not refrigerate, because it will change the texture.)

For the rolls
1. Cut the avocado in thin ⅛ in (3 mm) slices and the surimi into long thin sticks.
2. Cut the cucumber in half lengthwise (the size of the nori sheet).
3. Remove the seeds with a spoon and cut into thin sticks.
4. Cut the nori sheets in half.
5. Before making the sushi, prepare a bowl with cold water, a clean moist cloth, and a bamboo sushi rolling mat wrapped in plastic wrap.
6. Put the half nori sheet on the bamboo mat.
7. Put a ball of rice on the nori and spread it a bit.
8. Using your fingers, push the rice to the edges to cover the entire sheet.
9. Flip the nori over, so the rice is in contact with the plastic wrap.
10. Put the avocado, surimi, and cucumber one inch from the edge of the nori sheet.
11. Roll the bamboo mat to form a cylinder.
12. Unroll the mat, remove the plastic, and roll sushi in the mat, pressing gently to make it firm.
13. Sprinkle it with toasted sesame seeds.
14. Dampen the knife and cut into 8 equal pieces.
15. Serve with slices of ginger, wasabi, and soy sauce.

Waiter! There's an Avocado in My Sushi!

Surprisingly, sushi traces its origins to China in the fourth century BCE. It only became known in Japan in the eighth century. Over the years, it developed into the dish we know today. In the nineteenth century, it was a form of fast food, meant to be eaten on the street with your hands.

Using avocado in sushi is relatively recent and more common in Western countries. When sushi was exported, it was usually made the traditional way. Other countries added influences of their own cuisine to appeal to local clientele.

One of these culinary hybrids gave birth to the California roll (also known as uramaki) in the late 1960s and early 1970s. Its origin is disputed between two Japanese chefs, who claim credit for creating it: Hidekazu Tojo of Vancouver and Ichiro Mashita of Los Angeles.

As local lore has it, when Hidekazu Tojo began making sushi in Vancouver, the Canadians didn't like raw fish wrapped in seaweed (nori). The chef opted to roll the sushi inside out: rice on the outside and seaweed on the inside, where it was almost invisible.

Originally, it was known as the Tojo-maki, but he changed the name to California roll, due to its popularity among visitors from Los Angeles.

On the flip side, the urban legend of Ichiro Mashita is like a fairy tale. One day, Mashita went to the market looking for ingredients to make sushi, but he couldn't find tuna belly (toro) anywhere. Searching for alternatives, he got the idea to replace it and thought the avocado—known as "forest butter" in Japanese—was a good option for its flavor and texture.

Which of the two is the true inventor of this sushi recipe? Perhaps we'll never know. What we do know is that since the 1970s, the avocado has been an indispensable ingredient in recipes for sushi in the West.

↖ Hidekazu Tojo, Japanese chef in Vancouver.

↑ The California Roll, the most universal sushi.

Guinness World Record for a Hawaiian Avocado

An average avocado weighs some 6 oz (170 g), but the Pokini family of Maui picked an avocado in their garden weighing 5.5 lb (2.54 kg)! This earned them the 2019 Guinness World Record certificate, exceeding the previous record for a 5.3 lb (2.4 kg) fruit.

The Pokini's avocado tree measures 20 ft (6.1 m) and is more than ten years old. When his son Lohoi was born, Mark Pokini planted it from a seed from his brother-in-law's tree. What was the secret of this enormous avocado? According to Juliane Pokini, they didn't water or fertilize the tree, they just decided to "let it grow on its own."

Giant avocados are no rarity in Hawaii and Australia. In 2018 they were already finding specimens that weighed more than 4.5 lb (2 kg) and that were selling for $8 each. The called them Avozillas in honor of the famous Japanese monster, Godzilla.

What happened to the Pokini's prize-winning avocado? It must have ended up in a massive guacamole that delighted the guests at a big party held in its honor.

HAWAII'S AVOCADO

Avocado consumption took off in the US only fifty years ago. In fact, when I was a kid in Chicago during the 1950s, hardly anybody knew about it. But today, avocados are very popular and as an expert, I get roughly thirty to forty calls a week from people who ask me about them.

Aloha, Here I Am!

Educating the consumer is extremely important. Even if we ask chefs how many types of avocados there are, they'll mention two or three varieties, but some might know up to twenty.

What's important to know about a good avocado is its oil content and quality. Hawaii cultivates the Kahalu'u, which has four times more oil than the Hass. Agricultural scientists are mapping the DNA of certain varieties that can be crossed to achieve even higher oil contents and tolerance to low temperatures.

The urgent question is: how can producers satisfy the enormous demand? Obviously, the Mexican avocado industry is the largest in the world. In fact, even if all the trees in Hawaii and Japan were replaced with avocado trees, the harvest wouldn't reach the 72,000 tons that Mexico exports to Japan. Other producers have tried to outdo the Mexican market with local varieties, such as South Africa's Maluma or Australia's Shepard. Avocados are even being produced in Japan and India, countries that lack any tradition of this cultivation, but the limited production is entirely for the local market. In Japan, most of the avocados that are imported and consumed are the Hass, Pinkerton, Bacon, and Fuerte varieties from the Americas, plus the Sharwil and Maluma from Australia and South Africa.

To incentivize local production, I'd recommend small producers prune their avocado trees to keep them low and minimize the need for labor. To support them, the consumer should go to farmers' markets and buy directly from growers, in any country in the world.

Ken Love is an expert in avocado species, care, and cultivation. He has had his own farm in Hawaii for forty years and has specialized in exporting the fruit to countries like Japan and Australia. He has always shown his willingness to share his experience and knowledge with others.

Spanish sailor Francisco de Paula Marín first introduced the avocado to Hawaii around 1810, when he came across the archipelago that was importing and exporting different varieties of fruit with the Americas. Botanists Wilson Popenoe and David Fairchild incentivized avocado cultivation in Hawaii during the early decades of the twentieth century. David Fairchild's book, *The World Was My Garden*, details his journeys around the world including how he introduced avocadoes from Chile to California. Wilson Popenoe worked for him in Central America and was known for traveling on horseback with an assistant riding a mule in search of avocados in the highlands of Guatemala and Mexico, like a modern-day Don Quixote and Sancho Panza in Mesoamerica. His granddaughter, Juanita Popenoe, called him the "Indiana Jones of avocados."

← Death of Captain Cook in Hawaii.

↑ Francisco de Paula Marín.

↗ Wilson Popenoe.

↗ David Fairchild in Ceylon, drinking coconut milk in 1926.

Top 10 producers in 2019 (in tons)

1. MEXICO
2,300,890

2. DOMINICAN REPUBLIC
661,630

3. PERU
535,630

4.COLOMBIA
535,020

5. INDONESIA
461,610

6. KENYA
364,940

7. BRAZIL
242,930

8.HAITI
231,720

9. CHILE
138,770

10. ISRAEL
138,770

A WORLD OF AVOCADOS

· ·

Latin America, known as the avocado *pacha mama* (mother goddess), leads production and export of fresh avocados. Eighty percent of the total global production is divided among ten countries.

For a Fortune

Buying an avocado in Madrid isn't the same as buying one in Berlin. International avocado prices are tied to competitive demand for this fruit, which surpasses current supply.

In Germany alone, the demand quintupled in ten years and costs may increase depending on the season. Autumn and winter see a decrease in prices, unlike spring and summer when prices skyrocket. In those months, a 7-oz (200-g) avocado can cost up to $3 each in foreign markets. During holiday seasons US demand soars and avocados can cost up to $8 apiece. Over summer months such as July and August, production is very low, and prices can reach annual highs, especially in Europe. So, if someone buys an avocado in Germany in August, they might pay $3–4 per avocado. In London, it would round off to $5, and in Tokyo you might have to pay between $6–8.

Avocado sales have an annual growth rate of 3.5 percent and demand continues to rise from increasing consumption. Before the boom in the United States, avocado consumption per capita didn't even reach 1 lb (500 g) annually. Thirty years later, each person consumes an average of 8 lb (3.5 kg) per year (two avocados a month).

From Its Birthplace to the Clouds

The Mexican avocado entered the United States in 1997, through the North American Free Trade Agreement, and since then, exports have increased. The high demand took producers by surprise, making it difficult to supply. In recent years the panorama has changed: Mexico can boast of being the number one avocado producer and global exporter with 2.3 million tons sent to thirty-four nations. Of course, the US is the foremost destination in the volume of imports, followed by Canada, Japan, and Spain.

In Golden Letters

In her 1962 novel, *The Golden Notebook*, Doris Lessing mentions the avocado: "*They had brought food enough for us all, and we feasted on paw-paw and avocado pear, and bacon and eggs and hot fresh bread and coffee. The windows were open and the sunlight was hot outside, and wind coming into the room was warm and smelling of flowers.*" *The Golden Notebook* is Lessing's most famous novel and has been hailed as a staple of feminist literature.

Neither Pineapple nor Mango

In 2030, the avocado will be the most widely sold tropical fruit in the world, leaving pineapples and mangos far behind. It's expected that the United States and the European Union will continue to lead the pack of importers—at 40 percent and 31 percent, respectively—although China and some countries in the Middle East have also entered the race and are buying more than ever.

The avocado will become one of the most valued fruits on the market. World demand and lucrative export prices drove this growth, although the creation of new cultivation areas might lower the CPI (Consumer Price Index). It's expected that in 2030, around 74 percent of avocado production will remain in Latin America and the Caribbean, its traditional cultivation zones.

↑ Graphic details in urban art.

Avocados From Mexico™
▲▼▲▼▲▼▲▼▲▼
ALWAYS GOOD

Jalisco: The Mariachi Goes Green

This meteoric rise in exports tripled earnings in the last seven years, with the Mexican state of Michoacán as the main producer. Following in its footsteps, avocado production began throughout Mexico, and now at least twenty-three of the thirty-two states in the country grow avocados. It's surprising that in the last ten years, avocado plantations have increased 511 percent in various regions in the State of Mexico, and more than 1000 percent in the state of Jalisco, which will join Michoacán in exporting Mexican avocados to the United States, starting in June 2022.

↑ During the Avocado Festival at Casa Popenoe, sweet and savory dishes made with Guatemalan avocado compete.

We're Gonna Party

The world has seen a surge of festivals and international conferences devoted to the avocado. Some are celebrations, and some are meetings that discuss the avocado as a product of mass consumption and its impact on agriculture and the food industry. Among the foremost festivals and conferences are:

Avofest of Uruapan (Mexico)
This festival was first held in October 2019, to promote smaller local producer and avocado consumption through events celebrating cuisine, music, and dance as ways of promoting traditions.

California Avocado Festival (USA)
Founded in 1986 in Santa Barbara County (the third largest avocado producer in North America), this festival offers avocado fanatics a chance to taste a variety of dishes that highlight the avocado. There are also contests such as the World Guacamole Champion and the biggest avocado.

Latin American Avocado Congress (Guatemala)
Held every four years, it's currently preparing its sixth meeting. Organized by Agexport (Association for Commercial and Sustainable Development of Guatemala), it focuses on six production sectors and services, with special attention to agriculture and exports for the country's economy.

World Avocado Congress (WAC)
Like the Olympics and the World Cup, the World Avocado Congress occurs every four years. Its aim is to connect the world to avocados through an array of activities, such as workshops and scientific presentations. This congress has been held in South Africa, the United States, Israel, Mexico, Spain, Chile, Australia, New Zealand, Peru, and Colombia.

Casa Popenoe Avocado Festival (Guatemala)
Chefs from the best restaurants in the city of Antigua and students from the School of Nutrition at Universidad Francisco Marroquín create different dishes featured at tasting events for attendees. Casa Popenoe belonged to the eponymous US botanist-agronomist who purchased the house and converted it into his residence.

Tancítaro Avocado Fair (Mexico)
With a decade of experience, this open fair celebrates cultural events, cuisine, and dances to showcase the municipality's cultural features. Of course, there's an avocado tasting event alongside other activities for kids and adults.

Mango and Avocado Festival (Spain)
It's held in the locality of Vélez (Málaga), a region that has recently become a major producer of both fruit. It's a unique event featuring the participation of ten local bars and restaurants that offer tapas prepared with mango or avocado, offering a prize for the best dishes.

Ica's Palta Festival (Peru)
It was first held in 2018, organized by the Regional Government of Ica, the Chincha Agrarian Agency, the Municipality of Alto Laran, and the Palta Producers Association. This festival features exhibitions, cooking demonstrations, recipes, and the sale of related products, like avocado honey, oils, and shampoos.

Fruit Attraction (Spain)
This Spanish international fruit and vegetable fair serves as a commercial tool for marketing a wide variety of produce. In southern Spain, the avocado holds a prominent place in farming; specifically for innovations in the agricultural market.

Avocado Territory (Colombia)
This congress-trade show takes place in Medellín. In 2021, its third installment was held to foster research and technology, promote investment, and strengthen the sector by connecting it to global trends and markets, with a special focus on Hass avocado exports.

MICHOACÁN, WORLD AVOCADO CAPITAL

Thanks to its fertile volcanic soil, Michoacán has good reason to boast. It's the number one avocado-producing state in Mexico. Its rich soil is ideal for growing many varieties of fruit trees, led by the avocado. The main variety cultivated in Michoacán is the well-known Hass, followed by the Creole variety that grows wild (not a hybrid and without grafting), and the Fuerte variety, originally from Atlixco (Puebla).

← Scenes from the avocado harvest in Michoacán.

Which Is the True Capital?

Two municipalities in Michoacán dispute the title of world avocado capital: Tancítaro and Uruapan. But which of them can claim the honor? It's still undecided. Nevertheless, what we do know is that their ongoing competition has made Michoacán the indisputable avocado capital of the world.

Tancítaro: Tierra Caliente

Things have changed a lot for this small community so far in this century. It started out with modest avocado production, but by 2020 it already had more than sixty-five hundred orchards and was exporting two hundred thousand tons. That's why it's number one in global avocado production.

In addition, it holds the 2018 Guinness World Record for the biggest guacamole in the world. Half the town got together for this event. Its aim was to break Jalisco's record of 2017, when it made an almost three ton guacamole in ninety minutes. They got to work and in only thirty-four minutes, they prepared a monumental guacamole that left the Jalisco record far behind. Ecstatic over this triumph, the townspeople savored their guacamole during the annual avocado fair, held every April.

↑ Monument to the avocado in Tancítaro, Michoacán.

A URUAPAN
DEL AGUACATE

Uruapan: Flourishing Fruit

The nearby town of Uruapan has grown bananas, sapodillas, mamey sapotes, limes, oranges, lemons, and avocados since viceregal times. Today, it's second only to the state capital, in part for its high avocado production. Despite the smaller scale of its overall yield, it´s the hub for most of the state's avocado packing companies.

↑ In 2017, Jalisco broke the Guiness World Record for the world's biggest guacamole, but was beaten next year (EFE).

75

Urani: From the Family Orchard to the Popsicle Shop

"The avocado, as it's said in the verse, 'tree of twelve fruit, fruit of twelve months, avocado you're worthy of the best.' I'd say: but avocados deserve an ode, a song, the avocado is a blessed fruit."

Alejandro Bautista speaks passionately about the avocado. Born into a family who has avocado orchards, today he sells fruit popsicles under the brand name Urani. His specialty, of course, are avocado popsicles.

"To add value to Mexico's quality products, we made a drink. My brother Enrique hired a chemist who developed a beverage. We called it La Guacamaya (The Macaw). It was a big hit at all the events we went to.

"We'd take the drink concentrate to the market and add water to prepare it. I'd eat this basic mix and say to myself: 'this is tasty, I don't know why we have to make it into a drink.' I began making avocado ice cream that I'd take to food exhibitions and a chef, I think it was in Missouri, asked me for the mix. I don't know what he did to it, but he made it much better. He added seaweed or something that gave it a very pleasing texture.

"That ice cream was a bit hit. My brother, an expert in industries, recommended I make popsicles. I got an alcohol machine and started to make little avocado popsicles with passion fruit and sold them to the Association of Avocado Producers, Packers, and Exporters of Mexico (APEAM). They paid me a dollar each for those small popsicles."

↑ Urani brand avocado popsicles.

Gratissima: Everything Avocado

Gratissima is a restaurant in Uruapan, Michoacán. All the dishes are made with the best quality avocados, because of the restaurant's cultivated relationship with local growers.
Its menu features typical Mexican breakfasts, lunches, dinners, and desserts, with a touch of avocado, of course. Avocado hotcakes, spaghetti with avocado sauce, avocado soup, avocado jam . . . They even produce four varieties of avocado beer! Gratissima is so devoted to the avocado, they also have a souvenir shop where you can find everything avocado: coin purses, earrings, keychains and more.

↑ Detail of the mural at Gratissima Restaurant.

← In addition to its original avocado dishes, Gratissima produces artisanal beer.

77

Avocado Water, a Michoacán Treat

Among the refreshing drinks we can enjoy in Mexico, avocado water is one of the most delicious, although it's a bit of a local secret. It's made of avocado and limes from Uruapan.

To prepare it, you need an avocado, a liter (qt.) of water, a liter of grapefruit soda, and lime juice.

Preparation

1. Extract the avocado pulp and mix it in a blender with lime juice and half a liter (qt.) of water
2. Put the remaining half a liter of water and grapefruit soda in a pitcher.
3. Add the avocado mixture and stir well.
4. To chill it, add ice or put it in the refrigerator.

Small farmers in Michoacán produce the majority of Mexico's avocado exports.

Each region of Mexico has its own avocado varieties that must be responsibly protected.

↖ Scenes of the avocado harvest in Michoacán.

Most productive states

State	Tons / 2020
1 Michoacán	1,800,021
2 Jalisco	248,193
3 México	118,268
4 Nayarit	69,985
5 Morelos	50,410

Traditional knowledge and scientific progress improve the crop's potential, strengthening conservation and putting resources to best use.

The states of Jalisco, State of Mexico, Morelos, Nayarit, and Guerrero are following in Michoacán's footsteps in avocado production volume.

↑ Avocados begin their journey around the world in crates.

Emblem of Michoacán

I'm from Michoacán, which means "fishermen's zone," but for years that has no longer been the case. I was born in Uruapan, I grew up playing "cops and robbers" in my uncles' avocado fields, so when people ask me, "what is it about your town that you brag about the most?" It's the avocado, more than carnitas (braised pork). Not only is it an ingredient, it's a local emblem. It's involved in all tasks in Michoacán's life. During my childhood, there were always avocados on the table, because they were a staple in the family cookbook: pozole (hominy soup) prepared for Christmas had avocados and carnitas. Everyone in my family is originally from Michoacán, my two grandmothers on my mother's and my father's side. I have uncles who cultivated avocados and even though they emigrated to the United States, their orchards stayed here in Uruapan.

For me, Michoacán is the "great paradox," an extremely generous and abundant territory with gastronomic, cultural, and agricultural wealth, but at the same time with high levels of poverty. This ambivalence is curious. We're one of the biggest producers of fruit consumed in the United States, which has become as expensive as a luxury product and has ceased to be accessible worldwide. We know that it has many aspects with a controversial, bittersweet side for its monocropping process, but it's our "green gold" and the main source of support for families around here.

It's a complex fruit that can be used in both sweet and savory dishes. To mention a couple of its qualities, the pulp has the texture of a sapote and the seed has fats that can be extracted. Not to mention avocado oil for cooking, which is one of the humble unexploited marvels of the avocado fruit, with just as many, if not more properties than olive oil. I cook a lot with avocado oil, but I never heat it. I use it in cold dishes. Some four years ago I had a restaurant—inspired by the cuisine of my ranch in Michoacán—that was called Seneri ("new corn" in the Purépecha language), and we always used avocado oil to make a sweet bread and other dishes, like salsas and ice creams. Today, people recognize Mexico for its great contribution to world gastronomy, and the avocado is one of the leading products that we have given the world. Not only as a food, but also as an essential ingredient of our culture.

Fernando Martínez, chef. See the "Smoked Trout and Avocado Tostada with Wasabi" recipe.

↖ Avocado packing plant.

GREEN AGENDA FOR MICHOACÁN

The APEAM (Association of Avocado Producers and Packers of Mexico) has developed an ambitious "green agenda" to achieve a higher level of sustainability in the industry and in Michoacán communities. It is an environmental, social, and labor sustainability plan that involves the entire avocado industry in Mexico and the impact of the extensive cultivation on local communities of small farmers and the avocado's traditional habitats.

To mitigate the drying out of aquifers near avocado farms, one of APEAM's strategies is reforestation and restoration of the areas bordering crops that might have been damaged, in order to protect and conserve the biodiversity of the cultivated lands.

The figures speak for themselves: between 2011 and 2020, more than 2.2 million new trees have been replanted in the state of Michoacán, which has permitted and will permit the regeneration of the zone's watersheds, like the Cupatitzo River, which contributes 70 percent of the freshwater to the locality of Uruapan. As part of the green agrochemicals project, there is a list of authorized pesticides that only contain the molecules permitted by the US, the leading importer country.

In addition to soil conservation, APEAM also strives to improve water quality through the reduction of harmful chemical products entering the water system. It has also promoted a type of sustainable irrigation that has resulted in 97 percent of the avocado orchards in Michoacán being maintained with natural or sustainable irrigation: 61 percent depend on seasonal rains and 36 percent use high-tech drip irrigation or micro-sprinklers, which reduce excessive costs.

Another goal is to benefit local communities and artisanal growers in Michoacán, rather than massive export companies.

For the most part, workers in this industry are small producers: 64 percent cultivate areas from 2.5 to 25 acres (1 to 10 ha). But in recent years, the strong growth in this sector has enabled about 100,000 families (55 percent of women and 45 percent of men) to return to this work, allowing them to stay in the land of their birth and halting the trauma of migration. In addition, the signing of the United States, Mexico, Canada Agreement (USMCA) on July 1, 2020, aims to protect labor rights and guarantee the competitiveness of the Michoacán industry. These measures have led to improvements of roads and infrastructure in avocado producing areas, better conditions for social development (such as access to education for children and adolescents) in rural zones, and less poverty than in other areas of Michoacán not covered by the APEAM green plan.

Water for the Avocado

Avocado orchards require a lot of water to grow: according to statistics, between 1,500,000 and 2,400,000 liquid gallons (6,000,000 and 9,000,000 liters) of water per 2.5 acres (1 ha) annually. This is bearing in mind that farmers have to strike a delicate balance—the tree cannot tolerate too much moisture in the soil, nor can it thrive without enough moisture.

According to the World Avocado Organization (WAO), water consumption has been optimized and reduced in recent years. Just in the last decade, technical improvements in irrigation and exhaustive control of growth have led to water consumption dropping to about 132-158 gallons (500-600 liters). It might still seem like a lot, but compared to the volume of water needed for other fruit crops, the avocado is clearly below the average.

What a Downpour of Fruit!

How many gallons (liters) of water per 2.2 lbs (1 kg) do these fruit need to grow?

Tomatoes	55 gal (210 l)
Oranges	148 gal (560 l)
Avocados	158 gal (600 l)
Bananas	209 gal (790 l)
Apples	217 gal (820 l)
Nectarines	240 gal (910 l)
Almonds	317 gal (1,200 l)
Mangos	475 gal (1,800 l)
Dates	600 gal (2,270 l)
Peanuts	713 gal (2,700 l)
Olives	792 gal (3,000 l)

↖ Avocado fields in Michoacán.

CATE DE MI CORAZÓN

The avocado is synonymous with Mexico. It is deeply rooted in popular culture in riddles, as an ingredient, and as a natural remedy. It's produced and consumed in every corner of the country. It also can be found in a version of almost all regional recipes.

**Agua pasa por mi casa
Cate de mi corazón
¿Qué es?**

Riddle: Water (agua) passes through my house, cate from my heart. What is it? Agua-cate (avocado)!

↑ Street vendors selling criollo avocados in Guanajuato.

Street Food
Chicharrón and Guacamole Taco

Ingredients
10 servings

- 10 corn tortillas
- 10 oz (300 gr) chicharron (pork crackling)
- 8 oz (200 gr) Mexican *queso fresco* (Mexican cheese)
- 3 medium tomatoes
- 4 tomatillos
- ½ onion
- 2 cloves garlic
- 10 cilantro stalks.
- 2 serrano chilis
- 1 fresh jalapeño chili
- 3 ripe avocados
- 1 tablespoon olive oil
- 1 lime

Preparation
1. Wash all the ingredients: the cilantro, tomatoes, tomatillos, chilis, onion, and avocados.
2. Finely chop the cilantro, tomatoes, and tomatillos into cubes and mince the chilis and onion.
3. Set aside.
4. Put the tomato, ¼ onion, and 2 minced serrano chilies in a bowl (or *molcajete* grinding bowl), add 2 teaspoons of minced cilantro, lime juice, a pinch of salt, and mix.

Plating
1. On each tortilla, put pieces of pork crackling, two heaping tablespoons of guacamole and roll it up.
2. If you want, you can add *pico de gallo*, avocado slices, and more lime juice.

↑ Selling the fruit in Yucatán.

87

P'aybil oon / Chopped Avocado

Ingredients
1 servings

- 1 ripe avocado
- juice of 1 lime or a bitter orange substitute
- ground habanero chili, to taste
- Salt to taste

Preparation
1. Cut the avocado in two lengthwise.
2. Remove the seed and the pulp from the peel.
3. Cut the pulp into small cubes.
4. Put on plate and add citrus juice, ground chili and salt to taste.
5. Mix well.
6. Serve.

↑ Addi María Ay Ché, traditional cook, Yucatán.

Ancestrally consumed and enjoyed in Yucatán, avocado recipes have been passed down from generation to generation like family treasures.

Addi María Ay Ché, a traditional Yucatec cook from Chichimilá (Yucatán) and finalist in the "What Does the Nation Taste Like?" contest, recounts when she was nine, she'd carefully watch her mom prepare food. That's how people learn to cook in Mexican villages: by watching their mothers and grandmothers. An enthusiastic defender of her maternal legacy, Addi María believes it's important for young people to preserve their family cooking traditions.

One of her mother's secrets is worth its weight in gold: every food has components in correct proportions. The first thing Addi María made were tortillas and *pimes* (a thick tortilla), made with corn freshly ground on an old grindstone. They also made an *atole* (cornmeal drink) known as *chokoj sakan*. But the first dish she prepared was *k'óol*, a pipian sauce made with *oon*, avocado in Mayan. For the Yucatecs, this fruit is one of their community's most representative foods, because you can use it to make quick and easy recipes, usually served with a side of beans.

Addi María Ay Ché is like millions of people who consider food a part of identity. Indigenous recipes like these are strengthened by native products like avocado and corn, now popular in all corners of the globe.

Mexican Cuisine, World Heritage

You can find avocados all over Mexican market stalls. On many a street corner, little Creole avocados sit on a piece of tarp on the ground. Plenty of street food stands serve avo-dishes: tortas with green or red chilaquiles with cochinita (pork), tostadas, ever-present tacos—with pork carnitas (BBQ), al pastor (spit-grilled), or barbacoa (slow-roasted), stewed meat, or a la canasta (varied fillings)—bean tamales. And of course, guacamole is ready to serve in small plastic cups.

The avocado has accompanied all Mexican traditional dishes for centuries. From salads and ollas podridas (hearty stews) of well-to-do nineteenth-century matrons during the age of Porfirio Díaz to the humble beans with cheese and avocado that of the "agachados" (the poorest in Mexico City), to the "designer" torta eaten by young professionals during a busy work day. Desired and loved by everyone in Mexico, avocados are ubiquitous and don't discriminate.

↘ Mexican street food is fantastic!

Pre-Columbian Green Mole

Ingredients
2 servings

- 1 lb (½ kg) tomatillo
- 4 serrano chilis
- 2 sprigs of epazote (aromatic Mexican herb)
- 1 avocado leaf
- 1 clove garlic
- 1 onion slice
- 1¼ cup (150 g) *pepitas* (pumpkin seeds)
- A splash of stock (meat or plant-based)
- Salt

Preparation
1. Roast the tomatillos and chilis on a griddle; grind the epazote, avocado leaf, garlic, and onion in a grinding bowl. Combine.
2. Toast the pumpkin seeds and grind them, then sauté them in a bit of oil for a few minutes. Add the tomatillo mixture and a little water or stock.
3. Cook over low heat for 20 minutes, until the mixture thickens slightly.
4. Stir it constantly to prevent it from sticking. Make sure it doesn't reach a boil because it can curdle the pumpkin seeds.

A typical homemade Mexican highland recipe from the states of Mexico and Puebla. Today, it is still prepared and served as a mole sauce for an array of traditional and signature dishes.

Source: Cristina Barros and Marco Buen Rostro, *Cocina prehispánica: Recetario, in Arqueología Mexicana*, special edition series.

↗ You can find little eateries on any corner.

89

The Avocado Cumbia

The Oaxacan singer/songwriter, Flor Amargo, composes a traditional folk song to pay homage to the Hass avocado: the flavor of Mexico.

Toss avocado in that grinding bowl
Toss in avocado
Avocado Hass, Hass, Hass
Toss onion in the pot
Toss in avocado
Avocado Hass, Hass, Hass
Guacamole, *chilpachole*, and pozole (Yeah)
It's pure delight
It's not fruit, or vegetable
And the Hass avocado is from my land
It's pure delight
Remedy for bitterness
Come and join the cumbia of the Hass avocado
I'm like the avocado
I'm a fruit and I'm a vegetable
How d'you like it (the little avocado)
Surely (in your little bread roll)
With a bit of chili (and *chicharroncito*)
Ay! Ay! Ay, how tasty!
Toss avocado
Into that guacamole
It's my thing, dance with love
And everyone together
Let's go to the market
And buy groceries
And avocado Hass, Hass, Hass
Hooow tasty!
Avocado, Mexican green gold
It's Mexican, it's Mexican
Avocado, Mexican green gold
Avocado, you left me
With a love letter
I know you love me
To put me in a bowl
But first I want to dance a danzon.

Performer: Flor Amargo
Guest artist: Amandititita
Album: La Cumbia del Aguacate
Release date: 2020

Should You Ever Cook Avocados?

Mexican chef, Gerardo Vázquez Lugo, recalls that once his mother, chef María Elena Lugo, told him of a conversation she had with Patricia Quintana (1946–2018), international promoter of Mexican cuisine, years ago at the International Gastronomy and Wine Festival. "Morelia on the Palate."

One morning, at breakfast in the Casino Hotel restaurant, she saw Patricia Quintana—who had been invited to speak at the event—approaching her table and asked if she could join her. "Of course I said yes. How could I refuse sharing my table with the grande dame of Mexican cuisine?" recounts María Elena.

Patricia told her an episode from a dinner the night before. A waiter set a dish of avocado before her—grilled and served as a garnish! Chef Quintana couldn't believe it; unable to contain herself, in a loud voice she repeated one of those unwritten culinary laws: "Never cook avocado."

As many chefs and cooks know, avocado doesn't respond well to cooking from the chemical reaction it produces. It's best to leave it fresh.

↑ Grilled Avocado.

The Ghost of Avocado Alley

Like all ageless heroes, the avocado has also been featured in oral tradition, spread through word of mouth. In the bustling borough of Coyoacán in Mexico City, there's an alley where a strange atmosphere captivates passersby: it's Callejón del Aguacate (Avocado Alley) in the Santa Catarina barrio. That narrow street has seen it all. As legend would have it, during the 1930s, a war veteran moved there, seeking a peaceful existence. He would take walks in the neighborhood in his full uniform. Often, he would encounter children, dazzled by his medals, who would ask him to play, which irritated him to no end. One day, in a fit of rage, he killed a little boy beneath a leafy avocado tree. Repentant, he had an altar built to the Virgin Mary at the corner of the alley to alleviate his guilt. The altar also served as a place where anyone can pray.

Some say they can hear the boy's moans if they stand under the tree. Nowadays, tourists and the curious wander the alleyway looking for ghosts.

↑ Mural on Callejón del aguacate (Avocado Alley), Coyoacán, MX.

TOSTADA

TACOS

SALPICÓN

POZOLE

HUARACHE

HAMBURGER

→ Typical Mexican dishes, served with avocado.

GREEN TRENDS

GREEN TRENDS

The avocado has won us over, but what exactly do we know about it? Let's debunk myths and reveal the truth about this green object of desire.

VEGETABLE, WITH SKIN AND SEED?

The biggest debate concerning avocados is whether it is a fruit or a vegetable. Some botanists and scholars have considered the avocado a drupe: a fleshy fruit, usually round, containing a single seed or stone, covered in a hard layer, like peaches, cherries, or olives. For other analysts, it's wrong to call it a drupe, because, given the hard outer coat of the seed, the avocado is like a monosperm berry: a fleshy fruit with a seed surrounded by pulp, something much closer to blueberries, cranberries, or strawberries.

Ugly Outside, Handsome Inside: Taxonomy and Characteristics

A standard avocado generally measures between 2.5 to almost 12 in (6 to 30 cm), long, 1.5 to 6 in (4 to 15 cm) wide and weighs about 7 to 14 oz (200 to 400 grams). Let's dissect it to see how beautiful the avocado is inside.

The pulp is composed of two adjacent layers: the mesocarp and endocarp (the thin layer next to the seed coat). The mesocarp is known as the avocado pulp, the fleshy, smooth, buttery greenish-yellow part. The pulp can have different characteristics and appearances; depending on the variety, it ranges from intense green to greenish yellow. The flavor also depends on the variety, although it's usually described as soft and somewhat anise-flavored.

Seed

The almond, stone, pit, or seed is composed of three layers corresponding to the seed cover, cotyledon, and embryonic axis. It represents 15% of the fruit's weight, ranging in size from .75 to 1.5 in (2 to 4 cm) and weighs from 1 to 2.5 oz (28 to 75 g), depending on the subspecies. It's egg-shaped and covered with a thin brown layer; while the surface of the core is pale pink, hard, and rough, with a groove that divides it into two, like a nut. It has high amounts of oleic acid, vitamins and minerals, and can produce a milky fluid that smells and tastes like almonds.

Peel

The avocado peel or skin (exocarp) can have a rough and bumpy or thin and smooth surface that is even edible in some varieties. Its texture and composition vary in color and thickness, depending on the environmental conditions of its growth. In some avocados, the skin is bright green and shiny, in others, a lemony yellow. In places with a cool climate, the peel is lighter, smooth, and fine-grained; whereas in warm settings, it becomes rougher. It contains an essential oil with an anise-like scent.

MORPHOLOGY

It's a very strong, fast-growing tree, with a straight trunk and smooth bark, which measures some 33 ft (10 m) tall, although some have been found in the wild up to 98.5 ft (30 m).

Kingdom:	*Plantae*
Division:	*Magnoliophyta*
Class:	*Magnoliopsida*
Order:	*Laurales*
Family:	*Lauraceae*
Genus:	*Persea*
Species:	*Persea americana Mill*

Leaves

The foliage is evergreen (i.e., it has leaves year-round), with alternating leaves that are shiny on the upper side and matte on the underside. Their color varies from red to dark green, giving them a leathery appearance. They measure between 5 to 10 in (12 and 25 cm) long. Leaf morphology is conditioned by the genotype: in the Mexican variety, they are small, hairless and glandless, with an anise-like aroma. In Guatemalan and Antillean species, they are larger with fine, soft, short hairs and no anise scent.

Roots

It's taprooted (i.e., it grows vertically downward), highly ramified with a radial distribution with multiple white feeder roots, which spread outward, staying close to the topsoil.

Fruit

The fruit is a single-seeded, edible flesh berry. Its shape can be round or pear-like. Its average size: about 2.5 in (6 cm) long and some 7 oz (200 g) in weight.

Flowers

They tend to be yellowish-green, six-petaled, and very small (about .5 in or 1 cm). They are dioecious, or hermaphrodites. But because nature is wise, they open at two different phases of the day to avoid fertilizing themselves. Bees serve as the main pollinator, helping the flowers blossom during late winter into spring.

Trunk and Branches

Its wood is moderately hard and rough. Young branches are light-colored, while older ones are grayish. The branching is straight, forming 60° angles with the trunk.

The taste of avocado is it **umami**?

The tongue's tastebuds distinguish between four tastes: sweet, salty, bitter, and acidic (or sour). But for Japanese people and others in Asia, there's a fifth flavor: *umami*, which means "delicious, tasty" in Japanese.

Umami was coined in 1908 by scientist Kikunae Ikeda, a chemistry professor at the Imperial University of Tokyo. He discovered that the amino acid known as glutamate provides that hard-to-describe flavor capable of activating salivation and stimulating the throat, palate, and back of the mouth. Based on this discovery, glutamate became known as Ajinomoto (the "essence of taste") in Japan, a flavor enhancer that can be found in jamón serrano (dry-cured Spanish ham), tomatoes, asparagus, cheese, and avocados!

Sour

Tart

Umami

Tart

Salty

Salty

Sweet

The fruit is rich in glutathione, the "master antioxidant" essential for cellular protection and oxidative damage that fights cellular aging and keeps the immune system strong.

Even though we're not used to identifying the umami flavor, we can discern it on more than half the tongue, while sweetness is noted at localized points and bitter in the back. Thus, our sense of taste is more than prepared to perceive the avocado's flavor on its entire surface.

What Is It?

At first sight, the avocado looks like a vegetable. But it's not that simple. Vegetables are defined as edible plants cultivated on a farm whose leaves, stalks, or roots can be eaten.

Based on this definition, the avocado isn't a leaf, stalk, root, or seed. It's the fruit of a tree. By definition, a fruit is the product of a tree or tree-like plant that has one or more seeds and can be ingested as food. It is obvious that the avocado meets all these requirements.

The confusion in Mexico might come from the idea that fruits are sweet, and the avocado tends to be savory. This ambiguity has earned this versatile fruit kudos in gastronomy, with an exotic taste. This fruit is even more highly esteemed when it's at its peak of ripeness, because when unripe, it lacks flavor, and its texture is unpleasant.

THE TASTE IS IN THE VARIETY

The Three Pioneers

Historically, the three best known avocado varieties are the Mexican, Guatemalan, and Antillean varieties. All three have been documented since the Spanish conquest. Some authors describe a fourth variety: the Costarricensis from Costa Rica. The morphological difference between them is obvious. And the avocado of Mexican origin is the smallest, the Antillean the largest.

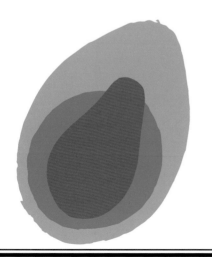

Antillean Avocado

Scientific name:
Persea americana var. Americana
In Nahuatl: Tlacacolaoacatl

Fruit quality	**Good**
Peel	**Somewhat thick, smooth and shiny**
Pulp and seed	**Abundant pulp**
Color of bud	**Green**
Flowering	**From February to March**
Anise-scented leaves	**No**
Maturation	**Summer and early fall**
Chlorosis resistance	**High**
Cold resistance	**Low (up to -1.8 °F [-1 °C])**
Salinity resistance	**Low**

Despite its name, it isn't from the Antilles, but from the Maya lowlands of Central America and the Yucatán Peninsula.

Evidence of this variety dating to 3000 BCE has been found in Peru, probably from trade between pre-Hispanic peoples.

It's the biggest of the three varieties, measuring 4–10 in (10–25 cm).

It's pear-shaped, and has light green, thick but flexible skin, so it's easy to peel.

The pulp is abundant with a slightly sweet flavor, not as intense as the Mexican variety, or as delicate as the Guatemalan. It has a subtle bitter aftertaste.

It's well-adapted to the moist lowland tropics, tolerant to high saline levels and chlorosis (a nutrient deficiency in plants).

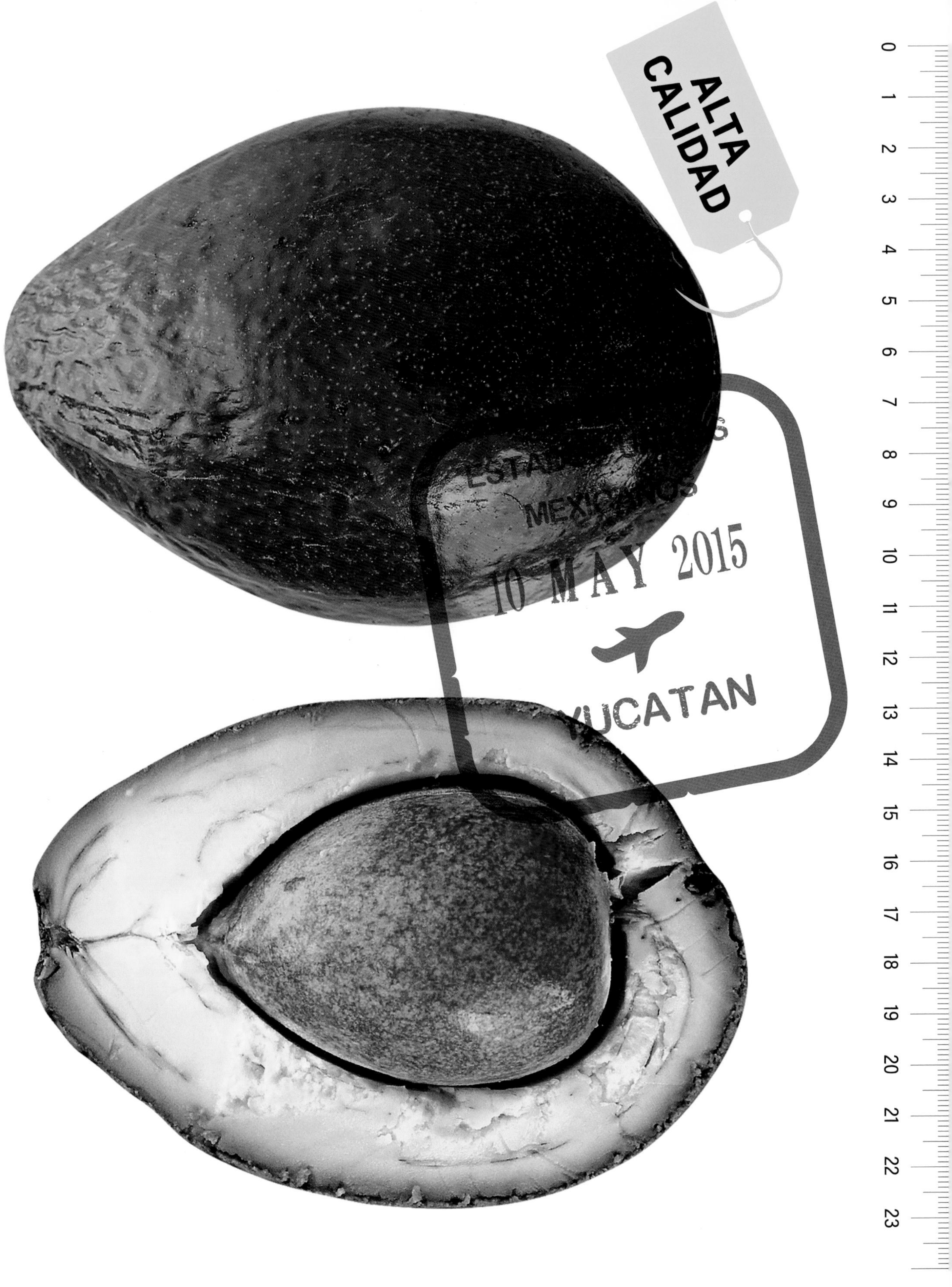

ALTA CALIDAD

ESTADOS MEXICANOS

10 MAY 2015

YUCATAN

0 1 2 3 4 5 6 7 8 9 10 11 12 13 14 15 16 17 18 19 20 21 22 23

Mexican Avocado

Scientific name:
Persea americana var. Drymifolia
In Nahuatl: Ahuacatl

Fruit quality	**The best**
Peel	**Thick, woody and rough**
Pulp and seed	**Abundant pulp, small seed**
Color of bud	**Violet**
Flowering	**From January to April**
Anise-scented leaves	**No**
Maturation	**Late winter and spring**
Chlorosis resistance	**Low**
Cold resistance	**Intermediate**
Salinity resistance	**Intermediate**

The Mexican avocado is the oldest variety of this fruit consumed by humans.

In Mexico, it's known as the "Creole avocado" and was domesticated in the central region of the country. It's well-adapted to the tropical highlands, so it's the variety most resistant to cold and is the origin of most New World varieties.

Its fruit is small, between 1 ⅝ – 4 ¾ in (4–12 cm), slightly elongated. It's covered by a fine, smooth, soft skin, so tender that it can be eaten.

Its pulp has an anise-like flavor. Its leaves are so aromatic that they're often used as a condiment in many Mexican dishes.

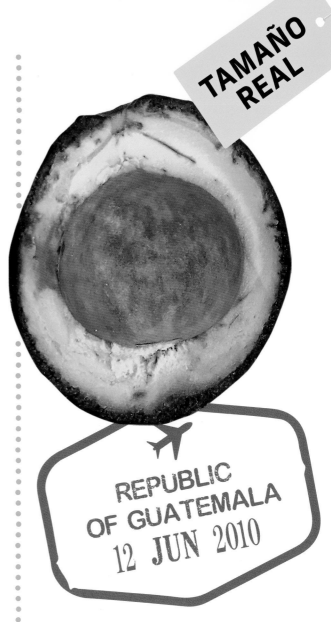

REPUBLIC
OF GUATEMALA
12 JUN 2010

Guatemalan Avocado

Scientific name: *Persea americana* var.
Guatemalensis
In Nahuatl: Quilaoacatl

Fruit quality	**Good**
Peel	**Very thin and smooth**
Pulp and seed	**Large seed and little pulp**
Color of bud	**Green**
Flowering	**From January to March**
Anise-scented leaves	**Yes**
Maturation	**Late summer-fall**
Chlorosis resistance	**Low**
Cold resistance	**High (up to -12.6 °F [-7 °C])**
Salinity resistance	**Low**

The variety that grows from southern Mexico to northern Guatemala.

Its shape is like that of the Mexican variety, compact and conical, with a mild flavor.

But it's the longest, between 4 and 7 ⅛ in (10 and 18 cm).

It has a more ovoid seed of a lighter color.

The skin is thick, rough, and withstands transport.

Guatemalan avocados are adapted to medium-range elevations in the tropics and are resistant to cold, for having grown in the subtropical highlands of the Americas.

MEXICAN VARIETIES

Aguilar
Mexican Creole variety. It was named in honor of José Aguilar Melchor, a researcher at CICTAMEX S.C. The fruit is relatively large: 5¼ in (13.5 cm) long and 3 in (8.5 cm) in diameter, weighing between 12.4 to 17.6 oz (350 to 500 gr). 81% of the fruit is pulp, 11% peel, and 8% seed.

Aguacatillo
Variety from the Mexican race, but it differs in that both the fruit and leaves of the tree are very small.

Aries
Considered a medium-sized tree, it has an average yield of 770 lb (40 kg) per tree. Each fruit weighs between 10.6 to 16.6 oz (300 to 470 gr) with an average length of 10¼ in (10.5 cm). The peel is dark green, the seed oval, and the pulp cream colored.

Ariete
Mature fruit are dark green, with cream-colored pulp and weigh between 12.4 to 13.4 oz (352 to 381 gr), with an elliptical seed. It averages 5 in (12.8 cm) in length.

Canelo
It's grown in the central part of southern Mexico. Immature fruit are dark violet, hence its name, which means cinnamon colored. Its average length is in (1 cm).

Fuerte
It was the most popular variety until the Hass appeared. It's a Mexican and Guatemalan hybrid, pear-shaped, and has fine, smooth light green, grainy, very flexible and peelable skin; with superb pulp. The seed is medium and the fruit usually weighs between 4.4 –17.6 oz (125–500 gr). It's considered to be one of the most flavorful. It's also good for cooking—containing more oil than other avocados—with a percentage of 23% and 27%.

Bacon
The Bacon variety is one of the most prized by chefs. It's a Guatemalan-Mexican hybrid that produces large fruit. It's adapted to colder environments, with more climatological complications. It can even resist windy zones. Its fruit is oval with smooth, fine, green skin, good quality pulp, and a big seed, with an average weight of 5.3–17.6 oz (150–500 gr).

Fundación II
Each fruit varies between 7 to 10.6 oz (250 to 300 gr). Its averages 4 in (10.4 cm) long. When it's ripe, the fruit is dark purple, with cream-colored pulp, and a round seed.

Jiménez II
It has black fruit with a rough leathery peel, not adhered to the fruit, with a small seed of floral type A.

Méndez
The thick, rough, green to dark skin is easily peelable, and the pulp is creamy and lacks fibers. It's seasonal and is the only tree variety that produces fruit when others don't. The name refers to its creator, Carlos Méndez Vega.

Despite differences in zone and altitude conditions, the different varieties of Mexican avocados can coexist and develop right next to each other, because of their similar genome. They are easily cross-pollinated. Hybridization has allowed numerous varieties to develop the three original Mexican avocado species. Every avocado variety descends from the Mexican avocado, but only these varieties can say they were "Made in Mexico."

Cimarrón

It's found at altitudes of 6560 to 9186 ft (2,000 to 2,800 m). Its distribution spans Veracruz to southern Mexico and Guatemala. It's mainly used as wood to make farming tools. The fruit is between 2½ and 3¼ in (6.3 and 8.4 cm).

Colinmex

It's dark green, with cream-colored pulp, weighing between 7.7 to 12.4 oz (220 to 351 gr), has a round seed, and is on average 4 in (12.5 cm) long.

Chinín

The color, texture, and size of its fruit vary, but it always has a thin skin or peel. It's used as a shade plant for coffee and macadamia crops. It has edible fruit and is highly prized in traditional markets. The fruit is 7½–11 in (19–28 cm) long.

De montaña

A species that can be found in southern Mexico and Guatemala that produces very compact, small fruit shorter than 2 in (5 cm) long.

Encinos

It comes from Hass seeds grafted with the Fuerte variety, planted in 1986 in Coatepec Harinas, Mexico. The pulp is light yellow, occupying 76% of the fruit, 18% peel, and 6% is the seed. The weight varies between 15 and 25.5 gr (425 and 725 gr) and measures 4¾ in (12 cm).

P. Longipes

Fruit with a very thin skin and more seed than pulp, so it's usually not popular with consumers.

P. Cinerascens

It's produced mainly in Michoacán and the State of Mexico. It's used for genetic enhancement for its roots resist rotting. It produces smaller fruit than all other varieties: only in (1 cm) long!

Puebla

A Mexican variety that withstands cold and frosts very well. The fruit are dark brown and oval and can weigh up to 7 oz (200 gr).

Rincoatl

Mature fruit are medium green; cream-colored pulp, weighing 12.7 oz (360 gr) on average; with a triangular seed.

Vargas

It has black fruit, 3 in (9.8 cm) long and 2¾ in (6.9 cm) in diameter, with a thin peel, weighing 9.3 oz (265 gr) on average, with a very large seed 1.4 oz (40.3 gr).

PINKERTON
AVOCADOS
$1.75/EA
OR
2 for $3.00

United States

Kenya

Italy

England

109

Bernecker
Relatively small in size, the fruit is pear-shaped, the seed is light and oval, the pulp pale beige. The peel is fine, soft and light green with darker points, separating easily from the pulp. It has an average fat content and tastes like egg yolk.

Brogdon
Ideal for cultivating in cold regions, it's a rapid-growth species with medium-large fruit of 14.1 to 24.7 oz (400 to 700 gr). Its dark green to purple skin is very thin, making it hard to peel. It's valued for its delicious buttery flavor.

Booth
It's a hybrid of Antille-an-Guatemalan origin. The advantage of this species is that it can be grown in climates where other types of avocadoes don't prosper. It has small to medium-sized fruit.

Maluma
Native to South Africa, where it was discovered in the 1990s, it's big, weighing between 5.29 to 14.1 oz (150 to 400 gr). Its skin is rough and wrinkled, dark purple even when it's completely ripe.

Mexicola
A California variety; very dark purple in color, practically black; its skin is thin and has a soft texture that is even edible. It has superb, very buttery pulp. It is plum-sized and has a high oil content. Its leaves are also eaten and used as a condiment.

Maoz
Pear-shaped, medium-sized, with hard leathery peel that turns violet purple when ripe; its pulp is sweetish and very low in oil. It's usually grown in Israel, where it's planted in saline or calcareous soils.

Carmero
Originally from the region of El Carmen de Bolívar, (Colombia), it has smooth, dark green skin that easily separates from the flesh. The pulp is creamy and lacks fibers.

Fuchs (fuchsia)
It has an oblong or pear shape, medium in size, with smooth skin and pale greenish yellow pulp containing 4% to 6% oil, with loose seeds.

Lorena
Elongated fruit, slightly oblique, with smooth, lustrous green skin marked by lots of dots. It's large, some 14.1 oz (400 gr) and has a 9% fat content. The seeds are medium, slightly adhered to the pulp. It's been grown in the Cauca Valley, Colombia, since 1957.

Lula
Originally from southern Florida, it's pear-shaped, with a large seed, almost smooth shiny dark green skin. Medium to large in size; its pale pulp is greenish yellow with a 12% to 16% oil content. It's Martinica's main crop export to France, representing 95% of the harvest.

Butler
It has a pear shape and is medium to large, with smooth skin and pulp that fits tightly around the medium-sized seed. It's usually grown in Puerto Rico.

Nabal
Its almost round shape distinguishes it from other varieties. The peel is hard and woody, which allows it to be kept for a long time. It mainly comes from Israel.

Ettinger
Fine, thin, shiny green skin, medium to large, its pulp is yellowish and very soft, perfect for smoothies. One of its main producers is Israel, where it represents between 25% and 30% of the avocados grown there.

There are many avocado varieties throughout the world; every producer thinks their variety is best. Each producer country can boast its own. To learn how to distinguish the types of avocados you find in the market, it's important to know their morphology, typology, and description. Between the 1950s and 1970s, the Creole variety was the Mexican favorite, but Californians preferred the Bacon and Reed varieties, and more recently, the Pinkerton and Gwen. And in first place, the super-famous Hass.

Choquette

A hybrid of the Guatemalan and Antillean avocado, it's originally from Florida. It's large and oval, with tender, shiny green skin. The pulp is very creamy and has a high water and 13% oil content. It has a loose, medium-sized seed. It can weigh from 18 to 409.4 oz (510 to 1400 gr).

Rincón

It has small to medium, pear-shaped fruit; the skin is very thin and smooth, but leathery. The pulp is very unctuous, with 15% to 26.5% oil content. Its seeds are medium. It is one of the six main types cultivated in California.

Pinkerton

Rincón and Hass hybrid. It has a long shape and rough, thick, green skin that is easily peeled. It has a small seed, delicious pale green pulp, is rich in oils, and usually weighs 8.8–17.6 oz (250–500 gr).

Reed

From Guatemala, it was developed in the late 1950s in Florida. Its large fruit is rounder than other types and usually weighs more than 17.6 oz (500 gr). It has tasty soft pulp, thick but pliable dark green skin, easily to peel, and a medium-sized seed.

Negra de La Cruz

It originated in the Valparaíso region of Chile, through the natural hybridization of the Mexican variety. With smooth, purple or carbon black skin, the medium-sized fruit is highly resistant to low temperatures.

Grande

Large and pear-shaped, it has hard skin and ranges in color between green and purple. Its seeds are medium-sized and are tightly packed together with the pulp. It's grown especially in California and Puerto Rico.

Hickson

It has an oval shape, is medium to small, and has slightly rough, thick, brittle skin, with pulp regular to good in quality, with 8% to 10% oil content. With a small, tight seed.

Russell

A type of avocado typical of Florida. It has a long shape and excellent pulp. It's a species fairly well-adapted to tropical climates and doesn't tolerate excessive cold. It produces a moderate yield.

Sharwill

The most important hybrid in Hawaii's production. Oval, medium-sized, with rough, thin skin; delicious greenish-yellow pulp, with 15% to 26% oil content and small seeds.

Susan

Medium in size, round, with an average weight of 8.8 oz (250 gr); smooth skin that peels off easily. Pale, cream-colored pulp with a delicate flavor; big, loose seed: the cover sticks to the seed.

Taylor

Pear-shaped, sometimes with a small or medium neck. Its skin is fairly thin, rough with small yellow dots. Excellent, tasty pulp, with 12% to 17% oil content and medium seeds, firm texture.

Trapp

Medium to large, round, golden yellow to green pulp, very close to the skin. Excellent in quality, but with a low oil content (3% to 6%). The large seed is loose in the cavity.

Zutano

Mexican-Guatemalan hybrid, pear-shaped, medium to small in size. The skin is pale green, very delicate, and leather. It has watery pulp, with 15% to 22% oil content, and a medium seed. It's cultivated in California and Australia.

111

OTHER SPECIES

ALPHA ANAHEIM
ASHIKAWA BEARDSLEY
BENIK BESHORE BONITA
CHRIS KELLY COBAIN COCKTAIL
FUERTE COLLIN 33 COOPER LATE
DAILY II DICKINSON DUKE
EDRANOL ESTHER FUJIKAWA
FUKUMITSU GANTER GOTTFRIED
GREEN GOLD HALL HAMACHI
HASHIMOTO HAYES HAZZARD HERMAN
HICKSON HULUMANU ILLIALU INFANTE
ITZAMNA IXTAPAN J-70 KAKAZU JAN BOYCE
JEANETTE JOHNSON KELLUM KANEKO
KAHALU´U KAMPONG LITTLE KADO LYON
KOSEL LEAL LINDA MASAMI MR.T
MALAMA MACARTHUR NARANJO NIMLIOH
MIT 13 MURASHIGE OHATA OTA
NISHIKAWA NORTHROP PRINCIPE
PANKAY PAPAIKO POLLOCK SAN MIQUEL
RODRIGUES RUCHLE RYAN SERPA
PURPLE SCHATTAUER SEMIL 34 SHIRAI
SCHMIDT SHARPLESS SHEPARD TAFT
SIMMONDS SOLANO SPINKS THOMPSON
TAMASHIRO TONNAGE YAMAGATA
TORRES TRINIDAD WAGNER
YAMANE WALDIN
WINSLOW

PRODIGAL CHILDREN

Among the many Hass avocado hybrids that have reached markets, these have the potential to steal the number one spot.

Carmen Hass
Identical to the Hass in appearance: pear-shaped, dark green on the tree, but it turns purple to black when ripe. The skin is medium to thick, with a rough texture. The seed is medium, with 66%–70% pulp of excellent quality, with a nutty flavor.

Gama 4021 y 4022
Variety from Chile; its ripening process is much like that of the Hass. It has similar yields and highly interesting quality, with a slightly larger seed than its predecessor.

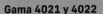

Gwen
It's another subspecies from California that resembles the Reed. It's round and more voluminous than the Hass. It has thick, rough green skin that doesn't blacken when ripe and is easy to peel. It has a high oil content, is creamy and very soft. The seed ranges from small to medium.

Lamp Hass
A common Hass variety, very large and round, with very dark skin that darkens as it ripens. It has lots of pulp with a very creamy consistency. It has a nutty flavor and small seed. It was designed to resist high temperatures, winds, and saline stress.

Gem
The grandson of Gwen and great-grandson of the Hass, it's one of the standard varieties of the California industry. It has all the characteristics of the Hass: creamy, almondy pulp, dark skin that turns pebbly when ripe. It's rounder and has an attractive outer appearance. It peels easily, almost like a banana.

↑ Atlixco Volcano.

How Cool, the Father Avocado!

The history of the Father, or Fuerte avocado, tells of the journey of a tree from Puebla to California. In 1911 Carlos Smith, a worker at the West Indian Gardens nursery in Altadena, arrived in Atlixco (Puebla, Mexico) on a mission: to find avocados of superb quality and the trees that produced them. He cut the best roots, numbered, labelled, and classified them, then sent them to California. However, most didn't adapt to the soil and the climate of California . . . except for sample number fifteen, which not only thrived, but managed to survive the great frost of 1913.

For its strength, resistance, and vigor, it was called the "Fuerte (strong) avocado.," as it is known in many places in Mexico. In thanks for this marvelous specimen, ten years later, the California Avocado Association planted a tree that they called the son of the Fuerte Avocado" in Atlixco.

Although the original tree died after contracting the disease known as "avocado sadness," it was replaced by another of the same species to honor its importance in the industrial and farming sector in Mexico and the United States. Some 110 years after the boom and decline of this new avocado species, production and consumption of its cultivation and commercialization was forgotten, due to its short shelf-life.

↖ The Fuerte variety is also known as the Padre (father) avocado.

113

NUTRITION'S CURE-ALL

People all over the world have written about the avocado's health properties, from Mexico to China. It's celebrated for its "good" fat content, protein, and caloric value. In this section, we'll take a closer look at the nutritional properties of avocados and demystify its superfood hype.

↖ All avocados into the water!

What's Good About Them?

Studies demonstrate that avocado consumption is associated with a high-nutrient diet, which implies lower risk for metabolic syndrome: high blood pressure and blood sugar, and abnormal cholesterol levels. The pulp, seed, and peel are rich in biocomponents, like vitamins, proteins, fiber, acids, and soluble fats.

Fiber

The avocado is rich in two types of fiber: soluble and insoluble. Roughly 30 percent is soluble, while 70 percent is insoluble.

Soluble fiber acts like a prebiotic, feeding the "good" bacteria of the intestine—playing a key role in the body's optimal functioning—helping stabilize blood glucose levels and preserve cardiovascular health.

Insoluble fiber improves the intestinal tract, which helps prevent constipation. At the same time, fiber-rich foods increase the feeling of satiety, so you feel full longer.

Half an avocado a day (about 3.5 oz or 100 gr of pulp) provides 27 percent of the daily recommended fiber intake. So, eating a 7 oz (200 g) avocado gives you half the fiber you need per day. That's not bad for a food you don't even have to cook.

Natural Antioxidants

Its green color denotes high antioxidant levels, mainly lutein and zeaxanthin, which help prevent cellular damage by slowing down natural oxidation. It also contains a sterol compound that keeps healthy cholesterol levels in check.

Good Fat, Bad Fat

Fat got a bad rap in the 1950s from studies that claimed saturated fat consumption implied a higher risk of heart disease. Although nowadays nutritional guides recommended moderate fat consumption, cardiovascular diseases continue to be the number one cause of death. However, fats are essential for daily nutrition and for our bodies to function properly.

A surprising piece of information is that the brain is composed of almost 60 percent fat and the body needs fat to regulate body temperature, produce hormones, protect vital organs, maintain energy reserves, and metabolize vitamins. But the right amounts in a balanced diet are important, because 0.035 oz (1 g) of fat provides 9 calories, while the same amount of proteins and carbohydrates provide 4 calories.

There's talk of "good fats" (unsaturated) and "bad fats" (saturated and trans fats). However, all foots rich in fatty acids contain a combination of both; therefore, it's essential to know the foods rich in beneficial fats to consume them more frequently.

The avocado is rich in fat, but the good kind: more than 80 percent of its fats are unsaturated, mostly monounsaturated fatty acids. According to the American Heart Association, this type of fat can lower LDL cholesterol levels, so-called "bad" cholesterol, and raise HDL or "good" cholesterol, which minimizes the risk of heart disease and stroke. Avocado oil is rich in oleic acid (omega-9), similar to olive oil. Avocado oils are recommended for diabetics because they don't substantially modify glycemic index. Also, they are highly resistant to oxidation from heat. That's why avocado oil can be a healthier option for cooking than other commonly used oils, like sunflower or industrial butters.

> **A surprising fact is that our brains are almost 60 percent fat, which our bodies need to regulate body temperature, produce hormones, and protect vital organs.**

We Cook with Good Oil Here

Cooking oils are derived from seeds or fruit. They're composed of saturated, monounsaturated, and polyunsaturated fats, which are classified depending on the type of fatty acid they contain and their organoleptic characteristics (smell, flavor, and color). Their caloric content is similar: one teaspoon provides 120 calories (9 kcal/gram).

Avocado oil is special. It contains digestive properties because of its high monounsaturated fatty acids with slightly less polyunsaturated and saturated fatty acids than other oils.

One popular belief holds that the most important factor in choosing cooking oils is the "smoke point" (how high a temperature the oil can tolerate). Avocado oil's smoke point is 520 °F (271 °C), higher than olive oil. But not all avocado oil is equal—it's best to choose virgin, cold-pressed, and unrefined avocado oil because industrialized processing can reduce its quality.

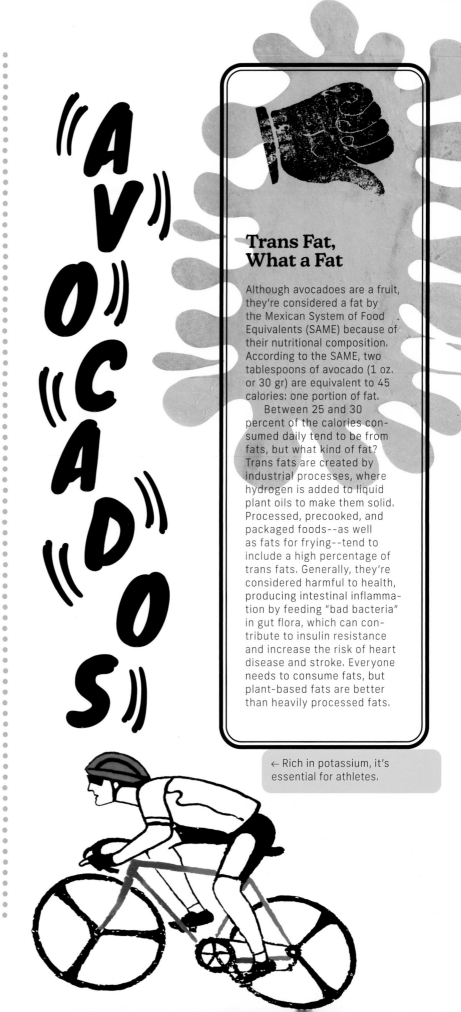

AVOCADOS

Trans Fat, What a Fat

Although avocadoes are a fruit, they're considered a fat by the Mexican System of Food Equivalents (SAME) because of their nutritional composition. According to the SAME, two tablespoons of avocado (1 oz. or 30 gr) are equivalent to 45 calories: one portion of fat.

Between 25 and 30 percent of the calories consumed daily tend to be from fats, but what kind of fat? Trans fats are created by industrial processes, where hydrogen is added to liquid plant oils to make them solid. Processed, precooked, and packaged foods--as well as fats for frying--tend to include a high percentage of trans fats. Generally, they're considered harmful to health, producing intestinal inflammation by feeding "bad bacteria" in gut flora, which can contribute to insulin resistance and increase the risk of heart disease and stroke. Everyone needs to consume fats, but plant-based fats are better than heavily processed fats.

← Rich in potassium, it's essential for athletes.

Rich in Nutrients

The avocado has a high potassium content that helps keep arterial pressure in check and block the adverse effects of salt. It can also prevent the development of kidney stones and loss of bone density. Magnesium relaxes muscles and helps the body focus on the distribution of cellular energy and protein production.

Avocados are rich in soluble and insoluble fiber, which promotes digestion.

Watch Out for the Leaves!
The leaves have been valued since Pre-Columbian times for their anise aroma, and these days because they are nutritionally packed with more protein, fiber, and minerals than the pulp and have less fat. It's been said avocado leaves are toxic; but their centuries-long food and medicinal use would seem to refute this.

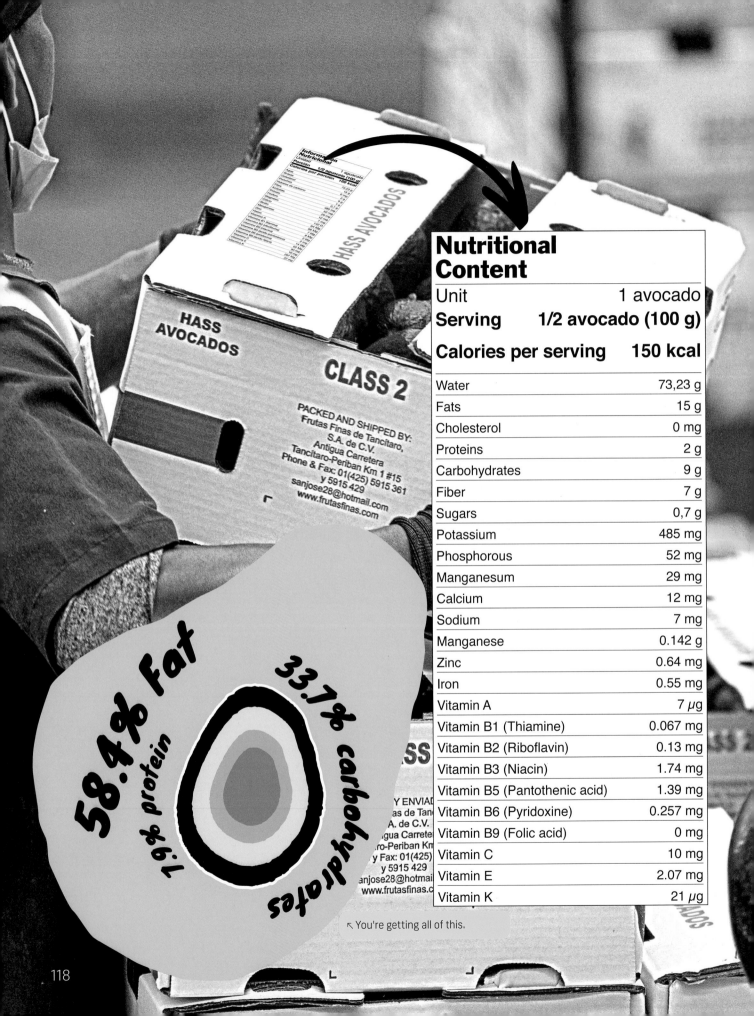

Nutritional Content

Unit	1 avocado
Serving	**1/2 avocado (100 g)**
Calories per serving	**150 kcal**
Water	73,23 g
Fats	15 g
Cholesterol	0 mg
Proteins	2 g
Carbohydrates	9 g
Fiber	7 g
Sugars	0,7 g
Potassium	485 mg
Phosphorous	52 mg
Manganesum	29 mg
Calcium	12 mg
Sodium	7 mg
Manganese	0.142 g
Zinc	0.64 mg
Iron	0.55 mg
Vitamin A	7 µg
Vitamin B1 (Thiamine)	0.067 mg
Vitamin B2 (Riboflavin)	0.13 mg
Vitamin B3 (Niacin)	1.74 mg
Vitamin B5 (Pantothenic acid)	1.39 mg
Vitamin B6 (Pyridoxine)	0.257 mg
Vitamin B9 (Folic acid)	0 mg
Vitamin C	10 mg
Vitamin E	2.07 mg
Vitamin K	21 µg

58.4% Fat

7.9% protein

33.7% carbohydrates

↖ You're getting all of this.

Remedy for All Evils, Avocardio and Avosafe

As early as the sixteenth century, Francisco Hernández, naturalist and court physician to the King of Spain, Philip II, documented the characteristics, uses, and medicinal properties of avocado seeds, attesting to Indigenous knowledge of the fruit by Pre-Columbian cultures. According to Hernández, these cultures used it for frying and also for bathing. Avocados were also considered a sort of aphrodisiac that allegedly increased the amount of semen. The oil from the seeds was used for curing rashes, improving scar formation, and preventing split ends.

But, how much of this is science is folklore? According to a study conducted by the Autonomous University of Zacatecas and the Ministry of Agriculture of Mexico, avocado oil consumption strengthens arteries, facilitates scar formation, controls cholesterol levels in the blood, and promotes skin hydration.

In the Biotechnology Center of the Tec de Monterrey, a group of researchers detected molecules in the avocado seed that can be extracted for a myriad of potential medical benefits. First, the research team developed a product using the seed's acetogenins called Avocardio, designed to work like aspirin. According to the researchers, the anticoagulant properties of the avocado seed's acetogenins thin the blood without side effects. The same team at Tec de Monterrey used this research to solve another problem: food preservation. Their second product, Avosafe, uses the same acetogenin technology to act as a preservative. This product was designed to replace conventional preservatives containing nitrites, which have been linked to cancer. Avosafe is intended to be used as a preservative for cold cuts and cheeses.

The avocado's healing properties have also been studied against one of the leading causes of death of our time: cancer. At the University of Waterloo (Canada) an avocado compound has been identified that might improve the treatment against acute myeloid leukemia (AML): Avocatin B, a fatty cell found only in avocados, attacks one of the key enzymes in cancerous cell growth.

↑ Traditional medicine healer.

Ancestral Secrets: Your Great-Grandmother Knew it All

The avocado's properties as an alternative medicine have been used for centuries—from the bark to the seed—but always consult a doctor before trying these methods for yourself.

Peel
It contains 3.5 percent of an anise-scented essential oil. The peel is used against intestinal worms or parasites in a tea consumed on an empty stomach for several days until the parasites are gone. It has been used as a remedy for warts, an antibiotic, and against dysentery.

Pulp
In the state of Michoacán, the pulp was used as an anti-inflammatory on the knee joint, covered with a hot bandage all night. It is also attributed with analgesic and anti-depressant effects, both as a tea and an oil for topical use.

Seed
It has 1.33 percent of a yellow wax that contains sterol and organic acid. It was used for muscular pain and arthritis, grated or soaked in alcohol. Teas were prepared to fight diarrhea and colds, with the finely ground seed and some crumpled avocado leaves boiled in water, sweetened with honey. It was also used to eliminate dandruff: ground up with castor oil and smeared over the scalp like a conditioner. The boiled seed also served to alleviate cavity pain.

Leaves
In Michoacán, avocado leaves were used in a tea to regulate menstruation, calm a cough from a cold, and prevent water retention. It was also recommended fresh leaves be chewed (without swallowing them) to eliminate mouth ulcers, for the juice has antibiotic effects. They are also good for making poultices for bleeding wounds and are heated and placed on the forehead to provide headache relief.

GREEN BEAUTY

Avocados are full of benefits, not only culinary, but also aesthetically as a coveted beauty product ingredient. Extracting the oil from its pulp yields almost 80 percent oleic acid, a popular ingredient known for its moisturizing and anti-inflammatory benefits.

Nature's gift, the avocado, is packed with Vitamin E, an effective antioxidant that fights off early signs of aging, as well as an emollient that softens and moisturizes skin. It can also provide temporary relief from mild sunburns. It's no wonder the avocado is a favorite natural, at-home beauty solution.

Home Stylist

Avocado oil can enhance the glossiness of your hair and it can make it seem softer. Its abundant plant oils also help strengthen the root and soothe the scalp.

Homemade Leave-In Conditioner

The scalp easily absorbs the fruit's fatty acids and vitamins, improving the hair's appearance. As a natural conditioner, it increases the hair's volume, shine, and sensation of softness. It's a good home remedy for treating split ends, a common problem with long hair overexposed to the sun.

To make this leave-in conditioner at home, you need a ripe avocado and a tablespoon of olive oil (.56 oz/ 16 g). Mash the pulp and mix it with the olive oil until it forms a smooth paste. Apply it to your hair when it's dry, gently massaging it from root to tip. Cover your head with a shower cap or towel and let it sit for 20 minutes. Then rinse your hair with lots of water. You can repeat this up to three times a week.

Anti-Dandruff Remedy

To make this all natural scalp scrub, use a ripe avocado and fresh rosemary, known to promote circulation in the scalp, making your hair grow quicker, and control your scalp's oils. Mash the pulp until smooth. Boil a quart (liter) of water and add the rosemary to make an infusion. When it boils, turn off the heat and let stand until it cools. Add the pulp and mix to form a uniform paste. Gently massage into scalp and let sit for 15 to 20 minutes. Then rinse thoroughly with warm water. You can repeat this process two or three times a week.

Avo All Over!

Rich in fatty acids and antioxidants, the buttery texture of avocado pulp can be used to make an emulsion that gives body to face creams, body milks, shampoos, deodorants, and other beauty and personal hygiene products. Avocado oil helps eliminate dead cells, reduce the appearance of dark circles and eye bags, in addition to moisturizing the skin. You can't ask for more from such a modest fruit.

No Impurities

A citrus-avocado mask is an effective remedy for skin impurities when it's applied to the face and neck. You need one ripe avocado, the juice of half an orange, a tablespoon of lime juice, and a tablespoon of extra virgin olive oil. The lime and orange juice help remove dead cells like a natural peeling, while the avocado and olive oil moisturize and prevent skin from drying out from the astringency of the citrus.

Cut the avocado into small pieces, mash it, and mix it with the other ingredients until it forms a uniform paste. Apply it with your fingers to your face and neck, avoiding the eye area. Leave on for 20 to 25 minutes and remove by rinsing with alternating cold and hot water. At the end, dry your face with a towel and apply a hydrating cream.

Glowing Skin

This recipe can be a moisturizing mask or an appetizing brunch. Finely grate the avocado seed, which is packed with antioxidants, to get two tablespoons of powder. Slice half a banana in rounds, add a teaspoon of honey and another of plain (sugar-free) yogurt, mixing it to form a dense paste, which is applied to the face. Leave it on for 15 minutes, then rinse thoroughly with water to remove all residue. You can repeat this process once every two weeks.

↑ Its cosmetic properties are many and endless.

Ironing out Wrinkles

Avocados can't perform miracles, but they can help smooth your skin. Use the pulp of a ripe avocado and a tablespoon of extra virgin olive oil to form a paste and apply it to your face, letting it set for 30 minutes. Rinse well and once your face is clean, apply a hydrating cream. Repeat once a week.

Goodbye to Undereye Bags

The avocado's antioxidants help diminish inflammation and poor circulation that can produce bags and dark circles. You just need half a ripe avocado and 4 round cucumber slices, mixed in the blender to form a thick cream. Carefully apply it around your eyes, without touching your eyelids and eyelashes, because it can sting. Leave it on for 20 minutes and repeat the steps every morning.

Hydrated Lips

The skin around the lips is extremely delicate. As we age, it can develop small wrinkles and easily become dehydrated, losing elasticity and firmness.

To repair your lips, make a mixture with half a ripe avocado, a round slice of papaya, and a teaspoon of extra virgin olive oil. Apply it to the area around your lips and leave it on for 20 minutes. Then rinse and repeat twice a week.

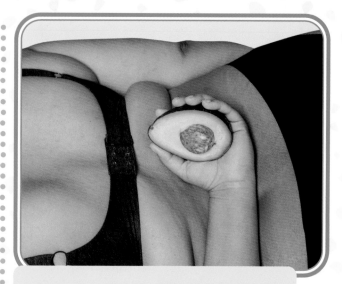

↑ Avocados benefit you inside and out, that's why it's important to always have an avocado on hand.

The Full Body Treatment

Avocados make us feel good inside and out. Omega-3s in avocados and avocado oil stimulate the production of collagen, which can help to diminish the appearance of stretch marks and cellulite, while their biotin content strengthens nails, cuticles, and hair. They also provide vitamin C, which activates blood circulation, and over time, promotes greater skin elasticity.

Minor Scars and Stretch Marks

The appearance of small scars or stretch marks can be diminished with a mixture of one ripe avocado and two tablespoons of almond oil. Prepare a small amount, and apply to the affected areas with a gentle circular massaging motion. Let it work for 30 to 45 minutes, then rinse.

Repeating this three times a week produces better results. The stretch marks will probably not disappear completely, but this massage will improve their appearance, while also promoting circulation and hydration of the skin.

Cellulite

With the pulp of a ripe avocado and two tablespoons of extra virgin olive oil, make an emulsion using a blender or molcajete. Then apply to the affected area with your fingers, massaging in a circular motion with gentle pressure for 15 minutes. At the end, rinse off your entire body with warm or cold water to activate circulation.

Green Manicure and Pedicure

To strengthen nails and soften cuticles, put half a ripe avocado, 10 drops of almond oil, 10 drops of avocado oil, and 10 drops of clove oil in a bowl. Mix until smooth and apply it with a Q-tip or cotton pad to clean nails. Ease into a spa mood, relax, and leave it on for 20 minutes. Rinse with warm water and repeat the steps once a week and you'll see the difference!

VINTAGE BEAUTY

Founded by François Coty, the father of the modern perfume industry, NYC-based beauty company Coty Inc. revolutionized the cosmetics world by blending artisanal production, elegant packaging, and reasonable prices. Like this avocado beauty milk, it couldn't be sold with more glamour.

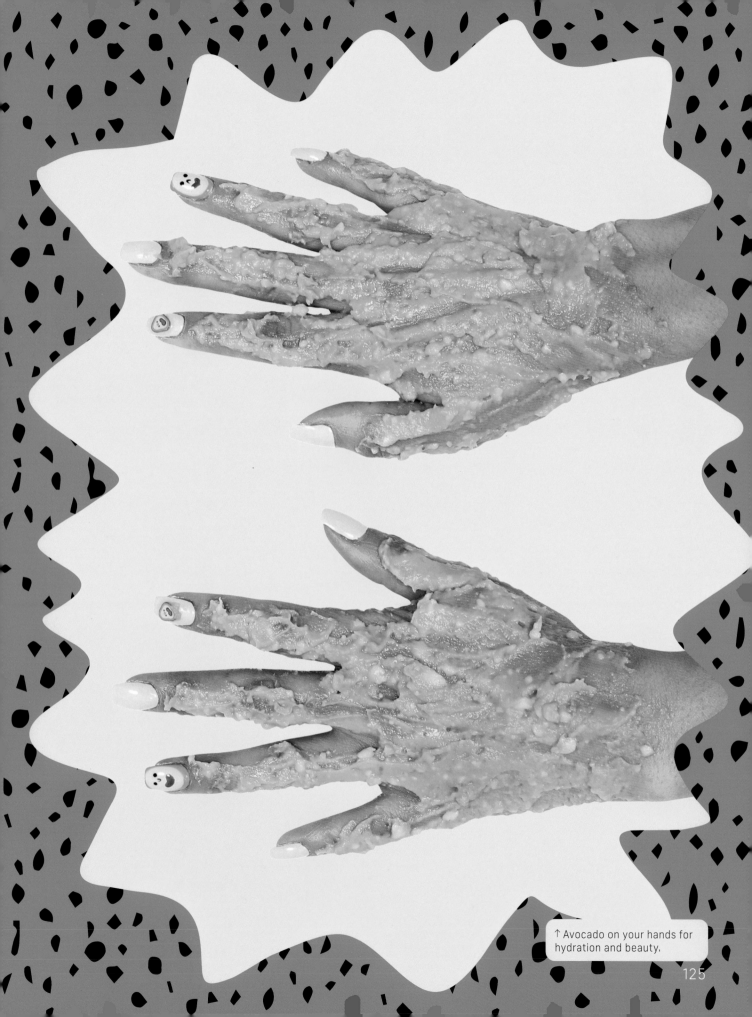

↑ Avocado on your hands for hydration and beauty.

12 o'clock

0 o'clock

3 o'clock

9 o'clock

6 o'clock

KEEP THEM GREEN!

Everyone prefers avocados when they're fresh and green. But why do they turn brown or black so quickly? It's due to the oxidation phenomenon that changes their taste and texture—the fruit's evolutionarily adapted defense mechanism.

Why Do Avocadoes Turn Brown?

This is a natural enzymatic process that protects the genetic material of most avocado species. It's like the rusty armor of a wandering knight—turning brown as it oxidizes. Oxygen activates an enzyme—polyphenol oxidase (PPO)—that alters the fruit's molecular structure making quinones: compounds that absorb radiation and produce dark tones.

However, this chemical phenomenon isn't the same as decomposition, spoilage, or rot. Although this brownish hue might not be the most appealing, quinones are effective microbicides that make proteins insoluble, therefore maintaining the pulp's rich nutrients.

That's why if an avocado turns black, it doesn't mean you have to toss it. Instead, it's part of the avocado's natural protection.

The Avocado Time Machine

In 2017, the Australian company Naturo Technologies launched an ingenious industrial machine called the Avocado Time Machine. It deactivates the enzyme that causes the pulp to oxidize, keeping the fresh for days. The company has kept the biochemical process of its invention secret and has patented two models of the antioxidant machine that can process 550 pounds (250 kg) and 1,102 pounds (500 kg) per hour, respectively.

Unfortunately, this industrial machine can't be installed in the kitchen of a normal home. So, there are other more affordable and portable inventions on the market to prevent the fruit from quickly turning brown. For example, silicon lids that "hug" the fruit, prevent the pulp from coming in contact with air. Silicon is a harmless polymer used extensively in pharmaceutical and food industries. It's flexible and nonstick and withstands temperatures between -76 °F (-60 °C) and 500 °F (260 °C) and can be used in microwaves, ovens, and refrigerators.

All the advice for extending the life of avocados at home has its pros and cons.

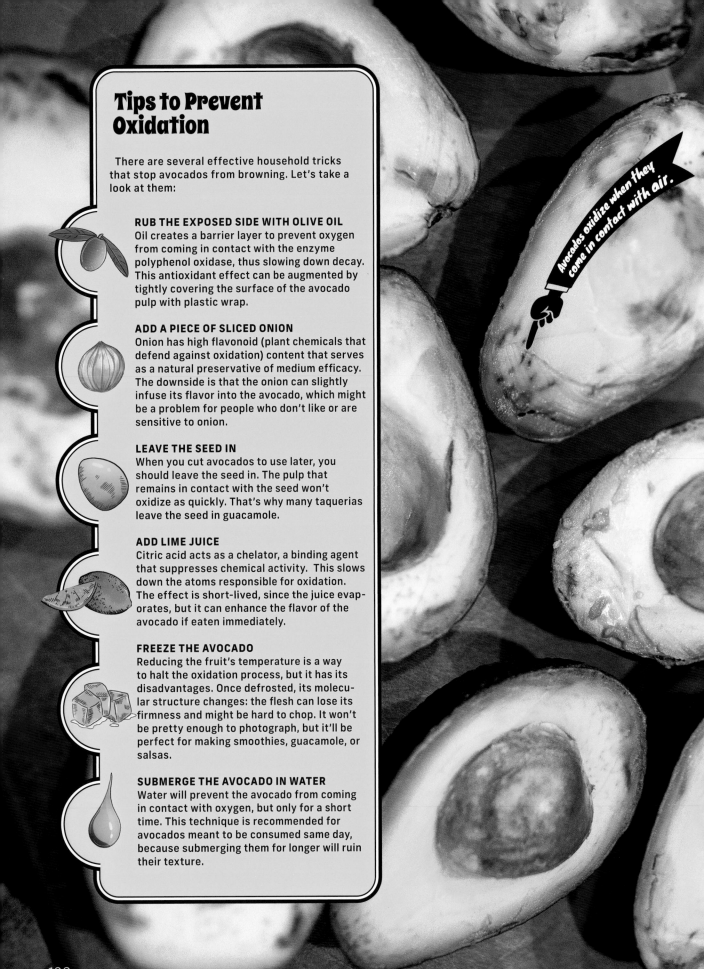

Tips to Prevent Oxidation

There are several effective household tricks that stop avocados from browning. Let's take a look at them:

RUB THE EXPOSED SIDE WITH OLIVE OIL
Oil creates a barrier layer to prevent oxygen from coming in contact with the enzyme polyphenol oxidase, thus slowing down decay. This antioxidant effect can be augmented by tightly covering the surface of the avocado pulp with plastic wrap.

ADD A PIECE OF SLICED ONION
Onion has high flavonoid (plant chemicals that defend against oxidation) content that serves as a natural preservative of medium efficacy. The downside is that the onion can slightly infuse its flavor into the avocado, which might be a problem for people who don't like or are sensitive to onion.

LEAVE THE SEED IN
When you cut avocados to use later, you should leave the seed in. The pulp that remains in contact with the seed won't oxidize as quickly. That's why many taquerias leave the seed in guacamole.

ADD LIME JUICE
Citric acid acts as a chelator, a binding agent that suppresses chemical activity. This slows down the atoms responsible for oxidation. The effect is short-lived, since the juice evaporates, but it can enhance the flavor of the avocado if eaten immediately.

FREEZE THE AVOCADO
Reducing the fruit's temperature is a way to halt the oxidation process, but it has its disadvantages. Once defrosted, its molecular structure changes: the flesh can lose its firmness and might be hard to chop. It won't be pretty enough to photograph, but it'll be perfect for making smoothies, guacamole, or salsas.

SUBMERGE THE AVOCADO IN WATER
Water will prevent the avocado from coming in contact with oxygen, but only for a short time. This technique is recommended for avocados meant to be consumed same day, because submerging them for longer will ruin their texture.

Avocados oxidize when they come in contact with air.

Because all avocados are unique and different, lids of various sizes are needed to adapt to the avocado's changing form. A solution has been devised by the Faberware company, which created a package containing a series of lids that can be stored like Russian nesting dolls, one fitting into the next. An ingenious, practical, and space-saving solution.

> It's a fruit that would never win a beauty contest, but it has won the heart of much of the world, conquering the most discerning palates.

Tried and True Results

In 2012, *HuffPost* conducted a home experiment to test the three most popular methods for preventing avocados from browning. For twenty-four hours, testers documented the behavior of four avocado halves: one without any manipulation as the control, another with the seed left in, a third with lime juice, and the last one, submerged in water.

The winner was the fruit with the seed: the worst was submerging it in water. But none of them kept the fresh green color intact.

In light of these results, it's clear that nothing can totally prevent avocados from turning brown. They should be eaten as soon as possible, shared, spread, or made into a beauty mask for face or hair. They're living proof of carpe diem: enjoy them while you can.

Houston, We Have a Superfood

In order to share the deliciousness of avocados with the colder regions of the globe, a company based in Uruapan (Michoacán) created an alternative called Avodehy.

Michoacán avocados are lyophilized (dehydrated, in powder or flakes, like astronaut food) that can travel to the other side of the world without losing their essential properties. In this way, they can be rehydrated with water or milk in their places of destination, whether Siberia, Alaska, or Greenland.

GENUINE OR IMITATION?

The huge global demand for avocados has not gone unnoticed by executives in the food and cosmetic industries, and plenty of companies have tried to cash in on a piece of this generous fruit.

All that Glitters Is Not Gold

Fast-food chains don't want to miss out on the avocado boom, and they've added it to their menus in all possible ways. Between 2016 and 2018, sales of foods packaged with avocado oil rose 31 percent in the United States, carving out a space between butters and other more traditional oils, such as olive and sunflower.

In the personal hygiene and cosmetic industry, avocados are becoming an essential element. On the shelves of any pharmacy in the world, we can find avocados in solid deodorants, body lotions, oils for all skin types, dry hand creams, hair masks, shampoos . . . There are even oils that promise to prolong erections like a natural Viagra.

But, when we check the product's list of ingredients that feature avocados on their labels, it's often surprising to find that avocado isn't even mentioned in the composition, nor is the percentage of its oils specified.

Fraudulent Labels

This lack of transparency by manufacturers has prompted high-profile scandals that have raised consumers' suspicions. In March 2021, a lawsuit was filed against a pet food company that claimed to contain a high percentage of minerals and vitamins from avocados. This wasn't really the case at all. The plaintiffs alleged that the formula contained scant amounts, far from the 100 percent claimed by the maker. That's not all: the company emphasized that their avocados came from California, information that was important because that state has strict regulations on pesticide and preservative use.

To make matters worse, according to the Pet Poison Helpline, avocados are a food that can produce mild intoxication in dogs and cats, due to the presence of persin, a toxin in the fruit's peel and seed. Although it's not a poisonous toxin, some dogs and cats are particularly sensitive to the avocado's components, which could trigger allergic reactions. Thus, avocados shouldn't be promoted as a food for all pets, given its potential side effects.

The Healthy Label is a Catchall

Research conducted by the University of California at Davis determined that 82 percent of the avocado oil samples in the United States were rancid before their expiration date or had been adulterated with other types of oil. In three of the study's samples, "extra virgin" avocado oil was actually 100 percent soy oil. The high demand for this product gave rise to

i'm the real thing!!!

Cases of product-related fraud that claim to contain avocado among their ingredients have prompted major distrust among consumers.

oil. And, as we know, refined oils, as well as processed and precooked products are toxic for our health for their high trans fat content (i.e., "bad" cholesterol).

However, many shopkeepers keep turning to the avocado's image in their products to imply that "they're healthy," despite doubts over their oil sources and quality. This ethical misconduct drew the scrutiny of the US Food and Drug Administration, which lacks regulatory standards for avocados as a product only recently introduced into American food culture. In contrast, products like peanut butter are strictly regulated; they must include at least 90 percent of the product to be sold. If they don't, the manufacturer will face strong backlash from consumers and the authorities.

Not Everything Is Fake Green

Even though there's lot of fraud in this sector, there are also products that offer exactly what they promise . . . and more. In the beauty sector, there are creams produced for personal care that contain decent amounts of avocado oils and nutrients. In addition, some brands and makers are ethically committed to purchasing fruit from responsible, sustainable farming projects. This trend toward fair trade is gaining traction, not only for the quality of an ecofriendly product, but also for supporting workers and small producers. In developing countries, the support of foreign enterprises with high export volumes makes it possible for workers to sell their products at true market value. Thus, the income generated by avocado production in small settlements benefit the community and domestic producers.

unscrupulous businesses taking advantage of consumers' trust, trying to pull the wool over their eyes.

There are many documented cases of such abuses in different countries. For instance, a Spanish company promoted a "light avocado." It claimed it was a supposedly low-fat natural variety and a rarity "exclusively cultivated for them." What is true is that it was a run-of-the-mill avocado from Florida.

This was also the case of some fairly well-known salsa brands, which were exposed when it was revealed that the product's green color wasn't a natural component of the avocado, instead it was an artificial dye. In fact, avocado wasn't even an ingredient. This controversy led to the discovery that other companies were also employing this fraudulent practice. They were not only lying about the ingredients, but were also claiming that their mayonnaises with avocado oil offered a balance of health and taste. However, of the .35 oz (10 gr) of fat in the product, 2 percent was from avocado and the remaining 98 percent from refined coconut

A Refreshing Ice-Cold Avocado Beer!

Although they don't taste like avocado, there are beers containing it. And we don't just mean the pulp, but also the leaves, which intensify its aroma. In Australia, beer is virtually the national beverage, and the avocado one of its preferred foods. It's calculated that each person in that country consumes an average of 8.8 pounds (4 kg) per year (Avocados in Australia Ltd.). In 2021, this love for beer and avocados led to the collaboration between Australian Avocados and the beer producers Grassy Knoll Brewing, specializing in limited edition beverages. The result was the Aussie Avo Cream Ale. It's an original beer made from Australian avocadoes with a hint of lemon.

Beer with avocado isn't new, nor did the Australians create it. Since 2012, Angel City Brewery has made a limited edition of Avocado Ale, a golden Kölsch-style beer prepared with avocados and a touch of honey, lemon, and cilantro.

Mexico couldn't fall behind when it comes to beer. The Tapatía brewery produces some 500 cases of Avocato beer, which are mostly exported to the United States, Japan, China, Canada, and Ukraine. In Guadalajara, the Dark Lord Brewery makes its own version of Blond Ale with 10% Hass avocado, transforming the fruit's fatty acids into sugar.

And, of course, in the avocado capital of the world, Michoacán, in Uruapan to be exact, there's Gratissima, The Avocado House, a restaurant established in 2017, dedicated to putting this fruit to best use in all ways possible. Gratissima, in collaboration with Cupatitzio Brewery, offers a complete line of avo-beers in Ale, Pale Ale, Blond Ale, and Kölsch styles, even avo-mead.

It's worth going to Uruapan just to taste them.

MUCH MORE THAN PULP

· ·

Nowadays, avocados have so many different and surprising uses—each part can be used in a myriad of ways.

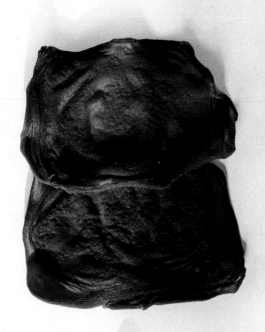

↖ Artist María Elena Pombo creates objects from *Persea americana* seeds. Besides extracting dyes to color clothing, she makes clay, leather, and even glass. This image shows the different tonalities of dyes she gets from the seed.

Fabric Dye... and it isn't Green

Using avocado seed dye on textiles isn't anything new. Pre-Columbian cultures knew that washing and boiling avocado seeds in plenty of water produced a natural dye, like the tannins in red wine, that could range from pink to red. The avocado's skin also serves as a natural dye, offering tones of purple or black.

Jennifer Gómez Menjívar, associate professor of Latin American Studies at the University of Minnesota, explained in an article in *The New York Times* that the Kuna community in Panama has long been using avocado seed dye to color their textiles. And further south, in the Andean region, archaeological remains attributed to Quechua groups confirm the seed was also used to pigment llama and alpaca wool.

Processing avocado seeds produces pink dyes used in the textile industry.

María Elena Pombo, a Venezuelan textile designer living in New York City, has ample experience applying this avocado seed alchemy to her work. She's crafted two collections, Ahvacatl and Rosa Terráqueo, with natural dyes. Boiling avocado seeds loosens the outer seedcoat—the endocarp—that colors the mixture in shades from ruby to pink. The result of these tones depends on the fruit varieties, and the water's mineral content, pH, and degree of purity. María Elena Pombo is also involved in La Rentrada project, which gives avocado seeds other industrial uses, like the production of adobe bricks, plastic substitutes, and dyes for leather and glass.

The American fast casual chain, Chipotle Mexican Grill, has also developed an inspiring sustainability project. Since guacamole is one of its star condiments,

↑ When avocado seeds are boiled, they release a colored dye ranging from ruby red to pink.

Chipotle requires massive amounts of avocados: in just one of their restaurants, they use five crates of avocados per day, more than 44,000 pounds (20,000 kg) a year. So, in 2020, the chain looked for a way to put the 300 million seeds discarded annually to good use. Experts knowledgeable about using these seeds as a natural dye created a limited-edition clothing line made from organic cotton dyed with avocado seeds: Chipotle Goods. According to Chipotle, each item from the "avocado dyed collection" uses five avocado seeds to produce that 100 percent natural unique pink tone.

↑ Chipotle Goods has a clothing line dyed with avocado seed.

THE SEEDS' LEGACY: A CONSUMMATE ART

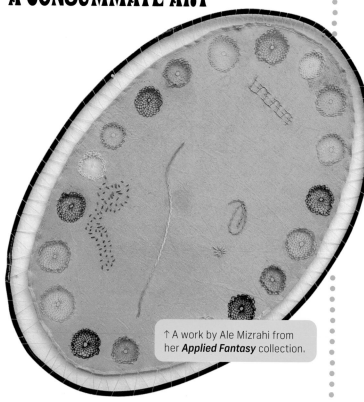

↑ A work by Ale Mizrahi from her *Applied Fantasy* collection.

Capture It on Canvas

Ale Mizrahi, an Argentine artist, participated in the collective exhibition, *Inside There's Nothing More than a Home*, on display in the Museum of Modern Art in Buenos Aires (MAMBA) with her *Applied Fantasy* collection. It consisted of canvases dyed with palta (avocado) seeds affixed to a stretcher, on which she rendered images from nature: flowers, bird silhouettes, nets catching empty space, lines going nowhere.

The process of her craft demands patience: waiting for the right color to materialize after days of boiling, drying, and cooling fabrics. From an imperceptible yellow emerges pink and with some luck, green colors that deepen with time. Then the artist soaks the cloth in starch, and once dried, it is stretched and heated with red-hot metal that singes and hardens the starch.

A Seed Jewel

The avocado isn't only good for dyeing. Some artisans and visual artists treat it like wood or ceramic. Ossaterra is a concept established in 2015 by French master craftsman Luc Varnier and his Mexican wife, Viridiana. In their work, avocado seeds and silver converge in pieces of jewelry that come with a lifetime guarantee. Each piece is a unique, worked avocado seed mosaic set in a handcrafted Mexican silver frame. Each fragment of avocado seed has a distinctive essence, so the process of creating these miniature mosaics is extremely laborious. It requires months of drying the seed, cutting, and meticulously filing, which must be done to perfection to assemble each one. Each creation is numbered and identified with a certificate of authenticity.

Each piece of jewelry is backed by an ethical, ecological, sustainable project. As Luc Varnier puts it: "In our creation and marketing processes, we prioritize environmentally friendly products and services, working with small Mexican companies and making a donation to the Rayuela Foundation (in the state of Morelos) that introduces Mexican children to arts, crafts, and sustainable disciplines like organic farming."

Trademarker Avocado

Luxury brands should take a look at the work of Mexican artist Balam Bartolomé. In his exhibition *Mexímoron* (2018), he set out to forge a dialogue between historical museum objects and his work in order to prompt a philosophical discussion. Avocados and their seeds are among his favorite materials, manipulated until they are almost unrecognizable, transformed into "seasonal ritual objects" or coins with axioms like: "Liberty-not-freedom."

In the Prime of Life

The prolonged and abundant blossoming of avocado trees permits the production of an exotic avocado flower honey. It's a dark honey with a subtle aroma and sweet flavor, with light acidic and salty notes. In some countries, it's recommended as a dietetic energizer and diuretic that helps cleanse the body. It's also considered a good food supplement for athletes, because it can prevent anemia and decrease hypertension. It's also used as a weight loss supplement for its high omega-3 fatty acid, iron, and fructose content. Its gastronomic impact is so great it's beginning to be called "the black gold of Mexican honeys."

RECYCLE IT

It's estimated that for every million tons of avocado that are harvested, half a million tons of seed and peel waste is produced. That's why different industries and countries have begun to put this waste to use on a massive scale. For instance, in Kenya, where the Fuerte avocado variety represents more than 80 percent of its production, the peel serves as a nutritional supplement for cattle. Because the avocado peel is rich in oils and minerals, cattle ranchers have substantially reduced the cost of feeding their animals.

A similar initiative has also been implemented in Mexico. Javier Germán Rodríguez Carpena, researcher at the Nayarit Center of Innovation and Technology Transfer (Cenit2), created a diet for pigs with avocado waste. This diet produced pork with a higher nutritional content and longer shelf life. "Nayarit, Mexico's fourth biggest avocado producer channels most of the crop for human consumption. But at least 10 percent is waste," notes Rodríguez Carpena.

The aim is to take advantage of those avocados that retain all their properties, but don't meet market standards because of certain "physical" defects. These can be purchased at a substantially discounted price. Processed in the laboratory, this fruit is turned into a nutrient paste that substitutes 30 percent of the protein in the conventional pig diet.

↑ To feed pigs, you have to give them the best.

Don't Throw Away the Peel

Avocado waste is being successfully used as compost or natural fertilizer. Researchers in Genetic Engineering and Synthetic Biology at the Center for Research and Advanced Studies at the IPN (Cinvestav) have explored this in experimental fields in Mexico, Hawaii, Venezuela, and Florida. Their aim is to create biomass by feeding organic avocado and banana peel waste to the bacteria E. coli, because both are rich in carbohydrates, potassium, magnesium, and B vitamins, to produce fertilizers and biofuel.

Scott Munguía—a chemical engineer from Guadalajara—conducted a university project with avocado seeds to explore the possibility of turning them into bioplastic. This led to his company Biofase, which employs a technology that extracts 60 percent of the biopolymer from the avocado seed, which is combined with 50 percent of synthetic organic compounds to produce biodegradable disposable utensils: cups, bottles,

↑ The peel and seeds can be given a new use.

Based on 100 percent Mexican technology: avocado seeds can be turned into bioplastic for cups, bottles, straws, and much more.

dishes, food containers, sheets, straws, and even ecofriendly pipes. These products are exported to the US, Spain, the UK, Belgium, Colombia, Scandinavia, and South Korea.

Another university researcher, Pamela Alexandra Márquez, in the Chemistry Department at the National Autonomous University of Mexico (UNAM), developed a bioplastic from avocado peel extract as an alternative to plastic wrap. She combined an organic cellulose derivative with avocado peel compounds, which are highly useful as fresh fruit containers for their antioxidant, antifungal, and antibacterial properties.

AN INTERNET IDOL

No need to poke around international markets to find every possible avocado variety. Just get on Instagram.

The #aguacate hashtag is home to more than a million posts and #avocado features more than 12.7 million, mostly photos and videos of fans showing how happy they are to be near avocados. They're labeled with a sweeping variety of names that tell you what's going on with avocado lovers: #healthy, #bio, #organic, #local, #sustainable, #veganlove, #glutenfree . . .

If you want to talk avocado media, check out two of the most sensational hashtags: #avoart and #avocadotoast. This latter features nearly 2 million posts, the numbers growing every day.

Food Art: To Eat or Not to Eat?

Instagram has become a showcase for every variety of food art, an aesthetic discipline that's been a trend for many years. Instead of carving into more traditional forms like wood or marble, food art uses fruits and vegetables to create whimsical,

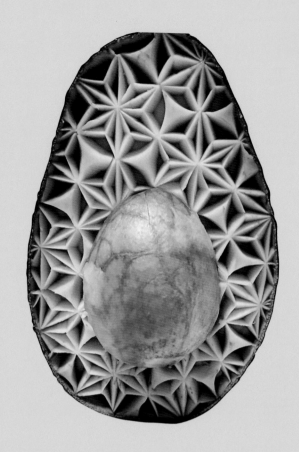

often fantastic forms. Avocado art is a popular type of food art, leading with their signature hashtag (#avoart), whose ranks include some of the world's most famous and admired artists.

In the work of Japanese chef and food artist Takehiro Kishimoto (Instagram: @gakugakugakugakugaku1), the creator synthesizes his love for cooking and his penchant for sculpture. Using an ancient Thai technique that melds with Japanese mukimono art, Takehiro creates avocado sensations, recreating the flavor of the four seasons with designs in sculptural relief and fantastic geometric patterns.

← The Japanese art of *mukimono* is to carve decorative designs into fruit and vegetables as garnishes.

Along those lines, Italian artist Daniele Barresi (@danielebarresi_artist) does delicate sculpture in the avocado's buttery texture in mind-boggling detail. His artwork—recognized worldwide—calls up Baroque, Venetian and French goldsmithing in forms inspired by animals and other natural shapes. With this extraordinary carving, the sculptor combines his two greatest passions: art and food.

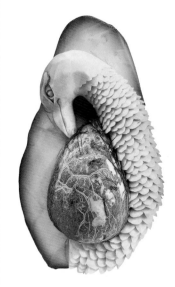

↖ Sculptures by Italian artist Daniele Barresi have a Baroque feel.

142

Jan Campbell, a miniaturist sculptor at Avocado Stone Faces (@avocadostonefaces), carves faces and characters, inspired by Irish and Scandinavian mythology, on avocado pits. He applies silverplate as a final, luxurious touch.

An Arm and a Leg

German artist Tim Bengel sought to immortalize our chic fruit by creating a solid-gold avocado bagel sandwich. It's formed of twenty-seven parts weighing 12 pounds of 18-carat gold. Just one avocado toast will set you back something like $14,000. With his bagel, the artist seeks to symbolize the dark spirit of our current cultural moment—the uncertainty of the pandemic amidst doomscrolling on catastrophic world events—under the title Who Wants to Live Forever? Christian Rother (Tim's gallerist) declares this avocado bagel has the potential to become an icon of our times. Time may not have a price, but this sculpture definitely does. It was offered for sale at Art Miami 2021, for a cool $2.9 million dollars. Just think of all the avocado toast you could bankroll with that!

↑ The price of this sculpture by Tim Bengel was set at $2.9 million.

→ Jan Campbell.

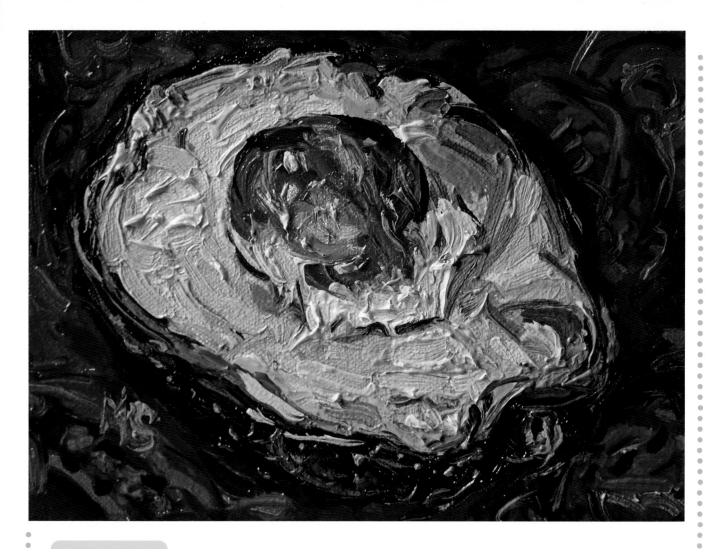

↑ Melissa B. Sarat.

When the subject of art comes up, most people think of painting first. In her downtown Manhattan studios, Melissa B. Sarat (@melissasarat) proposes ripe avocados to celebrate the fruit she reckons a culinary delicacy. At the same time it evokes nature's marvelous freshness.

→ Melissa B. Sarat.

Cooking as the Ninth Art

Caminos y Cocinas (*Roads and Kitchens*) is an interdisciplinary visual arts and anthropology project. The program created an online recipe and oral history archive for Colombia's traditional cuisine in a neighborhood known for its many immigrants. It's sponsored by the Moravia Cultural Development Center, a community center dedicated to the culinary arts where richness and enchantment derive from a melting pot of personalities, customs, colors, and tastes. The project aims to celebrate traditional foods throughout Colombia, with support from local cooks who take pride in their culinary heritage. It's an exhibition showcasing five dishes accompanied by stories of their makers, telling of their origins, life stories, and food traditions. Designing an aesthetic inspired by advertising and graphic design, these five appealing still lifes highlight the starring-dish at center-image, surrounded by the ingredients that make up every recipe. Naturally, avocados are commonly featured.

↖ Cristian Torres, photographer Jefersson Andrés Giraldo, chef Filled *Patacones* (fried plantains).

← Cristian Torres, photographer Nidia Moreno, chef Rice with *Longaniza* (pork sausage).

↓ *Orphanage for Tehuanas*, by Pedro Friedeberg, 1969.

↖ With basic care and a bit of love, any tree thrives.

SOW YOUR OWN AVOCADO SEEDS

Planting and cultivating this fruit is an art, but with some simple tricks anyone can grow their own avocados.

Before Planting

You need to bear in mind some features of the location and external conditions that will promote the tree's optimal growth.

A Good Seed

You need to carefully select the avocado variety you're going to plant. The varieties most resistant to cold have a higher probability of success in temperate regions: the Stewart, Mexicola, and Zutano avocados are highly recommended.

The Substratum

For the avocado plant to grow healthy and strong, the soil must have good water retention and mineral elements with low salt content. A lot of this comes down to the kind of substratum your plant lives in, or the foundation of soil below the surface. Some of the most common substrata in high production crops have a mix of peat moss, coconut fiber, and earthworm castings, which is very rich in nutrients.

The Type of Container

For planting in a pot, choose the widest possible container you can fit into your space. The ideal size is at least 19¾ inches (50 cm) deep, with large holes in the bottom. You can add coarse rocks to the bottom layer to ensure good drainage.

If you plant in a soil substratum, it needs to be a place that gets lots of sunlight most of the day, but it's better if it's not exposed to strong winds or drastic temperature drops.

The Right Temperatures

For trees to flourish, your avocado plant shouldn't be exposed to extremes: either winter frosts or blistering direct sunlight. The minimum temperature should be between 50 to 62.6°F (10 to 17°C), and the maximum temperature should be 82.4 to 91.4°F (28 to 33°C).

To plant avocados indoors, time of year doesn't matter much, because indoors the temperature tends to be relatively constant and controlled.

However, when you plant them outdoors or transplant a small tree, it's best to do so between late spring and early summer, roughly between March and June in the Northern Hemisphere. If it's done in winter, it's likely that the young avocado tree won't survive the low temperatures; and in summer the tree might not be able to absorb enough of the water for its young age and the high temperatures.

HOW TO PLANT IT

Preparing the seed:

1. Remove the seed, wash it completely, and let it air dry.

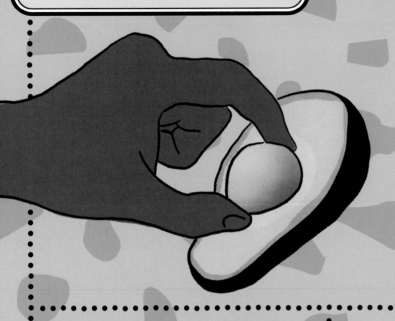

2. Insert three or four toothpicks evenly distributed around the widest part of the seed in a T-shape, slanting slightly upward.

3. Get a container that allows you to set the toothpicks on the rim of the vessel, so the seed is suspended.

4. It's important to make sure the narrower upper part of the seed is on top (where the sprout will grow) and the flat part (where the roots will grow) is at the bottom.

5. Add water to cover the bottom half of the seed.

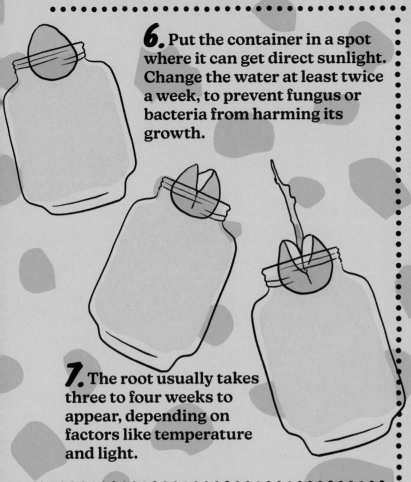

6. Put the container in a spot where it can get direct sunlight. Change the water at least twice a week, to prevent fungus or bacteria from harming its growth.

7. The root usually takes three to four weeks to appear, depending on factors like temperature and light.

8. When the root reaches around 4 inches (10 cm), remove the toothpicks from the seed.

Planting the seed:

1. Make a hole in the substrate that's deep and wide enough for the roots to fit and cover the seed with dirt, gently pressing down the soil around it. Be careful! The seed must be in the same position as in the container: the root side beneath the soil and the upper part above the soil.

2. Put the pot in a place with lots of sunlight, but if the sunlight is very intense, protect it with a bit of mesh for shade. Normally, the first leaves appear a month or a month and a half after planting.

Care and Observations

Water it once or twice a week, until moist but not damp.

To know if it needs more water, check whether the upper soil layer is dry. Insert a toothpick into the pot and if it comes out covered with dirt, it's time to add more water.

Fertilize the substrate in spring and summer because the avocado will need extra support. You can apply a new layer of earthworm castings, an ecological soil enricher. When the tree is about 23 inches (60 cm), you can do the first pruning to encourage growth. Otherwise, the tree will get very tall, which might cause space problems.

It usually takes at least five to six years for avocado trees to mature and produce fruit. After your first harvest, it tends to produce annually. Caveat: trees grown from ordinary seeds usually don't bear fruit; purchased seeds are a better bet.

Here Come the Pests!

Various harmful insects can damage avocado trees in a domestic setting. These bad bugs include:

Thrips

Usually appearing in the spring, they perforate the upper layer of leaves and drink their juice until they dry out. We know they're there when the leaves turn brown.

Red spiders

One of the most common avocado pests, these small reddish arachnids drink the juice and sap from the leaves, which turn brown and can fall off. In cases of serious infestation, spiderwebs can be seen among leaves that the insects climb to get to other branches.

Grain weevils

The larvae of these insects get inside the fruit, boring a tiny path through the pulp to reach the seed that they feed on.

Avocado scab

Disease produced by the Sphaceloma persea fungus, it attacks stalks, leaves, and fruit. Leaves turn a sickly brown, while fruit develops round brown splotches and no longer thrive.

Avocado sadness

A disease caused by parasitic organisms, commonly known as 'avocado sadness' affects the tree's roots, drying out the tall branches and making leaves lose their green color, decreasing their capacity for photosynthesis. The fruit becomes small, and the tree can end up dying.

Shoo, Bugs!

To combat the most common avocado pests in the home, here are some easy ecological remedies you can make at home:

Garlic insecticides

It's an effective remedy against aphids and ants. Let several garlic cloves sit in a container with a quart (liter) of water for twenty-four hours. Then boil the garlic and water on low heat for fifteen minutes. Let it cool and empty it into a spray bottle. Spray the leaves on both sides.

Milk insecticides

This is useful against mites and funguses because the lactic acid acts as a fungicide. To make it, mix half a cup of whey with two to four quarts (liters) of water (depending on the size of the tree) and three and a half cups of wheat flour. Pour it into a spray bottle and apply it all over the plant.

Chili insecticides

Insecticides using spicy products are highly effective against a wide range of pests. Toss six to ten chilies into a blender and add two cups of water. Blend for two minutes and let the mixture six overnight. Then add another cup of water and pour it into a spray bottle and apply.

Tobacco insecticides

They're useful for keeping insects away from plants. Mix the tobacco from three or four cigarettes in half a quart (liter) of water. Let it sit for two days. Filter the mixture, pouring it through a fine sieve, bottle it, and spray it on the plant.

Nettle insecticides

They're useful for keeping insects away from plants. Mix the tobacco from three or four cigarettes in half a quart (liter) of water. Let it sit for two days. Filter the mixture, pouring it through a fine sieve, bottle it, and spray it on the plant.

Tomato-plant insecticides

They're very effective against aphids, caterpillars, and worms because their leaves are rich in alkaloids. Mash the tomato leaves to fill two cups, add two cups of water, and leave them overnight. The next day, add two more cups of water and mix well. Pour into a spray bottle and apply.

Eggshell insecticides

These are useful against snails and some caterpillars. In addition to their high concentration of calcium carbonate, nitrogen, and other nutrients, they increase soil fertility. Crush eggshells until they're pulverized and sprinkle that into the pot around the base of your plants, creating a barrier.

Curiosity Killed the Insect

Paradoxically, the avocado pit is itself an effective sustainable insecticide against common pests, woodlice, and silverleaf whiteflies. It's easy to prepare:

Ingredients for 5 quarts (liters) of insecticide
- A large container
- One avocado seed, dry
- 5 quarts (liters) of water
- A grater.

Instructions
1. Boil two quarts (liters) of water to purify it.
2. Finely grate the avocado seed. Don't use a food processer or electric grater—the mechanism is too powerful and you'll lose vital components of the shavings.
3. Put the seed shavings into a container. Once the water boils, turn off the heat and pour the grated seed into the pot. Let sit overnight.
4. The next morning, strain the extract to eliminate impurities and dilute it in the three remaining quarts (liters) of water. Let it sit twenty-four hours before using.
5. Apply it to the underside of leaves in the afternoon, avoiding the sunniest, hottest hours of the day. This remedy protects plants in the germinating stage when the first leaves are growing.
6. In cases of a major infestation, you can use this insecticide once a week until it's eliminated. Keep the remainder in the fridge or use it all the same day.

→ Many pests can affect the tree.

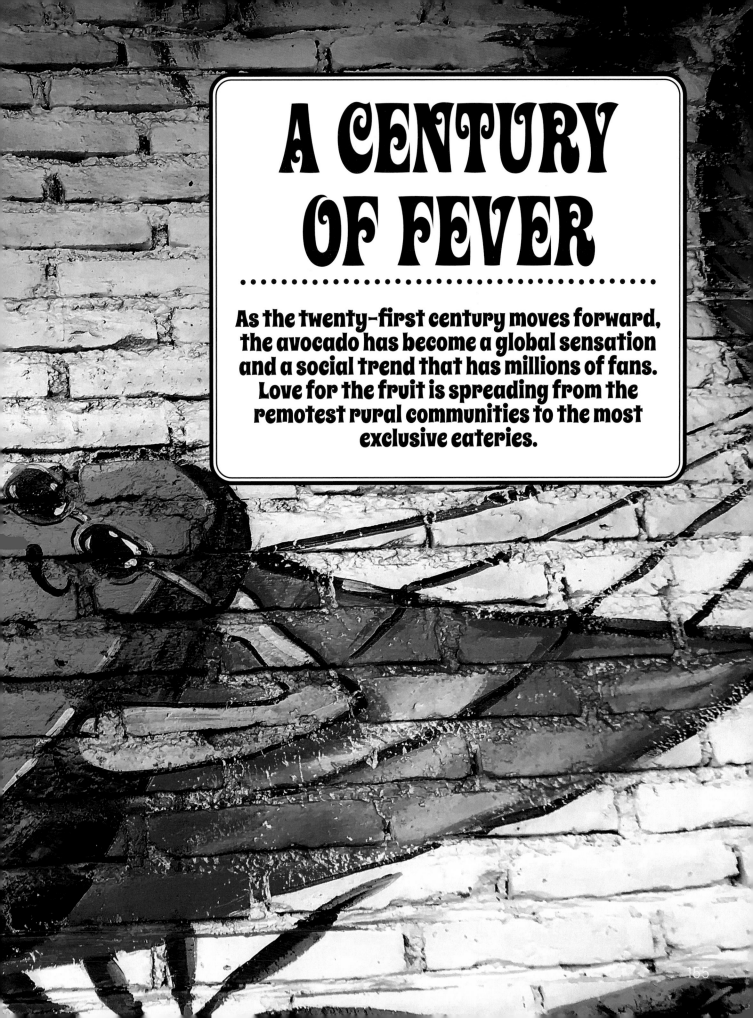

A CENTURY OF FEVER

As the twenty-first century moves forward, the avocado has become a global sensation and a social trend that has millions of fans. Love for the fruit is spreading from the remotest rural communities to the most exclusive eateries.

Personal History: Davocadoguy

Restaurants in New York City are big avocado consumers that need to be supplied daily and promptly. In 2014, Miguel González began to sell avocados to small food venues. He went all over town, personally delivering avocado crates. Word got out that he had the best avocados and the business took off in the blink of an eye. He's now got 120 restaurant clients in New York, from holes-in-the-wall to Michelin-starred celebrity tables. They say he's the biggest secret in the city, and—like every masked hero—he's known by his nickname, "Davocado guy" (i.e., the avocado guy).

Balanced diet fans eat it because it's vegan and you use it to make salads or smoothies rich in vitamins and minerals. There are hundreds of recipes and videos online. Just going as far as *Bon Appétit's* website will give you fifty-four. The official Avocados from Mexico website is home to 250 avocado and sixty recipes just for guacamole.

For some people, the benefits are overhyped by dieticians and Hollywood stars' personal trainers; for others, it's a bona fide super food. It's not hard to get in European capitals, or at a cute brunch spot where they serve avocado toast, which makes for such enviable pictures on Instagram. *Elperiodico.com* (July 2020) humorously commented that in Barcelona, "it's easier to find a menu with avocados than a tourist flat." The global culinary supply is fast becoming avocado, avocado pizza, avocado ice cream, avocado waffles, and even agualatte, i.e., a latte served in the avocado peel that doubles as a disposable cup. Fast and tasty is the word of the day.

Avocados from Mexico . . . in New York?

The number of foods and drinks you can make with avocados is a challenge to chefs' versatility, offering them a world of possibilities. It's curious that the appearance of monothematic avocado restaurants has been largely in Europe and New York. Avobar in London, Avocadoshow in Amsterdam, or the Avocadería in the Big Apple. While this trend popped up in these capitals, nowadays there are restaurants with similar specialties in other US and European cities. A study *Avocados from Mexico* did in 2016 about trends in avocado consumption among 3000 participants revealed that 80 percent of them are willing to pay more if their plate included avocado and fresh ingredients, because they associate that with a higher-quality restaurant.

Mexico is synonymous with avocado, so it would be impossible to think that this wave of monoavocadist restaurants wouldn't go back to the place where it all began. In almost every restaurant in Mexico, at least in

↗ Food gentrification reinvents forms of consumption.

the last third of the twentieth century and the early years of the twenty-first, avocados were eaten as a garnish on the plate or in guacamole to be shared. That is until the gentrification wave began to make its way into kitchens.

What Is Taste Gentrification?

In general terms, gentrification is what we call the progressive displacement of a central, working-class neighborhood to make room for a class with higher buying power that will modernize and revitalize that area.

The notion of "food gentrification" was used for the first time in spring of 2014, in a tweet from blogger Mikki Kendall, who declared that this phenomenon reflects the consequences of the sudden transformation of traditional food from poor communities into the latest fashion. It's a modification in consumer habits that influences health and urban lifestyles.

In the case of the avocado, food gentrification has reinvented the way we consume it. A simple piece of toast with avocado slices named avocado toast sounds sophisticated and adds to its value, attracting new diners that can pay a premium for a "gourmet" dish.

Whether it's a passing marketing trick or a true food trend, what's for sure is that this phenomenon shows we're standing before a fruit whose versatility offers infinite creative possibilities. And while diners continue to enjoy them, and pay for them, we can imagine that avocados will be loved by consumers for a long time to come.

Eccentricities Spread

The avocado as a social and globalized tree has astonishing ramifications at every level of society, since it affects ordinary citizens as well as celebrities on the red carpet.

Oprah Winfrey—the media magnate and timeless influencer of American public opinion—declares she loves avocados so much she's planted her own avocado trees in the land surrounding one of her mansions. Her passion goes further than that. She has declared in numerous interviews that when she travels she takes avocados from her own groves, and the idea that people pay for avocados strikes her as ridiculous . . . could she get through airport security?

Anything to declare?

Oprah's parcel is just a little garden compared to the almost 6 acres (2.5 ha) of avocado cultivation that singer Jason Mraz and his partner have, both avowed vegetarians. Their passion is so intense that before each concert, Jason takes his avocado portion with him, to prepare smoothies that help fine-tune his vocal cords.

Actor Tom Selleck, famous for an '1980s series *Magnum P.I.*, is also on the avocado bandwagon, even if in this case it's a bit curious. He does almost all the work and maintenance in his avocado fields in Ventura, California. He loves seeing the fruit grow and taking care of the trees. He confesses that for him, it's a way to relax and meditate. Paradoxically, he doesn't like the flavor of avocados and doesn't eat them. This doesn't keep him from looking happy when others eat them . . . and pay for them, of course.

Speaking of Eccentricities

In July 2015, on the eve of July 4 celebrations, Miley Cyrus showed the whole world the avocado tattoo on her left forearm, and declared a pledge of devotion: "Dear Avocado, I love you so much." That same year, after her performance at the MTV Music Awards, she handed out avocados to the press instead of making any statements. On her Instagram page she has dozens of avocado-based diets, masks, and beauty routines.

Following the electric current Miley generated, the avocado is becoming the new icon in romantic love, knocking out the now-squeezed-to-death, orange-half metaphor. Visually, it gives you a lot to play with. Half the avocado holds the seed, the other doesn't have any. The perfect symbol for people who are made for one another.

This fruit's cult goes way beyond nutrition, tattoos, or buying avocado themed attire. It's

↑ *Dear avocado, I love you so much.*
-Miley Cyrus

now reached the level of Marian devotion. In Minako, a rural settlement in Uganda, a handful of children insisted they'd seen the Virgin Mary appear atop an avocado tree. As soon as accounts of the apparition started spreading, a crowd occupied the area near the tree, trampling and not maintaining social distance against coronavirus. From the diocese at Arua, they're investigating if the Virgin Mary was real or something the kids made up. Many say the people who approach the tree miraculously feel an immense calm. Perhaps, among the avocado's benefits, we should add "certain mystical effects."

Go to Sleep, Avocado, Go to Sleep

To celebrate World Avocado Day (July 31), the hotel reservations platform Booking.com had an idea to promote a unique lodging: the Avo-Condo, a round dwelling with themed decorations dedicated to the avocado. It accommodates two people, features AC, a living room, and bathroom. There's a welcome basket with amenities made of avocados. It's right on an observation point at Campbell's Cove

Lookout, on Circular Quay in Sydney (Australia) with splendid views of the bay and the city's emblematic opera house. The cost of a stay is one hundred Australian dollars per night. Recommended only for #avofans.

↑ Avocado-shaped trailer, available at Booking.com

Don't eat avocado if you're angry: it can make you sick.

This adage couldn't be further from the truth. After you get angry, you might have an upset stomach from increased acid secretion and adrenaline that gets into your bile duct. So, some people might have indigestion from the bile in their digestive system. Anyone who has frequent temper tantrums will have a tummy ache no matter what they eat: whether avocados, mole sauce, or even chewing gum! They say that eating a *bolillo* (bread roll) can calm stomach acids, but it won't do the same for a hot temper.

For avocados, my avocados.

ALLIGATOR PEAR LOVERS

At the beginning of the twentieth century, avocados were little known in the United States. They were marketed with the dubious moniker "alligator pears," since the texture of avocado peels resembles a reptile's wrinkly green and black skin. The name—that went back to the late seventeenth century—created a resistance among producers, distributors, and consumers—an "alligator pear" was a hard sell. It was time for a rebrand.

Gwyneth Paltrow's Avocado Toast

The guru of healthy diets and perfumed candles suggests a number of recipes for ideal avocado toast. When she included her famous toasts in the cookbook *It's All Good* (2013), it caused a major furor among followers. One of them, an avocado toast with bacon and almond butter, stands out for its originality. This surprising combo has sparked the curiosity of many avocado lovers, who usually concentrate on one main flavor in a recipe, but in this case, sweet and savory come together. And what a delicious idea. The hardest thing about this recipe is toasting the bread!

The Most Eaten Toast

Besides guacamole—the MVP of avocado dishes—avocado toast was the first avo-recipe to win over the world.

In Peru, Colombia, and Israel, avocado toast is a common breakfast for everyone. But Australia is thought to be the hub, at least when it comes to marketing. The story began in 1993, when chef Bill Granger, proprietor of the restaurant Bill's of Sydney, began serving up a quick, cheap avocado toast: grilled bread, avocado slices, a sprinkle of lime, oil, and salt. That was it.

The snack's popularity and consumption exploded when Hollywood movie stars fell in love with it and shouted their devotion to the four winds, their mouths overflowing with breadcrumbs. Today the biggest names in showbiz skip Breakfast at Tiffany's and go straight to their hip brunch spot for their favorite avo-toast.

Jennifer Aniston, star of *Friends* and 1990s It Girl, touted avocado toast in a 2015 Instagram takeover with haircare brand Living Proof—selling us on her diet-friendly avocado toast with tomatoes and poached egg. Actress turned businesswoman Jessica Alba, alongside her friend Lizzy Mathis (of the Cool Mom Co), broadcast a video that showed her

Hugh Jackman ✔
@RealHughJackman

Whomever said that avocado toast is passé hasn't tried THIS version. This has been my personal public service announcement. Good morning.

Traducir Tweet

7:09 a. m. · 31 ene. 2017 · Twitter for iPhone

710 Retweets   **146** Tweets citados   **7.627** Me gusta

What do Salma Hayek, Hugh Jackman, and Miley Cyrus have in common? They all love avocados!

making three avocado toasts: vegetarian with gluten-free bread, another with tomatoes and a pinch of jalapeño (if you put too much "it can ruin your life," she says), and the third one with avocado and poached egg.

Even Hugh Jackman, Wolverine himself, ardently defended the famous breakfast after allegations that it had lost its cool. Jackman uploaded a photo of a mega-avocado toast that included almonds, stewed tomatoes, pomegranate seeds, green onions, and a poached egg. The caption read, "Whomever said that avocado toast is passé hasn't tried THIS version."

An Enchanted Pear

These days, the avocado is lauded everywhere. *BBC Good Food* magazine—the number one UK publication on nutrition and cooking—defends avocado-eating for its nutritional value and low saturated-fat, as well as being good for your heart, since it regulates appetite with high fiber content that leads to sensations of satiety.

Social media influencers, the real leaders in digital pop culture, are well aware of such benefits. If they love something, their followers will love it, too. One example is Mexican actress Aleida Núñez, who recommended her fans eat avocado instead of getting the increasingly popular Brazilian butt lift (BBL). She disclosed her secret by showing off her *derrière*, claiming that, "Avocados really help you keep your *pompas* high. It's protein, natural protein, and if you eat a lot of avocados . . . well . . . take it from me, [it's] going to grow one way or another." If you consider that more than 70 percent of an avocado is water and offers no muscle development, it's a little bit hard to believe. But just one more avocado never killed anyone, after all.

If the subject is carefully sculpted celebrity bodies, the Kardashians always come to mind. In her health and fitness website *Poosh*, Kourtney published her famed breakfast smoothie recipe in a 2020 edition as a post workout snack. It's as simple as combining avocado with banana, a handful of spinach, and almond milk. Blend and serve!

Alligator Skin

Avocados go down easy, but they're also must-haves for the beauty regimen. We've already seen avocado cosmetic uses from hair to feet (see the "Green Beauty" section). Well, both Thalía and Salma Hayek turn time and again to avocado face masks with the signature fruit, olive oil, egg, and honey as well as oleic-acid-rich emulsions. And you've got to admit both actresses have gorgeous hair and enviably perfect skin, thanks to avocados (or, maybe, some of the genes they inherited too).

In fact, Salma is co-founder of a BIY smoothie service (AKA "blend it yourself"), with a selection of twelve preparations delivered in bottles and ready to be enjoyed with just a smidge of water or nut milk. In addition to being a beverage, the smoothie packs double as beauty masks. Salma insists these recipes were born in her kitchen, inspired by her grandmother who, she says, "was like a witch doctor, a cosmetologist. We'd be having breakfast and she would take the leftovers —papaya, yogurt, honey, nuts—and blend them all together, then she'd start putting them on her face." Her papaya and avocado mix is designed to "renovate" dull skin. And no one can deny that her skin sparkles like the (movie) star she is.

Pears Didn't Go Over Well in the UK

The famed British emporium Marks & Spencer introduced avocados to their retail locations in 1968 with the name "avocado pears." Tradition-loving Brits demonstrated very little interest in the exotic fruit—they didn't understand how to eat them or what they were good for. One woman lodged a complaint after trying to cook them like traditional pears, serving them with proper English cream! Facing customer incomprehension, the stores had to start selling avocados with educational owner's manuals.

They backed up the strategy with coverage in local papers. In 1974, the *St. Michael's News* ran an item entitled "Different and Delicious... Avocados." The piece left aside the pears' "surname" and centered on nutritional values and a brief history. Most importantly, it presented plenty of ways to prepare avocados, such as stuffed, cubed for salads, in a dressing, and a quite singular recipe for guacamole with cream, paprika, Worcester sauce, lime, and wine vinegar, all to be eaten atop saltines. There was also a dessert recipe, avocado tutti-frutti, said to be a proto avocado ice cream—a dish ahead of its time!

↑ Don't squeeze the avocados.

CAREFUL WITH THAT KNIFE!

For a Mexican, Colombian, or Chilean, finding an avocado on your plate is as common as cracking an egg or squeezing a lime. It's part of those nations' diets and opening it up is as natural as it is simple. That said, avocado-cutting is not an easy matter for everyone.

Avocado Hand Exists

Starting in 2010, the avocado boom meant thousands in the US and Europe were hurting themselves because they didn't know the proper way to carve an avocado. This phenomenon is known as "avocado hand."

The unfortunate wound gained visibility when a handful of celebrities admit being avocado hand victims, which turned them into unwitting ambassadors of shameful clumsiness. It filled the internet with memes and jabs. In 2012, the most talked-about case was what happened to Oscar-bait actress Meryl Streep, who let herself be seen at a movie promotion, with her hand bandaged. With her wonted sense of humor, she blamed an avocado for the inconvenient injury.

The same thing happened to Joy Behar, a co-host on *The View*, and to Andi Dorfman, one of the stars of the reality show *The Bachelorette*. In 2018, she uploaded a photo from the hospital after reassembly surgery for her tendons and nerves, all from an unfortunate encounter with a slippery knife. That same year, Tom Brady, quarterback and a known avocado ice cream lover, appeared with his hand bandaged just days before the Super Bowl. The press speculated that it had to do with the dreaded avocado hand, but his spokespeople never confirmed.

Avocado hand appears to be quite common, and with increased consumption in countries that aren't yet used to dealing with the fruit, injury numbers keep going up. Surgeon Simon Eccles, Secretary of the British Association of Aesthetic and Reconstructive Plastic Surgery, disclosed that in 2017, every week brought an average of four patients to London's Chelsea and Westminster hospitals for injuries related to pulling out avocado pits. On the other side of the pond, researchers at Emory University (Atlanta) calculated between 1998 and 2017 a total of 50,413 victims of knife cuts were injured on their hands in avocado-related incidents; more than half took place between 2013 and 2017, when avocado sales skyrocketed in the United States. The numbers rise to inconceivable levels on Super Bowl Sunday, the biggest avocado-eating day in the country. On that Sunday—no one knows if it's a sporting event or a snacking event—emergency rooms put aside extra bandages, splints, and slings to attend to hands that come in bloody, damning their craving for guacamole.

→ In 2012 Meryl Streep fell victim to avocado hand.

TUTORIAL: HOW TO SAFELY CUT AN AVOCADO

Online, they've got hundreds of videos and tutorials with millions of views explaining how to cut an avocado. This is a good indication of the fear they produce in consumers who do not know how to adequately manipulate this fruit. Certain authorities on the issue—the Mayo Clinic, the Avocado Growers Association of California, Martha Stewart, a communicator on wellbeing issues, and the mediagenic British chef Jamie Oliver—have contributed their two-cents-worth explaining how to do it.

Although there are many ways to cut open an avocado, the simplest and safest can be summed up here:

1. Be sure your avocado has ripened but is still firm to the touch. If the flesh is too hard, it can be difficult to cut or lead to an accidental injury. Not least of all, a fruit that hard is not ready for eating.

2. Wash the fruit with soap and water to prevent germs, bacteria, and microbes from coming in contact with the knife and therefore the avocado flesh.

3. Lay the avocado on a cutting board and hold it down with the tips of your fingers. Choose a medium point lengthwise on the fruit to make a deep incision.

4. Sink in the knife until it taps the pit lightly and trace the cut around the entire circumference of the seed.

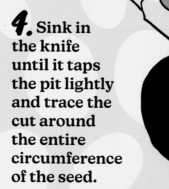

6. Separate the two halves; the avocado will open in all its verdant splendor.

5. Put down the knife and take the avocado in both hands, one at each extreme of the central cut. Then gently twist both parts like you're opening a jar.

7. If you're going to eat the whole fruit, you'll have to remove the pit.

8. With a great deal of care, strike the knife blade into the center of the pit so it will be stuck. Twist the knife over the pit's axis to extract it from the flesh and remove it completely.

As absurd as it sounds to those who grew up with knives in their hands and avocados in the other, avocado hand is a measurable reality that affects thousands annually. Consumers need to be in the know.

To please those most unwilling to use sharp objects, food distribution chains like the Colombian packer Frutexpo, which export avocados all over the world, have started selling vacuum packed, peeled, and ready-to-eat avocado. This might be the right solution for the clumsiest knife-wielders, but it sure does take away from the glamour. Some rituals are worth keeping, right?

That's it! Hands intact and avocado for everyone.

HANDLE CAREFULLY

The Avo Hand Drama

A small or shallow cut can be remedied at home by pressing down to stanch bleeding, washing the wound with copious soap and water, as well as wrapping the hand in sterilized gauze to keep away airborne infectious agents. If the wound does not stop bleeding, is too wide, or has sliced through a joint, it's likely to be a case of muscular, nerve, or tendon damage. Recovery time will depend on how severe the cut is, everything from a few days in the least severe cases, to months of physical therapy, or even one or more reconstructive surgeries. In the worst cases, 100 percent mobility may not be restored, leaving victims disabled for life. The knife a *New York Times* reporter's wife was using slipped from her hand and the surgery bill amounted to $20,000. Dinner was very expensive for that lady.

Don't Even Talk about Cutting

The hardest thing is removing the center seed since the peel's firmness coupled with the slipperiness of avocado flesh make it easy for the knife to slide toward the vulnerable hand. That's why dozens of contraptions for opening avocados and pulling out their pits without hurting yourself have been released. All are fairly similar and are made up of three principal parts. There's a plastic blade at one end, a ring to pull out the pit at the center of the device; at the other extreme, there's a grate with slightly sharp blades that slice the fruit. Some even resemble a human hand.

Since 2017, the United Kingdom's Marks and Spencer grocery stores have been selling a stone-free variant, the so-called "cocktail avocado" (or "date avocado"): a variety that was never pollinized, typically cultivated from the Fuerte subspecies and to a lesser degree Pinkerton and Bacon species. It's a definite perversion; since there is no pit the fruits are longer, like a medium-sized pickle. In terms of flavor, they emit an intense piñon-nut vibe, characteristic of the Fuerte variety. Grown in Spain, they're only available in December and largely exported to the United Kingdom.

As strange as it seems that there could be an avocado without a heart, it became an alternative not only in Britain but Switzerland and Canada, too. In spite of the fact that its price is a bit higher, the whole thing is flesh and some people insist the flavor is richer than better known varieties. As Jonathan Crane, a researcher at the University of Florida Horticulture Studies Department said, "a 100 percent flesh avocado is a natural miracle that must be enjoyed."

Guacamole
Kevin Johansen

Sittin' on a bencho, waitin' for the teco guacamole
Carne con frijole', carne con frijole...
Waitin' for the sun to shine, hopin' for the chicken yakisoba
Hope there's some left over, hope there's some left over...
Ay, mami, qué está haciendo, dónde va?
Ay, papi, no sé, pero vete ya!
Even when the pompan takin' on a holey, guacamole...
Samarranch, Havelange, Copa Mundo, UEFA de la FIFA
Just like Queen Latifah, hope she got some reefah
Solitaire, happiness, joie de vivre just' a like Lola
Hope she' there sola, hope she' there sola
Guacamole, Si Señor, Por Favor!
Ay, mami, qué está haciendo, dónde va?
Ay, papi, no sé pero voy pa' allá!
Even when the pompan takin' escabeche
Uy, café con leche!
Vamos a comer a lo de Beto, que nos hizo guacamole!
Carne con frijole', carne con frijole'!
Cuchufrito, habichuela, hot tamale, trucha al escabeche,
Con café con leche, con café con leche...
Chimichurri, zucundún con chequendengue, Caraguatatuba
Y uma caipiruva, y uma caipiruva...
Un poquito de manteca, cuatro cucharada e' milanesa
Queso con frambuesa, pongan bien la mesa!
Boca Juniors, River Plate, Chacarita, Diego Maradona
Diego no perdona, Diego no perdona
Solitaire, happiness, joie de vivre, just a like a Lola
Hope she there a sola, hope she there a sola...
Ay, mami que esta haciendo, donde va?
Ay, papi no se pero voy pa' alla!
Even when the pompan takin' on a lilly
Don't be so silly...
Guacamole, guacamole, si Señor, por favor!

Music & lyrics: Kevin Johansen
Publisher: Warner Chappell Music Argentina S.A.
(P) & (C) 2010 Sony Music Entertainment Argentina S.A.

To put the kibosh on knife accidents, there's a mini, pit-less avocado variety, the so-called "cocktail" or "date" avocado. But what's an avocado without a heart? A pickle!

↑ Different gadgets have been invented to help cut avocados.

Cellphone case

They say an ounce of prevention is worth a pound of cure. So, to prevent seeing your cellphone fall and shatter to bits, a silicon case with an avocado protector is both cute and functional.

Cloth hat

To avoid overheating, a cloth hat lined in a green pulp color with jumping avocados facing the sun is a fun accessory for summer or guacamole season.

Compressed face masks

Masks take up space unless they're compressed and vacuum-packed. This way, you can take a handful to any trip, party, or weekend escape. They sneak into any corner of your suitcase.

Masks

Tape dispenser

Sturdy tape to fix small jobs around the house and post notes on the wall is an essential for any office or home desk. With avocado, of course.

AVOCADOS EVERYWHERE

In fields like design and commercial promotion, the range of avocado products and knickknacks is huge: from clothing accessories capturing the joy of summer, to underwear, pet items, and decorative accents.

Earbuds

Music is like strength: it goes everywhere with us. To avoid losing the musical thread and protect earbuds from being smashed, tangled, or forgotten, a silicon avocado case is handy and weighs almost nothing.

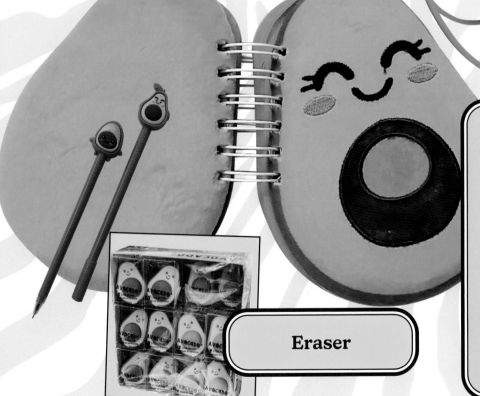

Notebook and pens

Taking notes on a cellphone is faster and easier than carrying anything else with you. But paper notebooks continue to have their own charm, especially if they have a fuzzy little avocado on the cover. And the pen isn't just for writing; it doubles as a stylus to avoid touching your cellphone screen.

Eraser

Socks

Head cool, feet warm. The secret to health or a mere proverb? Recalling the avocado's long journey from prehistory when donning these socks is bound to give you a boost, or at least a chuckle.

Pajamas

Competing with avocado leaf tea, these pajamas might not make you sleepy, but they'll raise your spirits when you look in the mirror. They can't be beat.

Cushion

T-shirts

Man or woman, boy or girl, with or without pineapple ice cream, but with avocados, please. It's a style trend that can't be missing from any closet: fresh and fun, like the fruit on your plate.

Tennis shoes

Here no one cares if the avocados are big or small. The size doesn't matter; it has the fruit of desire in its design. Running, jogging, or just walking can be a delicious experience with avocados on your feet.

Keychains

Backpack

Carrying several pounds of avocados might not be so hard for the Incredible Hulk, but for a person on foot, it's a lot easier to carry stuff on your back with a fun, warm, furry backpack.

Coin purses

What thief would imagine there's money in an avocado or smiling green pulp? Maybe it's not the most efficient safety measure, but as coin purses go, it's certainly original.

Handbags

Plush toys

Although many people no longer sleep with teddy bears, this fluffy avocado cushion might act as an anti-insomnia plush toy, supporting tired backs or raised feet. A remedy for all ills...

¡SANTO GUACA-MOLE!

HOLY GUACAMOLE!

· ·

There can be no question that guacamole is one of the greatest contributions Mexico has made to global cuisine. Both the name—and the guacamole—come from Nahuatl. The ancient name, *ahuacamolli*, is the combination of *ahuacatl* (avocado) and *molli* (stewed food or salsa). No (reasonable) Mexicans sit at any table without considering at least a small order, with tortilla chips or chicharron for dipping to their heart's delight.

→ Guacamole in a holy *molcajete*.

From its birth to the present day, the "true" guacamole recipe has been a cause for discussion. For some, you make it with crushed avocado, in a *molcajete* (grinding bowl), mixed with water, period. Others throw in tomato, others chili and lime juice… but everyone agrees that cilantro, pepper, garlic, and onions only arrived to become "Mexican" food on Spanish galleons.

From sixteenth-century friar Bernardino de Sahagún, we know there were people who cooked and sold "very flavorful *cazuelas*" (stewed dishes), and that one of these delicacies might be "avocados mixed with chili that burns a lot," perhaps a guacamole that had a detectable piquancy. In viceregal times, guacamole evolved with new ingredients from Europe, Asia, and Africa.

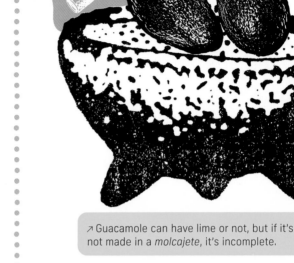

↗ Guacamole can have lime or not, but if it's not made in a *molcajete*, it's incomplete.

How to Make a Spicier Guacamole

1. Cube the chilis into small pieces, add a couple garlic slices, and a slice of chopped onion.
2. Mix everything in a blender, *molcajete*, or just smashed in a bowl with a fork until the mix is smooth.
3. Add the chopped tomatoes and salt to taste.
4. Put everything in a blender or a *molcajete*.
5. Add the avocado and grind again until the "guac" has a mousse-like consistency
6. Chill guacamole in a bowl or receptacle.

Plating
1. Put chicharron strips in every tortilla, plus two tablespoons of guacamole and roll up the tacos. Pico de gallo, sliced avocados and more lime make great garnishes.

Though it has always been a part of the Mexican diet, its supersonic flight didn't take off until the twentieth century. Once the Mexican Revolution ended, one of the most influential cookbooks of the day, *Recetas de cocina y platillos sencillos* (1918), published by Alejandro Pardo, declared guacamole was a salad. In the 1930s, amidst a hyper-nationalist environment, love and respect for the meaning of Mexican symbols was strengthened. Back then, everything was tricolor (green, red and white) as an analogy for the federal flag and even food had to do its part. There was green guacamole (with chile), white onions, and red tomatoes. Don't forget the cilantro, which set sail from the north of Africa and landed in fresh, spicy guacamole. Finally in the mid-twentieth century it had acquired its definitive recipe.

In recent decades guacamoles have become a gourmet dish, as reflected in an urge to make it more "sophisticated." We may happen on ingredients as unusual as pears, pomegranates, mangoes, wheat germ, yogurt, and a Mexican sort of Greek yogurt known as *jocoque*. These days, as a global food, the rules are no rules for preparing a decent guacamole, even if there is a traditionalist faction that insists if you don't chop it up in a *molcajete*, the outcome is not guacamole.

Classic *Molcajete* Guacamole

Ingredients
2 servings

- ½ white onion, minced
- ½ cup fresh cilantro, chopped finely
- 1 teaspoon granulated salt
- 2 avocados, peeled
- 2 teaspoon olive oil
- A few drops of lime juice, to taste, and to prevent the guacamole from turning brown

Preparation

1. Throw a tablespoon of onion, a tablespoon of cilantro, and the salt into the *molcajete*.
2. Grind everything to reach a pasty consistency, add the avocado and keep mashing.
3. Add the remaining onion and cilantro.
4. Season with olive oil and lime juice.
5. Serve with tortilla chips, or *chicharron-style* crackling, or even roasted crickets called *chapulines*.

You'll always be my avocado and together we are guacamole.

MOLCA... WHO?

You can grind any kind of seed, herb, and condiment, mixed with liquids or spirits.

The *molcajete* pestle is also called *tejolote*, which means "stone doll" in Nahuatl.

The perfect grind is done with circular movements in a spiral, or from one side to the other in a straight line.

Its design has remained the same for millennia. And it keeps working perfectly.

They can be made in different sizes, of diverse materials like porous stone, clay, or ceramic, with decorations or plain.

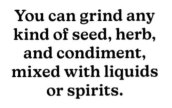

Work that Pestle

It's simply a Mexican mortar and pestle. This kitchen utensil was commonly used in pre-Hispanic cultures. It was also the secret weapon for making the best guacamole, for its volcanic stone gives it that unique mineral flavor that can't be reproduced with modern kitchen appliances. So it's essential for all making all traditional salsas like grandma used to make.

Chichamole or Pea Guacamole

Ingredients
12 servings

- 1 lime, peeled
- ½ teaspoon hot sauce (optional)
- Half of 1 small yellow onion, peeled and halved once more
- 2 peeled garlic cloves
- ½ teaspoon ground black pepper
- 4 cups (640 g) cooked peas

Preparation
1. Combine all ingredients with a quarter cup (60 ml) of water in a blender—in the above order—and cover tightly.
2. Turn the blender on low and blend at highest speed.
3. Mix for 45 seconds, using a spatula to push the ingredients down into the blades.
4. Transfer the guacamole to a large bowl, serve immediately or refrigerate until serving.

That's not right, dude!

No, You Can't

We witnessed a landmark in guacamole's political life on July 1, 2015, when then US president Barack Obama responded to a far-from-protocol-related question on Twitter.

Does guacamole call for green peas or not?

The debate had begun hours earlier, when Melissa Clark of *The New York Times* shared a guacamole recipe with green peas, warning it was "a radical move": but it could add a twist to the classic recipe. The discussion was still fresh, and journalists took advantage of a trending topic to attract audiences. They got them.

President Obama's response, "I respect the *New York Times*, but I'm not buying peas in guac. Onions, [yes], garlic, hot peppers. Classic," got 12 thousand retweets. Ex-President Bush's son also joined the conversation. "You just don't put peas in guacamole." This represented a landmark accord between Democrats and Republicans. Even the Texas Republican party social media accounts tried to be funny, joking that New York had declared war on Texas by suggesting that guacamole include green peas.

What now seems clear is that guacamole—with or without green peas—adapts to every culinary culture, thanks to the fact the fruit combines very well with myriad flavors. Top Chef Masters winner Rick Bayless, also a champion of Mexican food in the United States, knows all this well. He makes his guacamoles with seasonal ingredients. Winter means porcini mushrooms and crab; spring invites strawberries instead of tomatoes; in fall he adds apples and fennel; and in summer it's corn and poblano chiles.

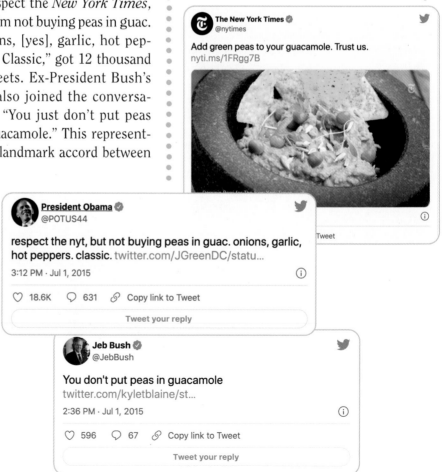

Red Guacamole

Ingredients
3 servings

- 3 big ripe avocados
- 1 big tomato, peeled
- ½ big onion
- 1 clove garlic
- 1 bunch cilantro
- 1 tablespoon oil
- 6 serrano chilis
- Salt

• •

Preparation
1. Peel and mash the avocados well with a fork.
2. Dice the tomato, onion, garlic, cilantro, and chilis, and add them to the avocados.
3. Mix well, adding the oil and salt to taste. To prevent it from turning brown, leave one or two avocado seeds in the mixture.

Magazine: *Arqueología Mexicana*
Pre-Columbian Food issue
Recipes, special edition no. 12
March 10, 2003, p. 35

Guaca Rocker
Botellita de Jerez

If your girl is a mix
of Janis Joplin and Lola Beltrán
and if it happens you squirm like Elvis
And the *pachucho* Tin Tan.
In your sneakers with spurs
You're like flying
And you put wings on your
party-loving problems.

Get with it
To get into guaca rock.
¡Guaca rocker!
If you mix up avocado in your taco
with a rock LP
And you add Chuck Berry,
To José Alfredo and a pinch of
blues.
If you dress up your look
Very jivey
With earrings and tattoos
Don't give up!
Get with it
To get into guaca rock.

Artist: Botellita de Jerez
Album: La venganza del
hijo del Guacarock

Chipotle™ Guacamole

Ingredients
2 servings

- 2 ripe Hass avocados
- 2 teaspoons lime juice
- 2 tablespoons cilantro, minced
- ¼ cup red onion, cubed
- ¼ tsp kosher salt
- ½ jalapeño chopped, including
  seeds

● ● ● ● ● ● ● ● ● ● ● ● ● ● ● ● ● ●

Preparation
1. Cut the avocados in half, remove
   the peel and seed.
2. Put the avocados into
   a bowl.
3. Cover them with lime juice.
4. Add the salt and mash
   Until smooth.
5. Add the cilantro, red onion and
   the jalapeño, and mix them.
6, Taste the guacamole and
   adjust the salt.

↑ Guacamole with seed to
slow down oxidation.

GUACAMOLE TOUCHDOWN

It's hard to imagine a time when avocados were undesirable, but in the not too distant past of the early 1990s however, avocados were branded as weird, oily fruits banned by the then-popular low-fat diet crazes. Something miraculous needed to happen to change the game for avocados—and there isn't a more anticipated game in the United States than the Super Bowl . . .

Mexico and other countries that follow the Super Bowl declared its "Latin flavor" has united millions in an emotional trance. But they forgot to name the dip that glues everyone to the screen—guacamole!
More than 126,000 tons of Hass avocado were eaten at Super Bowl 2021. And the numbers get bigger every year.
What better way to promote a healthy snack than on Super Bowl Sunday?

↗ Guacamole should be served in a Big Bowl.

↑ For younger generations, guacamole has always been part of the Super Bowl.

Everyone in Front of the TV!

To Americans, the Super Bowl might as well be a national holiday. It was February 7, 2021. John Smith, a typical American guy born in 1997, was excitedly watching the game in the living room of his California residence. Anxiously anticipating the events of the game, he knew one thing for sure: there would be Tom Brady, and there would be guacamole. But it wasn't always that way.

A Green Touchdown!

The Super Bowl was the biggest marketing move the avocado ever made. Not only is it the most important annual television event in the US; it's also become the biggest snack holiday for Americans.

There was another advantage. The football championship is played in the winter, when a lot of avocado harvests have already ripened. Advertisers got the idea to get players involved, asking them for their guacamole recipes; the public votes to elect the winner. The plan worked. In the last twenty years, guacamole and the Super Bowl have been inseparable.

A media phenomenon and an advertising crown-jewel in the United States, known as the Guacamole Bowl, started to come together beginning in 1993, by a dynamic avocado lobby that

Puebla's Guac, on chalupas

By the viral popularity of guacamole, we can safely say it has become a celebrity. Our favorite gringo friends love giving *Cincoh Day Mayoh* parties at home and have all but appropriated that once-minor-in-Mexico celebration. Although, in order to be up to the fiesta, they should know how to prepare the most basic of guacamoles. The preparation is so simple that even a rookie can swing it.

Ingredients
2 servings

- 2 ripe avocados
- 1 garlic clove, finely chopped
- 1 onion, chopped
- 1 small tomato, chopped and cubed
- 1½ tablespoons of lime juice
- Salt and pepper to taste
- 1 portion tostadas or chalupas

Preparation
1. Halve the avocados and use a large spoon to scrape out the flesh.
2. Use the same spoon to transfer the avocado to a large bowl, or preferably a Mexican molcajete mortar or indeed any mortar; add the garlic clove, onion, tomato, lime juice, salt and pepper.
3. Beat everything firmly until you get the right texture.
4. Add salt and black pepper to taste and stir once more.

Fake Guac
A tweet from @karligrafia published in 2019 that broke millions of Mexican hearts asked:

Karligrafia®
@Karligrafia

¿Que edad tenían cuando se enteraron que la salsa de 'aguacate' de los puestos de tacos no tiene aguacate sino calabacita cocida que le da el color y la textura?

10:29 p. m. · 3 jul. 2019 · Twitter for Android

321 Retweets **211** Tweets citados **1.160** Me gusta

never scrimped on campaigns: commercials with NFL players promoting the product, and of course, national TV commercials during the game. This is the world's most expensive ad space, with high quality requirements since its messages reach nearly 100 million viewers in the US alone.

Those responsible for changing the rules of the game were players from the Avocados from Mexico brand, the main spokesperson for the Mexican avocado all over the world since 2013. This organization's goal is to globally promote the avocado, specifically with their northern neighbor, the US, with a strategy focused on educating consumers and expanding demand. They scored their first goal with American consumers thanks to their funny TV commercials.

But let's get back to the game. We're getting close to the end of the fourth quarter and John Smith is hugging his entire family, his girlfriend, and his friends. His idol has just made history.

But there's another champion in the shadows that has made more money in a single day, much more than a star football player. Now the bowl that was full of guacamole is empty. John sees this and something in his tender gringo heart is crushed. Achingly, he cries out, "Guys, there's no more guac?"

Broccomole??

What started in the depths of Twitter and the fringes of YouTube has now taken social media by storm. This new phenomenon has incited rage in the general public and outcries around the globe. The travesty is of course, is none other than "mock guac."

Imitation guacamole recipes are all over the internet now. It's believed that street taco stands were the first to serve guacamole sans-avo because they couldn't afford the real thing. Restaurants, too, have replaced traditional avocado guac with cheaper alternatives, citing skyrocketing costs.

One of the most widespread recipes is "broccomole." It has all the ingredients of a traditional guacamole (tomatoes, cilantro, garlic, chilies, lime, and salt) but it replaces the avocado with broccoli and has a touch of cream cheese for a smoother consistency.

In some restaurants, they make guacamole with fava beans, like at the Handle Bar, a UK brunch restaurant that posted a dip with favas, mashed peas, and a touch of lime, mint, and cilantro, on its Instagram page. Also in London, Mexican chef Santiago Lastra created a faux guacamole option with pistachios and fermented currant. In Canada, another Mexican chef, Aldo Camarena, introduced an alternative you make with squash and pumpkin seeds. An even more sophisticated choice is edamame guacamole. This "mock guac" is made with the edamame (shelled), plain Greek yogurt, olive oil, tomato, and lime juice. Or try a Japanese-inspired recipe by throwing in powdered onion, cumin, white miso, and lime juice.

Since guacamole is now a global favorite, the variants are vast. Among the most interesting we found was "tropical guacamole," that calls for mango and pineapple chunks in addition to the traditional ingredients; apple guacamole, which calls for red onion and green apple chunks; or guacamole with hard-boiled eggs, which is very common in Honduras, Nicaragua, and other Central American countries.

← Tweet's translation: How old were you when you found out the "avocado" salsa at taco stands doesn't have any avocado, but is made of cooked zucchini to give it that color and texture?

Life is like a torta,
you have to fill it
with the best of ingredients.

AVOCADO RECIPES FROM AROUND THE WORLD

There is a reason why avocados are so popular. Their flavor and texture make a magical ingredient that complements nearly any dish. From a simple sandwich to the most sophisticated gastronomy, this versatile fruit has crossed every geographical border to delight the world's most discerning palates.

Ingredients
12 to 15 servings

Guacamole
- 4 ripe Hass avocados*
- 1 small tomato, minced
- 2 tablespoons diced onion
- 3 tablespoons diced cilantro
- 1 seedless serrano chili, diced
- Salt to taste
- Lime juice to taste

Fried Dough Shells
- 1¾ cups (.25 k) all-purpose flour
- ¼ teaspoon salt
- ½ tablespoon unsalted butter, softened
- 1 small egg
- 3 tablespoons pulque (Mexican fermented agave beverage)
- Oil for frying
- 1-inch wide tubes (cannoli forms), or make the forms yourself with aluminum foil

Preparation

Guacamole
1. Mix all the ingredients on the list in a medium bowl.

Gaznates**
1. Mix the dough ingredients in a food processor, blender, or with a beater and slowly add the water until it forms a malleable dough.
2. Wrap it in cloth and let it sit for two hours.
3. Roll out the dough as thinly as possible and cut out 4-inch squares. Cover each cut tube form with the dough and moisten the edges slightly to close them. Fry in hot oil.
4. Remove the tube form. Fill each fried dough shell with the guacamole.

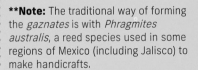

Maru Toledo Vargas

Researcher and Cook
Jalisco, Mexico
@marutoledovargas

Since 1997, Vargas has devoted her life to researching the Indigenous cuisine of Jalisco. She has written twenty-four books on it, receiving the Gourmet Awards 2017 prize in the Traditional Cook Trajectory category and the "Ricardo Muñoz Zurita" Medal at the Jalisco COME (Eat) Festival. She is a leading figure in the food world, creator of the "Women of Maize" project that promotes ancient culinary culture and foodie tourism. On the Santina de la Covadonga Ranch, in the community of Teuchiteco de Ahualulco del Mercado (Jalisco), she opened Maru Toledo, where she serves lunches, and holds workshops and demonstrations featuring traditional cuisine.

Her story with this dish
The recipe was born in Oaxaca as a dessert, named *gaznate* (colloquial word for throat) because of its cylindrical shape. The traditional preparation is with merengue, but for this savory version with guacamole filling, I use a strong pulque to give the shells character.

*Tip: If you want to prep your avocados for the guacamole, you can place the pulp in a bowl and cover with water—this will prevent oxidation. When ready, drain off the liquid, and finish preparing it.

**Note: The traditional way of forming the *gaznates* is with *Phragmites australis*, a reed species used in some regions of Mexico (including Jalisco) to make handicrafts.

Lemon and Avocado Mousse Tart

Ingredients
8 servings

- ¾ cup (100 g) macadamia nuts, toasted
- ⅔ cup (100 g) cashews
- ⅓ teaspoon (2 g) salt
- ⅓ cup (30 g) grated coconut, grated
- 1 scant teaspoon (4 g) coconut oil, melted
- 1 scant teaspoon (5 g) agave nectar

Filling
- 3 dates (soaked in ⅔ cup [150 ml] hot water for 30 minutes)
- 1 ripe avocado
- 4 ⅛ teaspoons (20 ml) lime juice
- 1 teaspoon (5 g) lime zest
- 2 ¾ teaspoons (20 g) agave syrup
- 1 teaspoon (4 g) coconut oil, melted
- ¾ teaspoon (4 ml) vanilla extract
- 1 pinch sea salt

Topping
- 1 cup (100 g) pistachios, ground
- ¼ cup (20 g) cranberries, dried
- ¼ cup (20 g) pistachios, toasted
- 5 pieces of pansies
- 2 sprigs fresh mint

Paola Garduño

Chef
Mexico City, Mexico
@chefpaolag

Garduño studied Culinary and Pastry Arts in Paris at Le Cordon Bleu. She has also taught classes at the Culinary Institute of America in New York. In 1991, she started her first catering company; in 2001, she opened Café O, and in 2003 she created Go Fresh, a chain of fast-casual shops. She has participated in publications related to pastry-making and has been a judge in gastronomy competitions.

Her story with this dish
Whenever I cook or eat avocado, I remember Mexico—although it's one of the few ingredients that doesn't taste the same to me if it's not grown in my country. As a child, I thought it was strange that it was a fruit, because it wasn't sweet. This raw-vegan dessert is a good example of how it can be used as a substitute for eggs in sweets.

Preparation

1. Pulse the nuts, salt, and coconut in a food processor until combined and fine-textured.
2. Add the oil and agave nectar to the nut mixture. Mix until incorporated.
3. Press mixture into a 6-inch (15 cm) diameter ring or tart pan to form a uniform base.
4. Refrigerate until ready to use.

Filling

1. Grind dates into a paste, either with a food processor or by hand with a mortar and pestle. Add avocado and grind until smooth. Add the rest of the ingredients and blend until creamy and smooth.
2. Pour into the mold and spread evenly.
3. Freeze for 3 hours until mousse is set. Unmold, and serve.

Topping

1. Sift the ground pistachio over the filling.
2. Place the cranberries, the toasted pistachios, the flowers and the mint.

Avocado Tlacoyo

Ingredients
4 servings

Refried beans
- 1 ⅔ cup (200 g) canned black beans (can be used with other bean types)
- 1 ⅛ tablespoon (10 g) garlic, minced
- ¼ cup (20 g) green onion (just the bulb)
- ⅓ teaspoon (2 g) salt
- 2 ⅔ tablespoon (5 g) avocado leaf*
- ½ tablespoon (5 g) lard
- ¾ cup (20 g) minced white onion

Lime juice dressing
- 10 teaspoons (50 ml) lime juice
- 1 teaspoon (5 ml) vegetable oil
- ¼ teaspoon (1 g) sea salt (best if Colima salt*)

To finish
- 1 ⅓ cup (40 g) quelites [pigweed] (or cilantro, verdolagas, amaranth or other leafy greens)
- ½ cup (80 g) or 1 Criollo avocado**

Avocado salsa
- 1 cup (150 g) or 2 avocados (keep the seed)
- ⅓ cup (75 g) tomatillos
- 1 ⅓ tablespoon (5 g) criollo cilantro
- 2 teaspoons (5 g) green Simojovel chili (or Piquín peppers)
- ¾ teaspoon (5 g) salt
- ¼ cup (60 ml) lime juice
- 2 teaspoons avocado oil
- 1 avocado seed

Tlacoyo
- 3 ¾ cup (300 g) corn masa
- 2 cups (150 g) refried beans

*Tip: Avocado leaf and Colima salt can be purchased online. Fresh corn masa can be found at some specialty grocery stores or purchased online. A popular brand is Maseca, but there is likely a smaller batch, local brand in your area.

**Note: Criollo avocados are known for their smooth green skin and large pit. This makes them easier to stuff, but you can use whatever avocado variety is available.

Preparation

Refried beans

1. Cook the beans in water, garlic, and the white bulb of the green onion for an hour until they are soft; add salt and avocado leaf and cook for 5 minutes. Remove leaf.
2. In a skillet, sauté minced onion in lard, add the cooked beans with a little of its juice/stock, mash until desired consistency, and keep for the tlacoyo filling.

Lime juice dressing

1. Mix all the ingredients with a wire whisk or blender and keep for garnishing.

Complements

1. Wash and place the quelites into a bowl and mix with the lime juice dressing.
2. Cut the Criollo avocado and grill for a few minutes to mark them, remove before they burn (less than a minute). Set both aside.

Avocado Salsa

1. Liquify the ingredients until you get a creamy consistency and aside.

Avocado seed

1. Remove the thin brown skin from the seed with a grater, then grate the rest and let it dry until it becomes crunchy. Set aside.

Tlacoyo

1. Make four tlacoyos (¼-inch oval patty) with 75 g of corn masa each.
2. Fill them with an eighth of a cup of refried beans and cook on a griddle or in a cast-iron pan.

Assembly

1. Put a tlacoyo on a plate and decorate with quelites and the grilled Criollo avocado.
2. Add 3 tablespoons of avocado salsa.
3. Decorate each with the grated dehydrated avocado seed. Finish with a pinch of salt.

Marta Zepeda Trujillo

Chef, Tierra y Cielo
San Cristóbal de las Casas, Mexico
@tierraycielorestaurante

Chiapas, her birth state, is the banner that characterizes this pony-tailed cook, who graduated from the Centro de Estudios Superiores de San Ángel (CESSA) university campus in San Ángel, Mexico City. In 2007, together with her business and life partner, Kievf Rueda, she opened the restaurant Tierra y Cielo, where they honor Chiapas cuisine, using almost all ingredients from the state. She was awarded the National Quality Prize in the category of Tourism and the "José Peza Fragoso" Entrepreneurial Merit Prize in Regional Cooking, among others.

Her story with this dish
The idea was to use every part of the avocado possible: we thought of tlacoyos that are part of everyday breakfasts or brunches in Chiapas—always with beans cooked with avocado leaf.

Avocado Mousse with Hoja Santa

Ingredients
4 servings

Mousse
- 2 tablespoons (8 g) cilantro
- ½ cup (130 g) cream
- 3 ½ cups (530 g) avocado
- 3 ½ tablespoons (50 g) lime juice
- 1 vanilla bean
- 1 ⅛ teaspoons (5 g) sea salt
- 2 ½ tablespoons (20 g) pectin

Tempura Hoja Santa* Leaf
- Almost 2 cups (240 g)
  all-purpose flour
- ⅓ cup (60 g) sugar
- 1 ⅓ tablespoons (20 g)
  baking powder
- 2 eggs
- 2 egg yolks

Yellow Lemon Purée
- 1.1 lb (500 g) yellow lemons
- 7 ⅛ tablespoons (100 g) butter
- ½ cup (120 g) lime juice

Preparation

Mousse
1. In a blender, combine the cilantro with the cream until it is smooth. Add the other ingredients and blend well; set aside in a rectangular mold.

Tempura
1. Mix all the dry ingredients with the eggs, then add a half cup of mineral water to produce a smooth mixture.
2. Dip leaf into mixture, fry in hot oil until light and golden.

Yellow lemon purée
1. Put the peel in cold water and heat to boiling. Repeat this three times.
2. Liquify the peel with the other ingredients.

Assembly
1. Put a bit of purée on the plate, then the mousse, or vice versa, and place the tempura leaf on top.

*Note: Hoja Santa is a peppery, anise-flavored Central American herb. You can also use fresh tarragon.

Nico Mejía

Chef, Mexía
Guadalajara, Mexico
www.mexiarestaurante.mx

A chef raised in Colima, Mejía is passionate about his roots. He is a teacher, researcher, and proud ambassador of Colima cuisine that unites Jalisco and Michoacán, his home state. After graduating from the Culinary Art School (Tijuana) in 2014, he became the creative head chef at the restaurant Cortez in Guadalajara, serving cuisine influenced by his state's roots. He won Best Casual Dinner of Mexico at the Gourmet Awards and was mentioned as one of the "Three to Eat in Jalisco" in *New York Magazine*. Today he is the creative chef at Mexía, a restaurant in Guadalajara, of the original Bar Social 1952, and La Sal restaurant in Manzanillo. He has written three books on recovering his state's roots and culinary secrets.

His story with this dish
Finding new ways to use avocados gives us the opportunity to celebrate the quality of Mexican ingredients. This recipe is part of our menu that we developed at Mexía, a restaurant that explores new ways of tasting Mexican ingredients while maintaining their essence. In this recipe, we play with texture—the creamy avocado with the crunchy, herbaceous tempura-battered hoja santa.

Tostada with Aguachile and Avocado

Ingredients
4 servings

Chili Water for the Aguachile
- 2 limes with seeds, juice
- ½ cup cilantro
- ¼ cucumber, seeded and peeled
- ¼ green serrano chili
- ¼ white onion
- 1 tablespoon olive oil

Tostada
- 4 blue criollo corn tostadas, toasted
- 2 avocados
- Artisan salt, to taste

Topping
- Purple margarita (daisy) petals

Preparation

For the aguachile
1. Liquify all the ingredients in a blender until they are combined. Season with salt.

For the tostada
1. Cut the avocados in thin slices and place them on the tostada.
2. Cover the tostada with the sliced avocado.
3. Finally, spoon dollops of the aguachile on the avocado and decorate with the margarita petals.

Lula Martín del Campo

Chef, Cascabel
Mexico City, Mexico
@lulachef

Chef and entrepreneur with more than twenty-five years in the industry, the author of twelve cookbooks, and collaborator for diverse print media, radio, and multimedia outlets; she seeks to promote Mexican food culture through what she considers the Mexico's culinary heritage. At her restaurant, Cascabel, she takes us by the hand through her menu with ingredients like endemic maize and bean species. In her new project, Marea, she focuses on seafood with a menu based on premium quality ingredients, with a keen awareness of the importance of local, sustainable consumption.

Her story with this dish
My history with the avocado has spanned a lifetime. I really enjoy the simple taste of a tostada with avocado puree [i.e., the original avocado toast!] and a touch of artisan salt. In my profession, although it might not seem true, sometimes it's hard for us to have regular meals. So, when I'm busy working and I need to eat, I have my tostada with avocado. It never fails me!

Sardine-Filled
Avocado Roll

Ingredients
1 serving

- 4-oz (120 g) can sardines, packed in olive oil
- ½ (40 g) small white onion
- 2 tablespoons (10 g) cilantro
- 7 tablespoons (50 g) slivered almonds
- ⅓ cup (50 g) avocado
- 2 Serrano Chilis
- Cilantro leaves
- Salt

Preparation

1. Clean the sardines and flake with a fork, removing the meat from the bones.
2. Cover the sardines with the olive oil and set aside.
3. Finely mince the white onion, serrano chili, and cilantro.
4. Mix the sardines with the minced vegetables.
5. Add salt. Season to taste.
6. Toast the slivered almonds and set aside.
7. Peel the avocado and cut the pulp into thin slices.
8. Arrange the slices vertically in a row on a sheet of plastic wrap.
9. Place the sardines horizontally in the middle of the row of avocados and fold over the plastic, firmly pressing it into a sushi-like roll. Put the roll on a plate.
10. Sprinkle the almonds on top and decorate with cilantro leaves.

Gerardo Vázquez Lugo

Chef, Nicos
Mexico City, Mexico
www.nicosmexico.mx

Trained as an architect and devoted to Mexican cuisine since 1996, he is heir to the cooking tradition of his parents. They founded Nicos sixty years ago, one of the best restaurants not only in Mexico City, but in all Latin America. Gerardo advocates the slow food philosophy, which not only promotes fully enjoying the dining experience, but also cuisine that is responsibly produced with social equity, working with producer coops, artisans, and farmers.

His story with this dish
Avocado shouldn't be cooked. This is a great lesson that Gerardo learned from his mother, chef María Elena Lugo Zemeño. Following the mantra, "nothing goes to waste in the Mexican kitchen," Gerardo uses fresh seasonal products to preserve the natural flavor of ingredients in traditional recipes made with loving care.

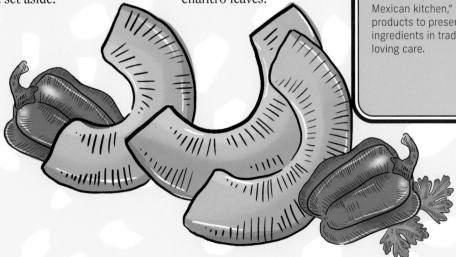

Lentil Hummus Pita with Tomato and Avocado

Ingredients
2 servings

Lentil hummus
- 1 cup lentils, cooked
- ¼ yellow onion, diced
- 2 cloves garlic, minced
- 1 serrano chili, deveined, minced
- Juice of 3 limes
- ¼ bunch of cilantro, minced
- 2 stalks celery, minced
- Pinch of fresh mint, minced
- 1 tablespoon tahini
- 1 tablespoon apple cider vinegar
- 3 tablespoons extra virgin olive oil
- 1 pinch of salt

Other ingredients
- 2 pieces of whole wheat pita bread

- 1 runny boiled egg (cooked 4 min)
- 1 large yellow tomato, thinly sliced
- 4 tablespoons bagel seasoning
- Olive oil
- Cilantro leaves

Avocado
- 2 Hass avocados
- Juice of one lime
- Salt and pepper to taste

Preparation

Hummus
1. Mix all the ingredients in a food processor. Place in a bowl and set aside.

Avocado
1. Mash the two avocados in a bowl.
2. Add the lime juice in drops, and salt and pepper to taste.

Pita bread
1. Heat and sear the pita bread in a frying pan with a little olive oil.

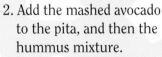

2. Add the mashed avocado to the pita, and then the hummus mixture.
3. In a circular pattern, arrange the yellow tomato slices. Sprinkle the bagel seeds, a pinch of salt, and the cilantro on top.
4. Finally, place the halved boiled egg in the middle.

Javier Plascencia

Chef, Misión 19
Tijuana, Mexico
www.chefjavierplascencia.mx

Born in Tijuana to a restaurant-owning family, he is a leading representative of the Baja California food scene. He studied in San Diego but returned to his birthplace to open his first restaurant in 1989. This was follows by Erizo (2007) with a Peruvian ceviche bar and Misión 19 (2011), inspired by the cuisine of his home state. In 2017, he inaugurated Jazamango under the motto "from the fields to the plate and from the plate to your mouth," Finca Altozano, restaurant-vineyard specializing in grilled meats, and Animalón, open-air dining under an oak. With one book published, he continues to promote the cuisine that he carries in his heart.

His story with this dish
Avocado fascinates me because it's an ingredient that is everywhere in Mexican cooking and throughout Latin American cuisine. I think that Mexican cuisine wouldn't be the same if we didn't have this precious fruit on our tables. It's a product that always wins; I've never met anyone who doesn't like avocados.

Green Curry Avocado Toast

*Tip: You can also buy milk bread at a Japanese bakery or some specialty grocery stores.

Ingredients
2 servings

Milk bread toast*
- 4 tablespoons
  (½ stick; 50 g) butter
- ¾ cup (100 g) cake flour
- ¼ cup (60 ml) fresh milk
- 1 lime
- Any kind of oil for deep frying

Avocado in green curry
- 2 creamy ripe avocadoes
- 1 ⅛ tablespoons (15 g)
  Thai green curry paste
- 1 lime
- ⅓ teaspoon (2 g) salt

Peruvian chalaquita
(Callao salsa)
- ¼ (30 g) red onion
- 1 red chili
  (aji limo chili peppers)
- 1 ⅓ tablespoon (5 g)
  fresh cilantro
- 1 lime
- ⅓ teaspoon (2 g) salt
- 1 teaspoon (5 ml) olive oil

Preparation

Milk toast
1. Mix the softened butter and flour to a sandy texture.
2. Mix the milk, two tablespoons of water and lime juice.
3. Combine the two mixtures until it reaches a liquid consistency.
4. Put a round mold (or cookie cutter) in a frying pan with oil over a low heat.
5. Pour 4 teaspoons (20 ml) of the toast mixture into the mold.
6. It will begin to form a porous toast that will stick to the mold.
7. Once it turns golden, take it out of the pan, remove the mold and let the toast cool.

Avocado in green curry
1. Mix all the ingredients in a blender and liquify until smooth.

Peruvian chalaquita
1. Mince the red onion, chili, and cilantro.
2. Mix them together, season to taste.

Assembly
1. Put the toast on a plate and add a generous tablespoon of the avocado curry cream on top.
2. Add a teaspoon of the chalaquita in the center of the avocado cream and place three thin slices of avocado on top.
3. Top it off with a pinch of the Maldon salt and cilantro leaves as decoration.

Francesca Ferreyros

Chef, Baan Perú
San Isidro, Peru
@francescaferreyros

She started out with chef Ivan Kisic in Lima, her hometown. Soon she went to work in other kitchens: in the United States with Niven Patel and in Spain at El Celler de Can Roca, Girona. Fascinated by their techniques and in search of new flavors, she moved to Bangkok (Thailand) to work with chef Gaggan Anand. Three years later, she returned to Peru and got involved with communities in the Peruvian jungle. Now, she hopes to open her restaurant inspired by the flavors of Southeast Asia and Peruvian ingredients.

Her story with this dish
The classic breakfast in all homes in Peru is bread with palta (avocado): you don't need anything more than the avocado, a little salt, and that's it. But this is an indigenous toast that is made like a fried milk dessert called *guevar*. I add salt and use it like a toast with the avocado Thai curry.

Note: For seafood lovers, you can add a couple strips of sea urchin of your choice. This combines the avocado's freshness and fat with the tostada's crunch and the creaminess and intense flavor of the seafood.

Sikil oon: Avocado with Squash Seeds

Ingredients
4 servings

- 1 Hass avocado, remove peel and seed
- 2 roasted amashito chilis, minced (or pequin peppers)
- 2.5 oz (70 g) toasted squash seeds, ground
- 1 teaspoons salt
- 2 tablespoons lime juice
- 1 ⅓ tablespoon (4 g) fresh chives, minced
- ½ ripe plum tomato, cubed
- 1 tablespoon fresh cilantro, minced
- ¼ (20 g) small red or other onion, diced
- 2 tablespoons water

Ricardo Muñoz Zurita

Chef, Azul
Mexico City, Mexico
www.azul.rest

One of the most active and highly respected food researchers in Mexico, he is the creator of Mexico City's Azul restaurants, where he serves dishes based on his research. He has published numerous books; his *Diccionario Enciclopédico de Gastronomía Mexicana* is a classic. *Time* magazine called him the "Prophet and preserver of culinary tradition," and he is one of the top chefs in Mexico and Latin America.

His story with this dish
The name *sikil oon* comes from Mayan, in which *sikil* means squash seed and *oon*, avocado. This is an everyday dish served as a garnish to accompany countless recipes; it can also be eaten on tacos or with pimitos (thick tortillas made of corn with salt).

Preparation
1. Mash the avocado in a bowl with the chili.
2. Add the rest of the ingredients and mix with a wood spatula to completely combine the ingredients.
3. Keep in the refrigerator until ready to serve.

Avocado Mole

Ingredients
4 servings

- 1 small onion
- 2 cloves of garlic
- 2 serrano chilis
- ⅓ cup (50 g) sesame seeds
- 4 tablespoons of olive oil
- Salt
- A pinch of cumin
- A pinch of oregano
- A pinch of pepper
- ⅓ cup (50 g) almonds
- 4 tablespoons olive oil
- 3 ripe avocados
- 2 cups vegetable broth
- ½ cup (30 g) cilantro leaves
- 2 bay leaves
- 4 small hoja santa
  (Mexican pepperleaf) leaves
- A piece of tasajo (dried beef)
- 1 oz (25 g) chorizo

Preparation

1. Add onion, garlic, chilis, seeds, spices, and nuts to a food processor. Grind until smooth.
2. In a deep pot or Dutch oven, add two tablespoons of olive oil and the ground mixture. Sauté on medium heat until the onion is translucent; season to taste.
3. Meanwhile, mash the avocados in a molcajete (stone grinding bowl). Add them to the pot and stir to combine.
4. Add vegetable stock to thin out the sauce. Taste and adjust salt.
5. Grind the cilantro, bay leaves, and hoja santa leaves and add them to the pot. Bring to a boil to let the flavors mature.
6. Serve this mole with tasajo (a cut of dried meat like cecina, a thinly sliced cured beef or pork) and chorizo (which must be fried).

Olga Cabrera Oropeza

Chef, Tierra del Sol
Oaxaca, Mexico
@tierradelsolrestaurante

A chef born in Huajuapan de León, Oaxaca. She was influenced by the women in her family, more than twenty years ago, she created the restaurant Tierra y Sol, known for its traditional recipes. Recently, she opened Masea, a bakery that specializes corn-based recipes, and an atole (cornmeal beverage) shop. Her projects seek to spotlight the grandeur of Mixtec, Oaxaca, and Mexican cuisine. She also launched the digital platform "Women of Fire," where she shares her colleagues' experiences.

Her story with this dish
This recipe goes perfectly with many proteins, including fish. We use tasajo and chorizo as they're typical meats you can find in the markets of Oaxaca. This recipe is a mash-up of the greatness of our moles with the creamy, delicious avocado.

Veracruz-Style Guacamole

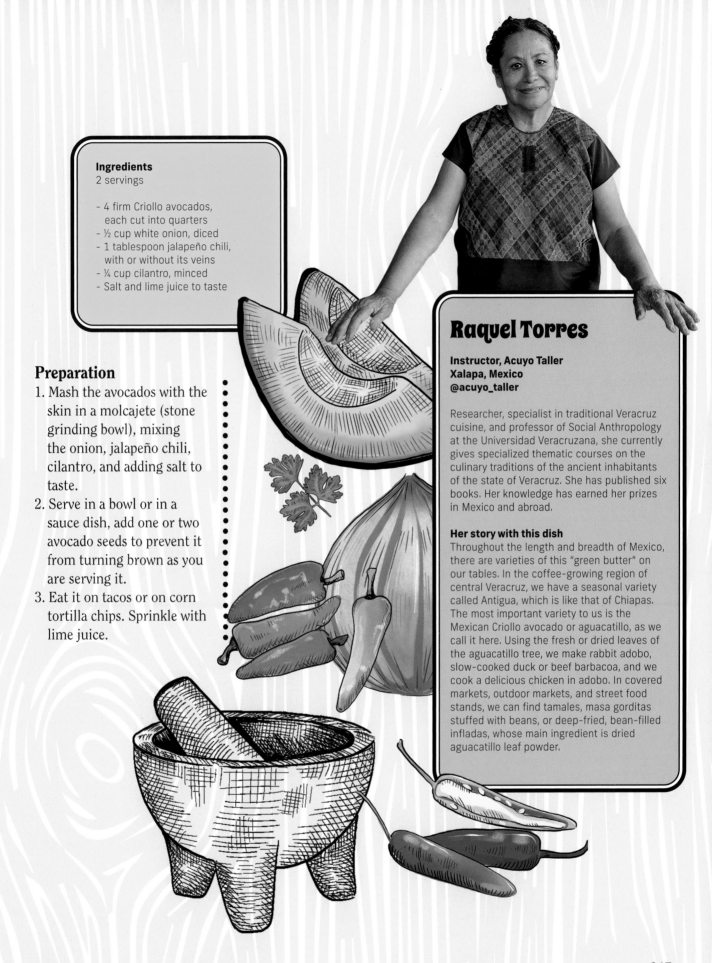

Ingredients
2 servings

- 4 firm Criollo avocados,
  each cut into quarters
- ½ cup white onion, diced
- 1 tablespoon jalapeño chili,
  with or without its veins
- ¼ cup cilantro, minced
- Salt and lime juice to taste

Preparation

1. Mash the avocados with the skin in a molcajete (stone grinding bowl), mixing the onion, jalapeño chili, cilantro, and adding salt to taste.
2. Serve in a bowl or in a sauce dish, add one or two avocado seeds to prevent it from turning brown as you are serving it.
3. Eat it on tacos or on corn tortilla chips. Sprinkle with lime juice.

Raquel Torres

Instructor, Acuyo Taller
Xalapa, Mexico
@acuyo_taller

Researcher, specialist in traditional Veracruz cuisine, and professor of Social Anthropology at the Universidad Veracruzana, she currently gives specialized thematic courses on the culinary traditions of the ancient inhabitants of the state of Veracruz. She has published six books. Her knowledge has earned her prizes in Mexico and abroad.

Her story with this dish
Throughout the length and breadth of Mexico, there are varieties of this "green butter" on our tables. In the coffee-growing region of central Veracruz, we have a seasonal variety called Antigua, which is like that of Chiapas. The most important variety to us is the Mexican Criollo avocado or aguacatillo, as we call it here. Using the fresh or dried leaves of the aguacatillo tree, we make rabbit adobo, slow-cooked duck or beef barbacoa, and we cook a delicious chicken in adobo. In covered markets, outdoor markets, and street food stands, we can find tamales, masa gorditas stuffed with beans, or deep-fried, bean-filled infladas, whose main ingredient is dried aguacatillo leaf powder.

Choco Guacamole

Ingredients
2 servings

- 2 criollo avocados, cut into cubes (1 Hass avocado)
- 10 g of cilantro or parsley, minced
- ¼ of a red onion, minced
- Stalks of criollo chives (to taste)
- Ripe pequin peppers, ground in a tamul (wooden mortar)*
- Juice of 2 limes
- Salt to taste

Preparation
1. Cut the avocado and put it in a bowl, adding the cilantro or parsley, onion, chives, and peppers, mixing well.
2. Add lime juice and salt.
3. Serve with tortillas or fried malanga (taro chips).

Nelly Córdoba

Cook, Cocina Chontal
San Isidro Comalcalco, Mexico
@cocinachontal

A traditional cook, Córdoba started out studying law and now has her own eatery, Cocina Chontal, in the Tabasco town of San Isidro Comalcalco, named one of the "20 Best Restaurants in the World" in Travel + Leisure and Food & Wine 2020. Her greatest teacher is her mother, also named Nelly. From the age of eleven, her mother taught her about the cooking traditions of the state of Tabasco, mastering fiesta and everyday recipes, such as this "guacamole."

Her story with this dish
The Criollo avocado is a large fruit, with a thin skin and soft, fleshy pulp that has high levels of moisture, simple and juicy. It is cut in large cubes to prevent it from breaking and releasing too much juice. It is generally eaten sliced alone or with beans and tortillas. Another way to taste Criollos is presented here, a simple guacamole accompanied by tortillas or fried taro chips. At other times, it is added to *puchero* (meat stew) or to boiled bean soup.

*Tip: You can use any kind of mortar and pestle, or even a spoon and a bowl.

Avocado and Basil Dressing

Ingredients
Yields 1½ quarts (1½ liters)

- 1 ripe avocado
- ¾ cup (200 g) queso fresco
- ½ tablespoon mustard
- 2 tablespoons basil leaves, minced
- 1 qt (1 l) neutral oil
- 1 tablespoon lime juice

Preparation
1. Blend the ingredients in a blender until a smooth sauce forms.
2. Chill in the refrigerator until ready to serve.

Hugo Soca

Chef, Almacén Hugo Soca
Puebla, Mexico
@almacenhugosoca

Hugo Soca is internationally known as the ambassador of Uruguayan cuisine, who has ten years of professional experience teaching patisserie at the prestigious Escuela de Gastronomía El Gato Dumas. A popular chef on TV programs like *De la tierra al plato*, *Recomiendo (lugares gastronómicos)*, or *Cena con mama*, and a frequent guest on radio programs, he is the author of the cookbook *Nuestras recetas de siempre*, which earned him first prize at the Gourmand awards, and third place in Best Chef Books in the World. His restaurant, Almacén Hugo Soca, was born in 2020 during the pandemic as the reinvention of a fresh, homestyle kitchen featuring organic products and prioritizing quality ingredients. Desserts occupy a prominent place on its daily menu: freshly baked breads, *alfajores* (filled cookies), pasta *frola* (pies), brownies, pear and crunchy apple tarts, all served in a warm, cozy setting.

His story with this dish
The recipe arose because I'm an absolute fanatic about avocados, which I consider a highly noble, versatile product, with lots of nutritional properties. It's good at breakfast, brunch, lunch, or dinner. That's why I wanted a recipe with a fresh avocado dressing to be able to enrich a dish as simple and everyday as a salad.

Avocado Gazpacho

Ingredients
4 servings

- 1.1 lbs (500 g) avocado
- 0.4 pounds (200 g) green tomatoes
- ½ of a large (80 g) green pepper
- ¼ green cucumber
- 1 white onion
- ⅛ of a handful of cilantro
- 1 clove of garlic
- ½ cup (120 ml) olive oil
- 1 tablespoon sugar
- 3 tablespoons sherry vinegar
- A pinch of salt
- ¼ cup (40 g) manchego cheese, thinly sliced
- A handful of pistachios, minced and toasted
- Few drops of lime juice
- Half a cucumber, cut thinly, lengthwise

Preparation
1. Put the avocados, green tomatoes cut into quarters, cucumber, green pepper, onion, cilantro, garlic and one cup of water into the blender.
2. Start to blend it and once it is a smooth consistency, pass it through a conical sieve and put it all back into the blender.
3. Start adding a thin stream of olive oil until it emulsifies.
4. Add the tablespoon of sugar, sherry vinegar, salt and lime juice.
5. Adjust the flavor and set aside.

Assembly
1. Individually roll the thin strips of cucumber so you have four or five cones. Place in a shallow bowl with the Manchego cheese slices, minced onion, and green pepper brunoise.
2. Sprinkle with minced toasted pistachios.
3. Pour the gazpacho over the ingredients in the bowl, leaving the cucumber slightly visible. Serve cold or at room temperature.

Eva Millán

Chef, Villa Valencia
Los Cabos, México
@evamillan_chef

Spanish chef Eva Millán burst onto the professional cooking scene after participating in the first season of the cooking competition show *Master Chef* (Spain) in 2013. She has studied haute cuisine at Le Cordon Bleu. A biologist by training with two master's degrees (in Food Quality and Nutrition), equilibrium in her dishes is her personal touch based on the careful balance of nutrients and calories, without compromising strong flavors. She was head chef at the restaurant Koba in the Club House at the Mayakoba Golf Club for four years, where she developed a fusion menu with Mexican products and Spanish techniques. Today, she is patron chef at Villa La Valencia.

Her story with this dish
Andalusia is my land. Gazpacho was a traditional dish that farmworkers used to make because it was loaded with all the vitamins, mineral salts, and hydration needed to continue their long work days. I have "Caribbeanized" it with local ingredients, like avocado, to redefine it as a more gourmet dish.

223

Aguacatillos Salad with Watercress

Ingredients
4 servings

- 6 Criollo avocados
- ¼ small red onion
- 2 tablespoons blueberry vinegar**
- 3 tablespoons extra virgin olive oil
- ½ teaspoon Soconusco pink salt*
- 1 big bunch of fresh watercress
- 1 pink of ground black pepper

Tip: You can use pink salt of choice, such as Himalayan.

**Note: Blueberry vinegar can be purchased online, but it is also easy to make—all you need is a pint of blueberries, white vinegar, sugar, and time.

Preparation

1. Cut the avocados into quarters and remove the seed. If you use Criollo avocados, you don't need to remove the thin, edible skin. Cut the red onion into thin slices or rings. Set them aside.
2. In a bowl, pour the blueberry vinegar, olive oil, and half the salt. Mix well to form a vinaigrette.

3. Put the watercress in a large bowl (using only the tender tips and removing any thick stems). Add the avocado, red onion, a little vinaigrette, salt, and pepper. Mix well and repeat twice more until all the vinaigrette is used.
4. Serve immediately with tortilla chips, freshly baked bread, or with main dishes.

Lesterloon Sánchez

Chef, Múcara
Xalapa, México
@mucara_veracruz

For several years, Sánchez has explored topics related to cooking and culture in Mexico. He published the books *Las Flores en La Cocina Veracruzana* and *Canasta Regional Xalapeña*. He has devoted his time to gastronomic tourism, taking groups to different regions of Veracruz to get to know its cuisine, markets, and food culture. Named gastronomic ambassador of Veracruz, he opened his restaurant, Nao, and three years later, Múcara, a restaurant in the Xalapa historic center where he presents a worthy compendium of popular Veracruz cuisine.

His story with this dish
When you visit Sunday markets in Xalapa and its vicinity, you can see the baskets overflowing with fragrant Criollo avocados, whose leaves perfume countless dishes. I always take advantage of them when they're in season to prepare a tasty salad with fresh watercress like how my grandmother used to make.

Avocado Ceviche and White Trout

Ingredients
3 servings

Ceviche
- ¼ cup (60 g) avocado purée and yuzu koshō*
- 5 cubes of avocado tempura
- 2 slices chargrilled avocado
- ½ cup (80 ml) avocado tiger's milk (recipe below)
- 4 oz (120 g) white trout (skinned, deboned, cut in cubes)
- 3 round slices of serrano chili, seeds removed
- Cilantro leaves and flowers to taste

Avocado and yuzu koshō purée
- ¾ cup (130 g) avocado
- 1 tablespoon (15 g) yuzu koshō**
- 1 tablespoon lime juice
- 1 pinch of salt
- Pastry bag (or plastic bag with one corner cut)

Green onion rings
- 1 green onion, cut in 15 rings
- Lime, juice

Tempura
- 2 egg yolks
- 3 cups all-purpose flour
- 2 tablespoons cornstarch
- ½ tablespoon salt
- 1 avocado

Chargrilled avocado
- 1 avocado

Tiger's milk
- 1 cup (250 ml) dashi** or fish stock
- ½ cup (80 g) avocado
- ⅔ cup (20 g) onion
- 1 clove garlic
- 2 ½ tablespoons (5 g) fresh ginger
- 2 ¾ tablespoons (5 g) cilantro
- ¼ cup (40 ml) lime juice
- ½ serrano chili
- Salt, as needed
- 4 ice cubes

Garnish
- 1 serrano chili, seedless
- Cilantro leaves and flowers to taste

Notes: Yuzu koshō is a Japanese condiment made from a chili paste, yuzu peel, and salt. You can find it in Asian markets. Dashi is a group of Japanese broths made from steeping various ingredients. At its simplest, dashi can be a cold-brewed kombu (seaweed) broth, or more complex with dried mushroom, dried shellfish, bonito flakes, and adzuki beans.

Preparation

Avocado and yuzu koshõ purée

1. Process all the ingredients in a blender to get a smooth purée.
2. Put into a pastry bag. Set aside.

Onion rings

1. Place the sliced onion rings in lime juice and a little salt to enhance the flavor and remove the strong flavor. Set aside as decoration.

Avocado tempura

1. For the tempura batter, whisk the egg yolks well over an ice bath.
2. Mix the dry ingredients and slowly add them to the yolks to avoid forming any lumps. Do not overmix and make sure batter is kept cold.
3. Cut the avocado into about ¾ in (2 cm) cubes
4. With chopsticks (or any other utensil), dip the avocado cubes into the tempura batter, covering them completely. Fry them in hot oil, drain and add a bit of salt.

Chargrilled avocado

1. Cut the avocado into thin slices. You can leave the skin on for more dramatic plating.

2. Arrange them on a tray and grill them with a cooking torch or put them into a hot frying pan and turn them over repeatedly.

Tiger's milk

1. Liquify all the ingredients in a blender shortly before serving to prevent the avocado from oxidizing.
2. If necessary, add salt, to produce a light, smooth, creamy consistency.

Assembly

1. Ladle one half cup of tiger's milk in a soup dish. Add five cubes of trout, seasoning them with a little salt. Put a dollop avocado and yuzu koshõ purée on each trout cube.
2. Arrange five avocado tempura cubes and two chargrilled avocado slices on top.
3. Finish the dish with five onion rings. Add three small rounds of serrano chili and cilantro leaves and flowers.

Mariana Valencia

Chef, Cocina M
Uruapan, Mexico
@cocinam

She studied at the International Culinary School in Guadalajara and has worked in major restaurants in Spain, the United States, and Argentina. Working at Andoni Aduriz's restaurant, Mugaritz was a watershed in her culinary vision. At her restaurant, Cocina M, her dishes combine Michoacán traditions and the culinary secrets she has gathered from all over the world. For example, her *gyozas* (dumplings) filled with *carnitas* blend Peruvian-Japanese techniques.

Her story with this dish
This dish doesn't have as romantic a backstory as many others. It was created for an important Mexican avocado association in the region. But I fell in love with the result. It represents a lot of who I am as a chef, as a person, and as an Uruapan.

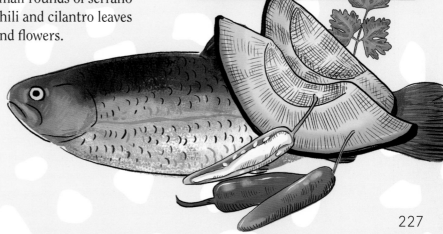

Avocado and Jumbo Shrimp Buñuelos

Ingredients
10 servings

- Sunflower oil or neutral oil for frying
- Edible flowers
- Turmeric powder

Buñuelo filling
- ¼ lb (100 g) jumbo shrimp, cooked
- 1 cup (150 g) avocado pulp
- 14 oz (400 g) cream cheese
- Juice of ½ lime
- Freshly ground black pepper

Buñuelo batter
- ¾ cup (100 g) chickpea flour
- ⅓ cup (50 g) corn flour
- ½ cup (50 g) rice flour
- 2 ¾ tablespoons (40 g) squid ink
- 12 oz (330 ml) light beer
- ¼ teaspoon (1 g) fine-grained salt
- ½ cup (100 ml) water

Avocado mayonnaise
- ¼ cup (10 g) spinach
- ½ cup (60 g) avocado
- Juice of ½ lime
- ¼ teaspoon (1 g) salt
- ¾ cups (200 g) mayonnaise

Ají panca (Peruvian red pepper) mayonnaise
- ¾ cups (200 g) mayonnaise
- 2 ¾ tablespoon (40 g) ají panca paste

Preparation

Buñuelo filling
1. Peel and clean the jumbo shrimp, cutting them in fine slices.
2. Cut avocado into cubes.
3. Mix shrimp and avocado with the cream cheese, lime juice, and pepper, forming small balls. Refrigerate for 4 hour.

Buñuelo batter
1. Mix the ingredients with a half cup of water in a blender, to make a smooth batter without lumps. Don't overmix; set aside.
2. In a large pot or Dutch oven, pour neutral frying oil into the pot until it is halfway full. Heat until 350F (180 °C)—the temperature may dip but should be kept in the 320-350 °F (160-180 °C) range.
3. Using chopsticks or other utensil, place each ball, one by one, into the tempura batter, then into the oil. Don't overcrowd. Fry until golden.

4. Put them on paper towel to remove excess oil.

Avocado mayonnaise
1. With a mixer, blend the spinach, avocado, lime juice, salt, and half the mayonnaise to form a smooth mixture.
2. Pour into a bowl and add the rest of the mayonnaise, put it into a squeeze bottle or a pastry bag.

Ají panca mayonnaise
1. In a bowl, mix the mayonnaise and the ají panca paste to produce a smooth sauce, and put it into a squeeze bottle or a pastry bag.

Plating
1. With the mayonnaise pastry bag, draw dots of different sizes on the bottom of the plate.

Borja Martín-Palomino

Chef, Kitchen Club
Madrid, Spain
www.kitchenclub.es

As a chef sensitive to gluten, he wrote *Cocina sin gluten, Recetas para triunfar* (Editorial Punto Rojo, 2018) in order to share inventive, gluten-free recipes. After having worked in many a professional kitchen, he now gives classes and cookery lessons at Kitchen Club, a culinary school based in Madrid and Santiago, Chile. It is a special place where unique gastronomic experiences are completely tailored and personalized for each client.

His story with this dish
This recipe is about the fusion of Latin American ingredients, like the avocado, and Asian cooking techniques, like tempura. The avocado is a highly versatile product that we can use both in sweet and savory dishes, while it also provides lots of health benefits.

2. Distribute the buñuelos on the plate and place a dollop of avocado mayonnaise on each of them.
3. Decorate with edible flowers and turmeric powder.

Avocado Cannelloni with Centollo

Ingredients
10 servings

- 1 lb (400 g) centollo meat, steamed*
- 1 ¼ tablespoons (20 g)
  centollo reduction (or fish sauce)
- ¼ cup (50 g) arrope de jitomate
  (slow-cooked tomato syrup).
- ⅓ lb (160 g) tomatoes
- ⅓ lb (140 g) green apple, with peel
- ½ (50 g) small onion, minced
- ¼ lb (115 g) asparagus, blanched
- ¼ cup (70 g) mayonnaise
- 5 turns of a pepper grinder
- 2.2 lbs (1 kg) avocado
- 1 oz (26 g) serrano chili
- Pickled radish
- ¼ teaspoon (5 g) salt

Preparation

1. If using centollo crab, make a stock with the crab shell and reduce it to 1¼ tablespoon. Skip this step if using fish sauce.

2. For the tomato syrup, boil ½ cup of water. Reduce heat to a simmer, then add the tomatoes and green apple. Cook over low heat until it forms a paste. Strain through a sieve to remove the peel and bits of tomato.

3. Finely mince the onion, cooked asparagus, and crab meat until it forms a homogeneous mixture.

4. Pour it into a bowl and add the mayonnaise, stock reduction (or fish sauce), salt, pepper, and mix.

5. Set aside

6. Remove the peel from the avocado and cut it into long, flat slices.

7. Place avocado slices on a piece of plastic wrap to form flat sheet. Make sure you have about 1-2 inches of plastic wrap clearance from the avocado (this will help with rolling the cannelloni later).

Assembly

1. Spoon the crab mixture onto the avocado, forming a line down the center. Less is more here—if you have any extra filling, you can use it on a salad or other dish later. Using the edges of plastic wrap, roll the cannelloni until it forms a tube. With hands at either opening, roll over so the edges are hidden. Place on serving dish, then remove plastic wrap and discard.

2. Decorate with the *arrope de jitomate* and mayonnaise, cilantro leaves, serrano chili, pickled radish, and salt.

Pablo San Román

Chef, Ekilore
Mexico City, Mexico
www.ekilore.mx

He was born in San Sebastián in the Basque country of Spain. His creative talent as a chef turned into a professional career that began at various hotels in San Sebastián and Palma de Mallorca, such as the María Cristina, Las Marismas, Cadena Sika hotels, and the restaurant Porto Pi. Stemming from this experience, he opened his restaurant Labeko Etxea in Irun, (Euskadi). After twenty-eight years, he inaugurated Ekilore in Mexico City; a Basque grill where you can savor dishes like this.

His story with this dish
The inspiration was Albert Adrià's avocado and brown crab cannelloni recipe, but we decided to adapt it to our Basque gastronomic tradition, and we fill it with a *txangurro* (baked crab) salad. For its dietetic and organoleptic characteristics, the avocado has become the essential ingredient to finish dishes on our menu. It's useful for both main dishes and as an ideal accompaniment for most of our recipes.

*Tip: Centollo crab (European Spider Crab) meat is revered for its intense marine flavor and smooth texture. If you can't find it, any crab meat can be used (though brown is preferred). Canned crab meat is often cooked already, but fresh crab needs to be fully cooked (boiled/steamed for 10-20 minutes).

Monument to the Avocado

Ingredients
2 servings

- 2 medium avocados
- Variety of grains and seeds (sunflower, squash, black and white sesame seeds, minced almonds)
- Salt and pepper to taste
- ½ lb (200 g) skinless red seabream, cut into 5/8 in (1 cm) cubes*
- ½ cup (100 ml) lime juice
- ½ cup (50 g) red pepper, seeded and cubed
- ½ cup minced ginger
- 2 tablespoons cilantro, minced
- 2 tablespoons fresh mint, minced
- 1 cup (100 g) seasonal fruit (watermelon, cantaloupe, mango, kiwi, grapes, pineapple), cubed
- 2 teaspoons parsley, minced

*Tip: If you don't find red seabream, ask the fishmonger for another seasonal alternative, like grouper, bass, etc.

Preparation

1. Cut the avocado in half, and remove the seed.
2. Toast the grain and seed mixture in a frying pan with a bit of olive oil and finish with salt and pepper.
3. To make the ceviche, season the fish with salt and pepper and let marinate for 10 minutes in the lime juice, making sure the fish is completely covered. Add the red pepper, ginger, cilantro, mint, and fruit.
4. Mix and season with salt and pepper; set aside.
5. Fill each avocado half with this ceviche, without going over the edge of the hole and place the other half on top to recover the original shape of the avocado.
6. Make sure the two halves fit together well and smooth over the division with a knife.
7. Cover the whole avocado with the seed mixture. It's important that the avocado is smooth for the seeds to adhere to the entire surface.
8. Serve each avocado on a bed of the seasonal fruit and minced parsley. Cut the avocado open in front of the guest and serve as is, or with the sauce of your choice. Garnish with parsley.

Michael Katz

Chef
Tel Aviv, Israel
@michaelkatzch

With thirty years of experience, he is one of Israel's culinary ambassadors. He has worked in two- and three-Michelin-star restaurants, was professor at the Cordon Bleu in London and Executive Chef at other outstanding establishments. For four years, he coordinated courses and taught at Dan Gourmet, the foremost culinary school in Israel. In mid-2022 he will open his own school for professional chefs.

His story with this dish
Many years ago, I saw a whole avocado covered with seeds somewhere on the internet. It captivated me and inspired me in this method, so it became one of my favorite techniques for serving ceviche. That's why I owe most of the credit to the person who inspired me and who is, to this day, anonymous to me.

Tacos with Deviled Scarlet Shrimp

Ingredients
6 servings

Guacamole
- 2 Hass avocados
- 1 white onion
- 2 teaspoons (10 g) cilantro
- Jalapeño chilis
- 3 tablespoons (50 ml) lime juice
- Avocado oil (to taste)
- Fine grained salt

Tacos
- 6 pieces of scarlet prawns
- ¼ cup (20 g) guacamole
- 6 small/medium corn tortillas
- 1 cup pico de gallo (onion, tomato, green chili, cilantro) to taste
- 6 lime quarters

Chipotle salsa
- 2 clusters of vine tomatoes
- 1 teaspoon oregano
- Splash of white wine
- 2 chipotle chilis
- 1 clove garlic, peeled
- Sunflower oil (or other neutral oil)
- Cinnamon stick
- Fine-grained salt
- ½ white onion

Preparation

Guacamole
1. In a grinding bowl, lightly mash the avocados.
2. Mince the onion, cilantro, and jalapeño chili.
3. Add the mixture to the avocados and gently stir.
4. Add the lime juice, avocado oil, and salt.

Chipotle salsa
1. Put all the ingredients on an oven try, except for the sunflower oil
2. Bake for 20 minutes until the tomatoes are slightly toasted.
3. Remove and mash.
4. Sauté mixture in a small pot with hot sunflower oil, until blended and fragrant.
5. Set aside.

Tacos
1. Cut the heads off the scarlet prawns a little below where the head meets the body. This helps to prevent the loss of juices during cooking.
2. Peel and devein the prawns and set aside.
3. Cook the prawn heads in a frying pan with sea salt and sunflower oil.
4. Cook the prawn in the chipotle salsa.
5. Heat the tortillas and top with guacamole and pico de gallo.
6. Put the prawns on top of the pico de gallo and spoon on the chipotle salsa.
7. Serve the prawn heads on the side and the lime quarters.

Roberto Ruíz

Chef, Barracuda Mx
Madrid, Spain
@RobertoPuntoMX

Established in Madrid for almost twenty years, Roberto is a Mexican creator of Mexican-Spanish fusion cuisine, without losing its roots, unique character, and traditional values. In a personal crusade through his signature cuisine, he has helped to change the idea of Mexican food as simple street fare to be appreciated as international gourmet food. His restaurant, Barracuda MX, features retro cuisine with Mexican techniques applied to major Spanish products. On his menu, 60 percent of the dishes contain avocado: ceviches, avocado cream soup, mashed avocado, lots of tacos, and his mestizo inspired guacamoles.

His story with this dish
I work a lot with the Hass and Bacon avocados . . . even though the latter isn't Mexican. Now, lots of avocados sold in Spain are from Granada or Málaga. Seventeen years ago, when I arrived, you could only get a good avocado in the Barrio de Lavapiés where there are Moroccan and Arab immigrants. There you could find 'exotic' products, and as they used to say: ethnic cuisine.

Avocado Agua Fresca

Ingredients
Yields 2 quarts (2 liters)

- 1 tablespoon chia seeds
- 2 ½ cups (360 g) avocado, peeled and seeded
- 1 (70 g) sweet lime**
- 2 sprigs fresh rosemary
- 2 qts (l) water
- ½ cup (40 g) sugar (or to taste)

Note: Sweet lime describes a variety of fruits generally with less acidity and more aromatic flavor. They can be difficult to find, so you can use any other citrus available.

Preparation

1. To begin, put the chia in water for two hours.
2. Separate and wash the avocado, lime, and rosemary leaves. Set aside.
3. In a blender, grind the lime (cut into quarters) together with a cup of water, until you get a pulpy consistency. Don't overgrind it because it will bring out the sour notes of the drink.
4. Pass the lime juice through a sieve into a pitcher.
5. Return the lime water to the blender and blend together with the avocado and another cup of water.
6. Pass the mixture through a sieve again, and add sugar, soaked chia, and rosemary to the pitcher, making sure the sugar is completely dissolved.
7. Refrigerate for 15 minutes and serve.

Rosalba Morales

**Cook, La Cocina Tradicional de Rosalba
San Jerónimo Purenchécuaro, Mexico
@rosalba_morales_bartolo**

This traditional cook was born in the Indigenous community of San Jerónimo Purenchécuaro (Michoacán). After performing many kinds of jobs and even moving to the United States on different occasions, she returned to settle down in her homeland in early 2000. Years later, she started La Cocina de Rosy and her culinary talent and fame spread. She was invited to competitions and was a steadfast winner. She was named as Master Traditional Cook of Michoacán by the state government.

Her story with this recipe
"This is a recipe that we always prepare at home because I have a garden where I have criollo avocado, and that's a privilege. But if you don't have a tree, use Hass avocado or any other kind you like. The recipe works well with any kind of avocado."

Avocado and Citrus Water

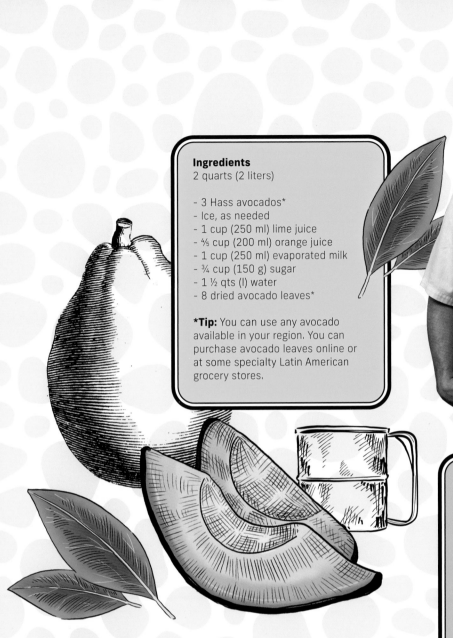

Ingredients
2 quarts (2 liters)

- 3 Hass avocados*
- Ice, as needed
- 1 cup (250 ml) lime juice
- ⅘ cup (200 ml) orange juice
- 1 cup (250 ml) evaporated milk
- ¾ cup (150 g) sugar
- 1 ½ qts (l) water
- 8 dried avocado leaves*

*Tip: You can use any avocado available in your region. You can purchase avocado leaves online or at some specialty Latin American grocery stores.

Preparation
1. Remove the pulp from the avocado (make sure they're not too ripe, they should be tender to touch but still firm).
2. Put two or three ice cubes, the lime and orange juice, evaporated milk, sugar, half of a quart/liter of water, and the avocado into a blender. Mix until smooth.
3. Add the rest of the water until desired texture. Adjust sugar to taste. Serve in glasses with more ice and decorate with a dried avocado leaf.

Juan Cabrera Barrón

Chef, Fonda Fina
Mexico City, Mexico
@fondafinamx

A graduate in Gastronomy from the Universidad del Claustro de Sor Juana in Mexico City, he got his degree in pastry arts from the Culinary Institute of America in New York. After graduating, he worked as head chef in the restaurants Pujol, Teo, Eno, and in catering for Grupo Enrique Olvera, in addition to other restaurants in Monterrey, Villahermosa, and Guadalajara. Today, he is executive chef and partner in the restaurant Fonda Fina in Mexico City and opened Casa Tijuana, his personal project, in Tijuana.

His story with this dish
It's important to seek other uses for the whole avocado that aren't too obvious. Recently, I experimented with an avocado beer. I consider using fresh avocado as a path that has always been in our cuisine, and even more if we use the leaves.

Avocado and Blueberry Yogurt

Ingredients
1 serving

- 1 ripe avocado
- 1 tablespoon honey
- ⅞ cup (200 ml)
  plain unsweetened yogurt

Assembly:
- Yogurt with avocado
- 2 tablespoons raspberries
- 2 tablespoons blackberries
- 2 tablespoons garambullos
  (bilberry cactus berries)*
- 2 tablespoons granola
- 1 strawberry
- 1 sprig fresh mint

Preparation
1. Put the avocado, yogurt, and honey into a blender and combine to form a smooth, uniform mixture. Set aside.

Assembly
1. In a tall glass or parfait glass, put a layer of yogurt, raspberries, blackberries, and bilberry cactus berries, and then a layer of yogurt followed by granola.
2. Repeat until you have used all the ingredients, or the glass is full.
3. Top with a strawberry and a sprig of fresh mint.

*Tip: These are small, dark red or violet berries harvested from the bilberry cactus. You can use blueberries as a substitute.

Alejandro Piñón

Chef, Los Danzantes
Mexico City, Mexico
www.losdanzantes.com

Alejandro's culinary career began at Los Danzantes in 1996, where he moved up from being a dishwasher to head cook, sous chef, and later head chef at Los Danzantes Oaxaca, later in Los Danzantes Coyoacán in Mexico City. Earlier, he demonstrated his leadership at Ricardo Muñoz Zurita's restaurant Azul y Oro, at the National Autonomous University of Mexico. In 2011, he joined the new Los Danzantes group, where his work focuses on the planning, training, and execution of all the group's menus, festivals, and special events.

His story with this dish
This recipe is ideal for breakfast for its easy assembly, bright ingredients, and freshness. The avocado and honey form an interesting synergy with the tartness of the raspberries and blackberries. We should remember that avocado is currency and fruit—a basic ingredient in Mexican cuisine, it's butter and color.

Avocado Cheesecake

Ingredients
8 servings

Cheesecake mixture
- 12.5 oz (360 g) cream cheese
- ¾ cup (96 g) sugar
- ½ cup (112 g) whipping cream
- 2 eggs
- 1 avocado

Crumble
- ½ cup (100 g) muscovado sugar
- 1 stick (100 g) butter, cold
- ½ cup (120 g) flour
- 1 avocado seed, grated*

* Tip: Toast it in a pan to remove the brown seed coating and then grate it.

Avocado ice cream
Yield 1 pint

- 4 egg yolks
- 1 cup (120 g) sugar
- 1 cup (250 ml) milk
- 1 cup (250 ml) whipping cream
- 4 avocado leaves

Preparation

Cheesecake mixture

1. In a bowl, cream together the cream cheese and sugar. Add the whipping cream and the eggs and beat to produce a smooth mixture.
2. Divide the mixture in half. Put one half in the blender with the avocado and blend until it is smooth.
3. Grease a round 11 in (28 cm) pan and coat it with sugar. Alternate the cheesecake mixtures, starting with the plain layer and then the avocado layer to create a marbled effect.
4. Place the pan in a container of water and bake at 350 °F (177 °C) for 35 to 40 minutes. Remove and let cool. When it is lukewarm, unmold it, and refrigerate for at least 4 hours or overnight.

Crumble

1. Put the ingredients in a bowl and mix it until they are barely incorporated in a sandy texture, without overmixing.

2. Put mixture on a tray lined with Silpat or wax paper and bake at 350 °F (177 °C) for 20 minutes, taking it out to stir occasionally in order to obtain a soil-like texture. Set aside.

Avocado ice cream

1. In a bowl, beat the egg yolks with the sugar until it is light, fluffy, and white.
2. Heat the milk with the cream and the avocado leaves. When it is hot, turn off the heat and gradually add the beaten egg yolks, beating constantly to avoid lumps from forming. Once it is all combined, return it to a medium heat and warm it until it coats the back of a spoon (nappe consistency). Pass the mixture through a sieve and set aside.
3. Put the mixture in a container and place in the freezer, stirring it every half hour until it produces a smooth ice cream.

Karla and Mario Papa García

**Chefs, Teté Cocina de Barrio
Guadalajara, Mexico
@tetecocinadebarrio**

These siblings form a team in the kitchen: Karla defines her style as a blend of traditions and techniques aimed at achieving the perfect balance of flavors, sensations, and memories; Mario has fifteen years of experience at establishments like Quintonil and was a student with mentors like the chef Alfredo Heredia. They opened the restaurant Teté Cocina de Barrio in 2015 with different tasting menus, one of them entirely plant-based.

Their story with this dish
We devised this dish to avoid wasting any part of the avocado: the cheesecake is made with the pulp, the leaf and toasted grated seed is for the ice cream. It's an exercise that shows the versatility of this Mexican ingredient.

Assembly

1. Cut the cheesecake into slices, put a slice on a flat dish, sprinkle with the crumble, and add a tablespoon of the crumble on the side of the cheesecake. Top with a ball of avocado ice cream.

Strawberries with Sweet Avocado Cream

Ingredients
6 servings

- 30 strawberries (2 pints)
- ⅜ cup (3 oz) orange liqueur (like Cointreau)
- 1 ¾ cup (250 g) avocado pulp
- ½ cup (100 ml) heavy cream
- ¼ cup (2 oz) agave syrup
- 1 yellow Eureka lemon*
- ¼ cup (20 g) grated parmesan cheese
- 20 fresh mint leaves

*Tip: Eureka lemons are sourer and tarter than other varieties, but you can use what is available in your region.

Preparation
1. Cut the strawberries in quarters and marinate them in the orange liqueur for two hours in the refrigerator.
2. About 15 minutes before serving, beat the avocado pulp with the cream and agave syrup to blend them completely into a smooth mixture (if necessary, pass it through a strainer for a smoother consistency).
3. Keep it in the refrigerator.

Assembly
1. In a bowl, combine the strawberries with the sweet avocado cream.
2. Spoon a layer of sauce in a bowl and add the marinated strawberries on top. Then grate some lemon zest on top and add a generous amount of parmesan cheese.
3. Decorate with fresh mint leaves.

Juan Emilio Villaseñor

Chef, La Cocinoteca
León, Guanajuato, Mexico
@lacocinoteca

A self-taught chef, he was born in Mexico City. For sixteen years, he has lived in León, Guanajuato, where he started the project La Cocinoteca with his family in their home kitchen. Since then, it has turned into a local landmark restaurant. Named chef ambassador by the state of Guanajuato, he has traveled to Asia, Europe, and North and South America. He also collaborates with the Mexican Grillers' Society as Fire Master, instructor in charcoal- and smoke-based cooking techniques. In 2019, he won the most traditional tapa at the Third World Championship of Pinchos and Tapas in the city of Valladolid, Spain.

His story with this dish
I used two products from my region—strawberries and avocados—to pay tribute to them. The silky flavor of one combined with the tartness of the other are the perfect contrast for a dessert.

Creamy Avocado Dessert

Ingredients
10 servings

- 3 teaspoons gelatin powder (6 gelatin sheets)
- 2 ½ cups (600 g) whipping cream
- ¾ cup (70 g) glucose syrup
- ½ teaspoon (2 g) kosher salt
- 2 teaspoons (4 g) agar
- 1 cup (250 g) Hass avocados (blended)

Avocado leaf syrup with vanilla
- 1 ½ cup (270 g) sugar
- 1 ⅛ cup (270 g) water
- .7 oz (20 g) dried avocado leaves*
- 1 yellow lemon (juice and peeled)

*Tip: You can buy online

Preparation

1. Mix three tablespoons of gelatin with ice water and set aside.
2. Heat the whipping cream, three quarter cup of glucose syrup, and salt in the pot over medium heat.
3. Bring the mixture to 200 °F (93 °C) and add the agar, vigorously mixing it with a wire whisk.
4. Remove the mixture from the heat. Add the gelatin to the avocado until it is dissolved.
5. Pass the mixture through a fine conical sieve and pour into silicon molds. Freeze the mixture in the molds and unmold them when they are completely frozen (usually overnight). Leave in the refrigerator until you are ready to serve.

Avocado leaf syrup with vanilla

1. Put one and a half cup of sugar, one cup and two tablespoons of water, and avocado leaves in a pot over medium heat. Cook for 30 minutes, stirring occasionally, until a syrup forms.
2. Pass through a sieve, add the lime juice, and let it cool.

Assembly

1. Put a serving of the creamy avocado in a bowl and generously spoon on the syrup.
2. Decorate with edible flowers.

Óscar Cortázar Cuilty

Chef, La Cocinería
Chihuahua, Mexico
@lacocinoteca

He studied at the International Culinary Center in New York and at the Apicius Culinary Institute in Florence. He has worked at Martin Berasategui, Spain; Aquavit and Crema Restaurante in New York. Today he is the owner and chef at the restaurant La Cocinería Bistro, in the capital of Chihuahua, as well as a partner in the cocktail bar Licorería Central. Today, the restaurant has its own garden and promotes ingredients from the region, such as pasado chili, chile de la tierra, ari, lamb, peaches, apples, nuts, Mennonite dairy products, and wild mushrooms.

His story with this dish
I decided to make a cold dessert with avocado, because when I was a child, my grandfather used to take me to his orchard near Ciudad Cuauhtémoc. There was a popsicle shop called Germania, and one of the most popular flavors was the avocado popsicle, so I wanted to try to capture that memory in this dish, adding avocado leaf to give it the dessert a more herbal touch.

Avocado Tarte with Strawberries

Preparation

Tarte base

1. Add all the ingredients to a bowl and combine with a mixer or food processer. Once they are just combined, stop mixing: you shouldn't produce a sticky dough; it should be crumbly.
2. Dump mixture onto a piece of plastic wrap and refrigerate for half an hour.
3. Roll out the dough and press into tarte pan(s).
4. Preheat the oven to 350 °F (180 °C). Bake approximately 25 minutes or until the crust is golden.
5. Set aside for the assembly.

Pastry cream

1. Boil the milk with half of the sugar, adding the vanilla and the cinnamon.
2. In a bowl, beat the egg yolks with the sugar until they change to a whitish color, then add the cornstarch.
3. When the milk has boiled, remove the cinnamon, and temper the yolks: in other words, add a third of the hot milk to the yolks, while stirring constantly to prevent them from cooking, to produce a smooth mixture.
4. Add the rest of the milk and lower the heat to prevent lumps from forming.

The consistency should be thick and smooth.
5. Remove from heat. Put a piece of wax paper on top of the mixture to prevent a crust from forming. Let cool.
6. Once cooled, add the mashed avocado to the mixture and beat with a hand mixer or whisk to produce a smooth mixture.
7. (Optional) Pour the mixture into a piping bag or plastic bag with one corner cut.

Assembly

1. On the crust, pipe or spoon the pastry cream, ¾ in (2 cm) away from the edge.
2. Cut the strawberries to decorate the tarte, arranging them as you please (you can also put sliced avocado), sprinkle sugar over them.

Ingredients
4 to 6 servings

Tarte base
- 1 ¼ cup (290 g) butter, softened
- ½ cup (40 g) sugar
- A pinch of salt
- 2 eggs
- 3 cups plus 2 tablespoons (500 g) all-purpose flour
- ½ vanilla pod

Pastry cream
- 2 ¼ cups (500 ml) milk
- ¾ cups (150 g) sugar
- ½ vanilla pod
- .2 oz (6 g) cinnamon stick
- ⅖ cup (120 g) egg yolk
- ¼ cup (35 g) cornstarch
- 1 ¼ cup (200 g) avocado, mashed

Topping
- 1 ½ cups (300 g) strawberries
- ¼ cup (50 g) sugar

Claudia Ruiz Sántiz

Chef, Kokonó
San Cristóbal de las Casas
www.kokono.mx

A woman with Indigenous roots, she has worked in various restaurants in Mexico City, including Pujol, Máxim, and DUO. In 2012, she published the recipe book *Ve'eliletik Chamo' (Chamula Recipes)*, written in Tzotzil and Spanish. In 2016, she opened Kokono' and joined the Alliance of Slow Food Chefs. She also inaugurated Albertina, a signature restaurant that uses local and seasonal products. She was one of the young talents named on the 50 Next, a list of promising young chefs in world gastronomy.

Her story with this dish
I consider the avocado a delicacy: as children we craved it, because it was hard to get. One of the ways we used to eat it was in a taco: a handmade tortilla, avocado pulp, and a touch of salt. We combined it with homemade beans and cheese or in a dish that my grandmother used to make: a pea soup with dried shrimp, served with tostadas. We also flavored it with charred bird's beak chili.

Avocado Ice Cream

Ingredients
Yields 1 ½ quarts (liters)

Custard sauce
- 4 egg yolks
- ⅔ cup (130 g) sugar
- 2 ¼ cups (500 ml) milk
- 1 ½ cups (30 g) fresh basil leaves

Avocado purée
- 2 ¾ cups (400 g) Hass avocado, firm, ripe, without blemishes
- ¾ teaspoon (3 ml) lime juice
- 3 tablespoons (50 ml) milk (approximately)

Topping
- 2 ¼ cup (500 ml) whipping cream, cold

Preparation

English cream

1. Put the egg yolks and sugar in a bowl, beat until the yolks take on a whitish color and the sugar has dissolved. Set aside.
2. Cook the milk and the basil leaves over a medium heat for 5 minutes.
3. Remove from heat. Strain, then place the bowl with the milk mixture on an ice bath to lower the temperature.
4. When the milk is lukewarm, add the egg and sugar mixture little by little.
5. Transfer the mixture back to the stove. Cook on a low heat, mixing constantly to prevent it from burning.
6. Continue mixing until the cream thickens. You will know when it is ready when it coats the spoon. When you run your finger over it, the spoon should be streaked (nappe consistency).
7. Set aside (if possible, leave the sauce in the refrigerator for 6 hours or more before using it).
8. Beat the cream until it forms peaks. Set aside.

Avocado purée

1. Liquify the avocado pulp, lime juice, and milk, until it makes smooth purée.

Assembly

1. Incorporate the purée with the custard sauce with a spatula. Add the whipped cream, mixing with circular movements to prevent the whipped cream from deflating.
2. When combined, put the mixture into an ice cream machine for 35 to 40 minutes, until it reaches the desired consistency. Empty into a container and keep it in the freezer.

Pilar Cabrera

Chef, La Olla
Oaxaca
www.laolla.com.mx

Pilar Cabrera is part of a family of Oaxacan women who love cooking. Born in Oaxaca, she was immersed in the legendary culinary culture unique to her state. In 1994, her own restaurant, La Olla, was born and in 1998 she founded Casa de los Sabores in order to teach traditional cooking classes. She has written books such as *Recipes from Pilar Cabrera and Casa de los Sabores Cooking School*.

Her story with this dish
When we think about avocados, savory things always come to mind. In this case, I thought about something sweet. To bring out other flavors from the avocado notes, I added basil to make it a little more interesting. I didn't want it to be so sweet. I chose firm, nice-looking Hass avocados. The avocado gives it texture and creaminess. To decorate it, the best thing is a little avocado chargrilled with a cooking torch and a sprig of basil.

Avocado and Vanilla Millefeuille

Chantilly cream
- 1 qt (1 l) liquid (whipping) cream
- 1 cup (120 g) powdered sugar, sifted
- 1 vanilla pod

Topping
- Dill sprigs for decoration.

*Tip: You can use what is available in your region, just make sure the pulp is creamy.

Ingredients
10 servings

Puff pastry
- 2.2 lbs (1 kg) puff pastry dough
- 1 cup (200 g) powdered sugar

Avocado pastry cream
- 2 cups (500 g) milk
- ½ cup (100 g) sugar
- ⅓ cup (100 g) egg yolk
- ¼ cup (35 g) cornstarch
- 1 vanilla pod
- 1 tablespoon gelatin powder (4 g gelatin sheets)
- 4 Hass avocados*

Preparation

Puff pastry

1. Preheat the oven to 350 °F (177 °C). Roll out the puff pastry with a rolling pin to ¼ in (5 mm) thick. Slice the puff pastry into identical rectangles.
2. Place the rectangles on a baking sheet and bake for 10 minutes.
3. Sprinkle a little of powdered sugar on top and bake again for 10 minutes. Prick the surface with a toothpick to make sure the dough is cooked through.

Avocado pastry cream

1. Heat the milk with half the sugar and the contents of the scraped inside of the vanilla pod. In a bowl, whisk the egg yolk with the rest of the sugar, then add cornstarch and mix. Separately, hydrate the gelatin in ice water (it's better to use gelatin sheets).
2. Pour the hot milk over the yolks slowly, mixing constantly to avoid clumps, and add the entire mixture back into the pot.
3. Over medium heat, reheat the mixture. Then when it begins to boil, wait for three minutes, then add the gelatin (with no excess water). Cool the pastry cream and keep it in the refrigerator.

4. Once the pastry cream has cooled, mash the avocado with a fork and pass it through a sieve to produce a smooth purée.
5. Mix with the pastry cream and refrigerate.

Chantilly cream

1. Mix the cream in a bowl with a wire whisk.
2. When it begins to thicken and expand in volume, add the powdered sugar, then add vanilla pod seeds.
3. Mix until stiff peaks form.
4. Pour into pastry bag (or plastic bag with one corner cut).

Assembly

1. Put a rectangle of the caramelized puff pastry dough on a plate, add two lines of avocado pastry

Regina Escalante Bush

Chef, Restaurante Merci
Mérida, Yucatán
@mercimid

This chef is inspired by the cuisines of Mexico, the United States, and France. She brings these influences to her home state of Yucatan, where her restaurant Merci Restaurante showcases her vision. Her path began at the age of seventeen, when she set out to study at the Institute Paul Bocuse in France. She worked in France at Michelin starred eateries, until in 2014 she opened her own personal project, where she serves breakfast, brunch, and dinner.

Her story with this dish
In this recipe, I use Hass avocado for its creaminess and sweetness that perfectly complement the vanilla notes and the puff pastry texture. All my childhood, I only ate avocado in savory dishes, however, it's an excellent ingredient for making desserts.

cream and again another puff pastry layer, the more cream.
2. Finally, add a third rectangle of putt pastry and add the Chantilly cream on top. Decorate with sprigs of dillweed.

Spinach Gelée with Avocado

Ingredients
10 servings

Spinach purée
- 2.2 lb (1.5 kg) spinach leaves

Spinach gelatin
- 1 cup (250 g) spinach purée
- almost 1 packet powdered gelatin (3.5 gelatin sheets)
- ½ teaspoon (2 ml) lemon juice
- Fine grain salt

Assembly
- 2 Hass avocados
- 8-10 marcona almonds, sliced in half
- ½ cup (100 g) sheep milk ricotta
- ⅓ cup (100 g) sheep yogurt
- 7 tablespoons (100 ml) squash seed oil
- 20 cilantro sprouts (or fresh cilantro, chopped)
- 4 limes
- 1 jar of tahini

Preparation

1. Liquify the spinach in a blender with enough water to make a purée.
2. Strain it and reserve the liquid spinach purée.
3. Hydrate the gelatin sheets with cold water.
4. Put a pinch of salt in the blender and add the lemon juice.
5. Dilute the gelatin in part of the puréed spinach over a low heat, not over 147 °F (64 °C).
6. Strain and combine with remaining spinach purée.
7. Pour 1 tablespoon and 1 teaspoon (20 g) of the purée onto a plate.
8. Cut each avocado lengthwise into 5 slices.
9. Put the peeled almonds on a plate covered with moist paper.

Assembly

1. On the top of the gelée, carefully place the avocado seasoned with the fine grain salt.
2. Carefully place the almonds on the outer part of the avocado.
3. Gently place two cilantro sprouts separated on top of the avocado.
4. On the left side of the avocado, put an elegant dollop of sheep ricotta.
5. On the right side, place the sheep yogurt and make a hollow with a small spoon to add a few drops of squash seed oil.
6. Cut the limes in quarters and on of side, add dry chili with salt or tahini.

Paco Morales

Chef, Noor
Córdoba, Spain
www.noorrestaurant.es

He is known for recreating Al-Andalus (Moorish Spain) cuisine, constantly researching, among other traditions, sixteenth century Spanish gastronomy. In 2010, he was awarded his first Michelin star with his Paco Morales restaurant in Bocairente, Valencia. In just over three years, he has earned two Michelin stars. In 2021, he was ranked 54th of 100 on the international Best Chef Awards. *Noor* (which means "brightness, light" in Arabic) puts to best use the value of the intermarriage of Arabic and Andalusian cuisine.

His history with this dish
For five years, we didn't use avocado. Now, I have transformed my old limitations into a recipe overflowing with imagination. This recipe combines the techniques of Al-Andalus cuisine with uniquely American ingredients, merging the Old and New Worlds. For me, it was exciting to experiment with combinations that emphasize the delicacy of texture, fusing plant flavors with fresh dairy and buttery almonds.

Scallops, Caviar, and Avocado Salmagundi

Ingredients
6 servings

Avocado Royal
- 1 tablespoon (5 g) agar
  (or cornstarch)
- 1 quart (1 L) pistachio milk
- 2.2 lbs (1 kg) avocado
- 3 ⅓ teaspoons (20 g) salt

Salmagundi base
- 5.25 lbs (2.4 kg) tomatoes
- .6 lbs (300 g) green bell pepper
- 1.1 lb (500 g) red bell pepper
- 1.1 lb (500 g) spring onion
- 5 ¾ teaspoons (35 g) salt
- 2 ½ tablespoons (35 g)
  sherry vinegar
- ½ cup (125 g) cider vinegar
- ⅓ cup (100 g) colatura di alici
  (Italian anchovy sauce)

Apple and cucumber disks
- 1 Granny Smith apple
- Herb water
- 3 Persian cucumbers

Pistachio milk
- 1 ¼ cup (300 g) pure pistachio paste

Fresh herb oil
- 3 ⅓ cups (200 g) parsley
- 3 ¼ cups (100 g) mint
- 1 ¾ cup (100 g) dill
- 1 ¾ cup (100 g) tarragon
- 2 ⅓ cups (500 g) virgin olive oil

Fresh herb water
- ½ lb (250 g) mint
- ½ lb (250 g) parsley
- ½ lb (250 g) chives
- ½ lb (250 g) spinach

Codium-infused "pil pil" sauce
- 7 oz (200 g) codium algae
- ⅚ cup (200 g) oil at 32.72 °F (0.4 °C)
- Salt
- Xanthan gum

Assembly
- Fresh scallops
- Extra virgin olive oil
- Green shiso sprouts
  (or other microgreens)
- 1.76 oz (50 g) sturgeon caviar

Preparation

Avocado Royal

1. Mix the agar with the pistachio milk in a pot on the stove until it boils.
2. Let the mixture cool to 176 °F (80 °C) and purée it with the avocado and salt in a blender.
3. Strain the mixture and spread it on trays, forming a five eighths of an inch (1.5 cm) layer.
4. Refrigerate until it forms a jelly.
5. Cut it into rounds 1 ⅝ in (4 cm) in diameter and make a hole in the center of each one with a melon scooper.
6. Set aside in layers of parchment paper in a container.

Salmagundi base

1. Grind the ingredients in a juicer and freeze.
2. Defrost on absorbent paper to produce a transparent liquid.
3. For each quart (liter) of fresh herb water, add one third teaspoon (one gram) of xanthan gum and one sixth of a cup (50 g) of colatura di alici (anchovy sauce) and mix.
4. Remove the air from the mixture with a vacuum packing machine.
5. Set it aside for when you are ready to serve.

Cucumber and apple disks

1. Cut the apples into very thin layers and then cut them into one sixth of a (2 cm) diameter disks.
2. Infuse the disks with fresh herb water in the vacuum packing machine until you are ready to serve them.
3. Do the same with the cucumber but set them aside plain.

The dressings

Pistachio milk

1. Grind the ingredients in a blender for 5 minutes.
2. Strain the mixture and put it into a superbag.

Herb oil

1. Grind the ingredients in a blender at 158 °F (70 °C) for 7 minutes and pass it through a fine strainer.
2. Cool the oil in a cold water bath and pass it through a fine strainer without touching it.
3. Set aside in squeeze bottles.

Herb water

1. Pull the leaves off the stems and scald them for 10 seconds and cool them in ice water, saving the water used to scald them.
2. Drain well and grind with 2 and one third cup (500 g) of the cool scalding water and 2 and one third cup (500 g) cold water. Pour through a cheesecloth and set aside.

Codium pilpil (sauce)

1. Grind the ingredients in a blender at 176 °F (80 °C) for 8 minutes.
2. Cool and pour into squeeze bottles.

Jesús Sánchez

Chef, Cenador de Amós
Cantabria, Spain
www.cenadordeamos.com

Jesús has a chef's soul and an artist's hands. Since 1993, he has been the owner and chef at the Cenador de Amós in Cantabria, a restaurant set in a beautiful eighteenth century building: the Mazarrasa Palace-House, which dates to 1756 with a spacious interior patio. In 2021, it was awarded three Michelin stars in Spain and Portugal. A second restaurant, Amós, is in Rosewood Villa Magna, the emblematic luxury hotel in the heart of Madrid.

His story with this dish
The idea arose from a traditional Spanish dish: seafood salmagundi. We wanted to make a translucent salmagundi water and contrast it with a fatty, plant-based element; that's why we picked avocado. To strengthen the seafood flavor, we used sea urchin and caviar.

Assembly

1. On the bottom of a wide soup bowl, place the avocado royal and put the sea urchin in the middle with drops of sea urchin extract.
2. On top of this, arrange the apple and cucumber disks overlapping slightly to form a circle. Put the caviar in the center.
3. Complete the dish with three dots of codium pipil, and at the table serve the salmagundi water together with some drops of herb oil.

Tostada with Cured Trout and Avocado Wasabi

*Tip: Salicornia (also known as glasswort or sea beans) is a member of the succulent family that grows in salt marshes and on beaches. When dried, it is commonly used as a Korean medicinal herb. You can purchase it online.

**Note: You can make your own chili powder by grinding the dried, toasted chilis of your choice (we recommend chiles de árbol and guajillo chilis for this recipe) in a molcajete (stone grinding bowl) or in a mortar and pestle.

Ingredients
4 servings

Cured trout
- 2 trout filets (2/3 lb [300 g] each)
- 1.1 lbs (500 g) sea salt
- 1 cup (200 g) sugar
- Zest of two yellow lemons
- 2 sprigs of rosemary
- 2 sprigs fresh oregano
- 1 tablespoon allspice pods, toasted
- 1 tablespoon black pepper pods, toasted
- 1 tablespoon dried juniper berries

Avocado and wasabi cream
- 2 medium avocados
- ½ (50 g) small onion
- ¼ cup (50 g) green tomatoes
- Juice of 1 lime
- 1 tablespoon wasabi paste
- 2 tablespoons olive oil
- 1 bunch of cilantro

Chilli powder
(can be substituted by pepperoncino)
- 3 chilis de árbol, toasted
- 3 guajillo chilli, toasted

Assembly
- 4 6-in (15-cm) tostadas
- Mayonnaise
- 1 avocado
- Olive oil
- Chili powder**
- Fresh pepper
- Fresh chives
- Salicornia (sea beans)*
- Fresh clover (watercress or mâche will also work)
- Ikura (salmon roe)

Preparation

Cured Trout
1. Mix the salt, sugar, lemon, spices, and herbs together.
2. Cover the two trout filets with the salt-spice mixture for six hours.
3. After six hours, remove the excess salt from the trout and rinse.
4. Cut into thin, sashimi-like slices. Set aside.

Avocado and wasabi cream
1. Mix the green tomatoes, onion, lime juice, and cilantro in a blender and strain through a fine sieve. Set aside.
2. In a clean blender, add the filtered juice, olive oil, wasabi, avocado, and blend until you get a smooth texture. Salt to taste. Set aside.

Assembly
1. Spread mayonnaise on the tostada.
2. Spread on the avocado cream.
3. Generously place the cured trout on top.
4. Cut half an avocado into thin slices and serve on the trout.
5. Dress with olive oil.
6. Lightly sprinkle on the chili powder and fresh chives.
7. Crown with salicornia, clover, and using a small spoon, carefully add a bit of ikura on top.
8. Serve with a salsa.

Fernando Martínez

Chef, Migrante
Mexico City, Mexico
@RestMigrante

Winner of the Chef of the Year in 2014, he headed the Mexico City restaurant Yuban, ranked one of the country's best culinary endeavors and included in the Mexico's Gastronomical Guide as one of the 120 top restaurants. Today, he leads two restaurants: the first, Migrante, in the Roma neighborhood, where the approach is inspired by cuisines, ingredients, and techniques from all over the world; and Casa Kun, where the focus is on the sea and regional Mexican food.

His story with this dish
I was born in Uruapan, which to me, is the world capital par excellence of the avocado. It's a mainstay of family cooking there. As we've seen the avocado rise in popularity, it has become even more of a symbol for us. It's what we show off the most, it's what we eat the most, and in terms of ingredients, it's what speaks to us the most, even more than maize.

Escamoles Stuffed Chargrilled Avocado

Ingredients
4 servings

Escamoles (ant larvae)*
- 1 ½ tablespoons (20 g) butter
- ¾ tablespoon (10 g) vegetable oil
- ½ onion, cut into cubes
- 1 teaspoon (3 g) serrano chili
- ¾ tablespoon (5 g) epazote (aromatic Mexican herb)
- ½ cup (100 g) escamoles
- Salt to taste

Pickled onion
- ¼ cup (65 ml) vinegar
- 1 tablespoon dried thyme
- 1 tablespoon salt
- 2 bay leaves
- 1 tablespoon dried oregano
- 2 black peppercorns
- 1 medium (200 g) red onion, sliced

Chiltepín salsa
- ½ cup (60 g) shelled unsalted peanuts
- ½ cup (100 g) tomatoes
- ¼ cup (80 ml) olive oil
- 10 chiltepin chilis
- 1 tablespoon salt
- 1 teaspoon (5 ml) vinegar

Assembly
- ½ Hass avocado
- Prepared escamoles
- Verdolaga (purslane) leaves (or any other tender green)
- Radishes, very thinly sliced
- 1 tablespoon pickled onion
- 1 teaspoon (5 ml) olive oil
- 1 tablespoon salt
- Chiltepín salsa

*Tip:. Edible ant larvae of the *Liometopum apiculatum* species, which is collected in Tlaxcala and Hidalgo. You can purchase edible ant larvae in Mexico.

Ángel Vázquez

Chef, Intro
Puebla, Mexico
www.introrestaurant.com

Since 2003, he has taken the flavors from Morocco, Thailand, and France to tables in Puebla. At his restaurant, Intro, his first gastronomic project became, from the start, a radical approach that offered new alternatives in a city dominated by more traditional establishments serving Pueblan or Spanish cuisine. An essential part of his professional training was his work at restaurants in New York, Paris, and Barcelona. Today he has other projects, including Augurio, focused on his roots in Puebla.

His story with this dish
It came from the intention to offer a different kind of dish for Lent. The texture of the escamoles together with the creaminess of the avocado give us a dish that tantalizes the palate. Hass avocado is recommended for this recipe because it is firm enough to serve as a container for the escamoles, and it can stand up to the chargrilling that we suggest.

Preparation

Escamoles
1. In a frying pan, heat the oil and butter.
2. Sauté the onion. When it becomes translucent, add the serrano chili and the epazote. Add the escamoles and cook until tender. Season to taste and set aside.

Pickled onion
1. Mix 1 cup (250 ml) of water, vinegar, herbs, and spices in a large shallow pan, then add the onion. Cook for 10 minutes over medium heat. Remove from heat before it reaches a boil. Check the taste and cool.

Chiltepín salsa
1. Toast the peanuts in a frying pan and set aside.
2. Sauté the tomato in some oil.
3. Combine the toasted peanuts, seven eighths (200 ml) of a cup of water, and sautéed tomato with the rest of the salsa ingredients in a blender. Season to taste and set aside.

Assembly
1. Peel half an avocado and remove the seed.
2. With a cooking torch, chargrill the outer part of the avocado until it produces a uniform black color.
3. Fill the avocado with the escamoles and decorate it with purslane leaves, radish slices, and pickled onion. Finish with a bit of olive oil on the escamoles and serve with chiltepín salsa.

Chinchayote and Avocado in Greens

Ingredients
4 servings

Cold avocado cream
- ⅓ lb (150 g) avocados
- 2 serrano chilis
- 5 tablespoons (10 g) criollo cilantro
- 2 ½ tablespoons (5 g) epazote (aromatic Mexian herb)
- 2 ½ tablespoons (5 g) hoja santa (Mexican pepperleaf)
- 3 tablespoons (50 ml) Colima lime juice
- 2 ice cubes
- ⅜ cup (100 ml) olive oil
- Colima salt to taste (or finishing salt of choice, such as fleur de sel)

Chinchayote
- .4 lbs (200 g) *chinchayote***
- A little olive oil

Cured *nopales* (prickly pear paddles)
- ½ lb (200 g) *nopal* leaves, cubed**
- 1 ¾ tablespoon (30 g) Colima salt

Ayocotes
- .4 lbs (200 g) *ayocotes***
- 1 cup vinegar
- ¼ cup (50 g) sugar
- 2 cups water
- 3 bay leaves
- Olive oil
- ¾ teaspoon (5 g) salt
- 5 Tabasco peppercorns

Xoconostle
- 1.5 lbs (750 g) *xoconostle***
- 1 cup (250 g) mirin**
- 1 cup (250 ml) Colima lime juice
- 1 cup (250 ml) rice vinegar
- Colima salt to taste
- ¾ cup (200 ml) olive oil

Assembly
- Cold avocado cream
- .4 lbs (200 g) *chinchayote*
- ⅓ lb (150 g) avocado, cut in cubes
- ¼ lb (100 g) cured *nopal*
- .4 lbs (200 g) *ayocotes*
- 10 epazote leaves
- ⅝ cup (20 g) criollo cilantro
- ¼ cup (70 ml) *xoconostle* vinaigrette
- 2 serrano chilis, cut into rounds

Preparation

Cold avocado cream
1. Combine the ingredients in a blender.
2. Check the salt and refrigerate it until ready to serve.

Chinchayote
1. Wash and peel the *chinchayote*.
2. Cut it into three eighths inch (1 cm) cubes, blanch them, and set them aside with a little olive oil drizzled over them.

Cured *nopales*
1. Put the *nopales* in salted water for half an hour, stirring every ten minutes.
2. After 30 minutes, rinse them with water to remove the slimy residue.

Ayocotes
1. Wash and cook the *ayocotes* over a low heat for 3 hours (the texture should be creamy on the inside).
2. Apart from the beans, boil the vinegar with sugar, water, bay leaves, olive oil, salt, and Tabasco peppercorn for 10 minutes.
3. Add the cooked beans and pour into a glass container with a vacuum seal. Set them aside. They will be ready in a week.

Xoconostle
You should make a large amount of this recipe because it takes a long time to prepare. One of the good things is that the longer you leave it, the better the flavor.

1. Toast them on a griddle, peel them, and remove the seeds of *xoconostle*. Cut the pulp into small cubes and set aside.
2. In a bowl, mix the mirin with lime juice, vinegar, olive oil (poured in a thin stream) and salt. Mix, preferably with a wire whisk.
3. Add the *xoconostle* and keep it in a glass jar.

Assembly
1. Mix all the ingredients together and enjoy it as like a ceviche or salad. For attractive plating, mix the cold avocado cream and the *chinchayote* in a bowl with the *nopales* and *ayocotes*.
2. Divide it into four parts, and with the help of a cylindrical cutting mold, arrange it so it keeps its shape.
3. Marinate the herbs with the *xoconostle* vinaigrette and place them on one side, like a fresh green side. Arrange the serrano chili rounds on top.

Fabián Delgado Padilla

Chef, Pal Real
Guadalajara, Mexico
@_palreal_

A self-taught professional chef, he uses Mexican cuisine as a narrative pretext to decode his tendencies. He cooks what he finds in many ways, always seeking fresh and seasonal ingredients. Partner and chef at Pal Real, in Guadalajara, this restaurant has become a mandatory destination for locals and visitors. Recently he opened an eatery called Yunaites in the IV Centenario municipal market in Guadalajara.

His story with this dish
For this recipe, I drew inspiration from the *chinchayote*, which in Jalisco is popularly cut into rounds, coated in egg batter, fried, and bathed in a tomato-oregano sauce, served with a local cheese called *adobera*. And speaking of avocado, it's best when it's in season, like the aceite avocado that I get from San Martín de las Flores, a community that preserves the customs and culture of Jalisco.

*Notes: 1. *Chinchayote* is the root of the chayote, a mildly flavored, bright-green squash that is easy to find at specialty grocery stores, but the root is harder to come by.
2. *Xoconostle* is a sour fruit found on specific varieties of prickly pear cactus; you can buy it online or at some specialty grocery stores.
3. *Ayocotes* are large black beans with a similar flavor to butter beans that you can buy online. *Nopal* are the flat green pads of Opuntia cacti. You can buy it online from a specialty store or market—nopales are best when firm and brightly colored.
4. *Mirin* is Japanese sweet rice wine, available at most grocery stores.

Avocado Salad with Insects

Ingredients
2 servings

- 1 medium criolla squash (round green summer squash), chopped*
- 2 green onions or white onion in half-moon slices
- 2 medium Hass avocados (if there are criollo avocados, leave the skin on, but cut diagonally)
- 2 tablespoons chapulines**
- 2 tablespoons chicatanas**
- 1 ½ cup (80 g) mixture of leafy greens and lettuce (cleaned)

Vinaigrette:
- 4 teaspoons (20 g) chintextle salsa**
- 1 teaspoon (1 g) oregano
- 1 small clove (2 g) garlic
- 6 toasted maguey worms**
- ¼ tablespoon (5 g) salt
- ½ cup minus 1 tablespoon (100 ml) apple cider vinegar
- 1¼ cups (300 ml) olive oil

Celia Florián

Cook, Las Quince Letras
Oaxaca, Mexico
@lasquinceletrasoax

Born in La Ciénega, Zimatlán de Álvarez in Oaxaca, Florián is proud of her Oaxacan roots and culture. In 1991, she opened Las Quince Letras in the downtown Historic Center of Oaxaca. She is well-known for her research on recipes, indigenous ingredients, and techniques. Since 2015, she has presided over the Association of Traditional Cooks of Oaxaca. Recently, her restaurant was chosen by France's La Liste, The World's Best Restaurants as the "Artisan & Authenticity Award Winner."

Her story with this dish
Moles, tamales, sauces and more recipes in Oaxaca use chapulines, maguey worms, chicatana ants and jumiles as the main ingredient. Foods that provide protein, calcium and fiber.

Preparation
1. Pan roast the squash, onion, and avocado to intensify their flavor.
2. Normally, edible insects are coated in salt to preserve them—so you need to rinse them before toasting in the oven or on the stove over a low heat. Roast until brown: this is what gives them their very special flavor.
3. Put the leafy greens on the plate, then add the roasted squash, onion, and avocado. Add the insects and pour on the vinaigrette.

Vinaigrette
1. Put the chintextle in a bowl and add the oregano (after toasting it in a frying pan).
2. Finely mince the garlic and grind or mash the maguey worms. Add both ingredients to the bowl with the others. Mix and serve.

**Notes:
1. Chapulines are edible grasshoppers, traditionally collected from cornfields.
2. Chicatanas are queen leafcutter ants—in Oaxaca, they are caught and toasted on a griddle over low heat until the feet and wings fall off.
3. Chintextle is a Mixe smoked pasilla chili ground with garlic, water, and salt, generally sold in markets in Oaxaca. If you can't find it, grind Mixe pasilla chili or chipotle, garlic, and salt.
4. Maguey worms, colloquially referred to as "tequila worms," are worms that live in the heart of different agave species.

Chargrilled Avocado Tartar

Ingredients
2 servings

Beurre noisette
- 4½ sticks (500 g) of butter
- 6 cloves garlic
- 3 serrano chilis
- 1 tapered sauce pan or deep sauce pot

Sherry vinaigrette
- 1 qt (l) olive oil
- 2 ¼ cup (500 ml) sherry
- 1 tablespoon salt

Spinach powder*
- 1.1 lbs (500 g) spinach
- Dehydrator

Onion powder
- 2.2 lbs (1 kg) white onion

Dehydrated sorrel
- 3 ¼ cups (100 g) green sorrel
- ⅕ cup (50 ml) banana vinegar*
- Vacuum-sealed cooking bag

Assembly
- Green kale
- ¼ Hass avocado
- Escamoles (ant larvae)
- Epazote (aromatic Mexican herb)
- Sherry vinaigrette (recipe)
- Spinach powder (recipe)
- Onion ash powder (recipe)
- White onion sliced into rings
- Serrano chili, sliced into rings
- Dehydrated sorrel (recipe)
- Lime zest to taste
- Salt

***Tip:** You can buy spinach powder and Banana vinegar online. You can also buy dehydrated onion powder, but it won't have the charred, vegetal flavor.

266

Preparation

Beurre noisette

1. Cook the butter in a pot over a very low heat, stirring constantly, while you mince the garlic and chilis.
2. When the butter has a dark golden color, remove it from the heat. When it is lukewarm, add the minced garlic and chili.
3. Set aside.

Sherry vinaigrette

1. Whisk half the oil with the vinegar. Keep adding the oil in a thin stream so it emulsifies. Season to taste, set aside.

Spinach powder

1. Wash the spinach well, dehydrate it overnight at 140 °F (60 °C).
2. The next day, mix in a food processor to produce a fine powder. Set aside.

Onion powder

1. Slice the onion very thin, and char in the oven at 572 °F (300 °C) for 20 minutes. You can also char on a grill. Blend it into a fine powder and set it aside.

Dehydrated sorrel

1. Clean the sorrel leaves and put them into a vacuum-sealed cooking bag. Pour the banana vinegar into the bag, making sure it covers the sorrel, but doesn't drench it.
2. Seal the bag and let it marinate for an hour. Then open the bag and cook the sorrel at 212 °F (100 °C) in a true convection oven for 20 minutes or until the leaves are dry, keeping an eye on them to prevent burning.

Assembly

1. Clean the kale and dry it, placing it on paper towels to remove excess moisture. Roughly chop and place onto a baking sheet. Massage with oil and sprinkle with salt. Roast in the oven at 300 °F until crisp.
2. Cut the avocado quarter into small cubes and chargrill it with a cooking torch; cook the escamoles with enough of the prepared butter, season them, and finish with the chopped epazote.
3. Mix the escamoles with the avocado, but without making a purée. Add a little sherry vinegar but keep the mixture thick. Add more salt if necessary.
4. Put a circle of spinach powder on the plate by using a sieve and do the same with the onion powder.
5. With a small round cutter, form a disc with the avocado mixture. Top with the rings of onion and chili, and decorate with the kale chips and sorrel, finishing it with lime zest.

Jorge Vallejo

Chef, Quintonil
Mexico City, Mexico
www.quitonil.com

After studying culinary administration and arts at the Ambrosía Culinary Center of Mexico, Vallejo spent time as chef on Princess Cruises. After that, he worked in the kitchens of restaurants like Noma and Pujol, and served as corporate chef for Grupo Habita. In 2012, he decided to open his own restaurant, Quintonil, with his wife Alejandra Flores. Since 2015, Quintonil has been on the list of The World's 50 Best Restaurants.

His story with this dish
Avocado is a fruit of Mesoamerican origin that I regard as a culinary treasure. In Mexico, it can be eaten alone or with a tortilla. It gives you a complete meal that can help to control cholesterol and blood pressure, nourishes you with vitamins, and takes you to another sensorial dimension its texture, color, and flavor. At Quintonil, it's almost always on the menu and is the star of one of the restaurant's emblematic dishes: avocado tartar accompanied by escamoles—another Mexican delicacy—and fried *quelites* (sorrel).

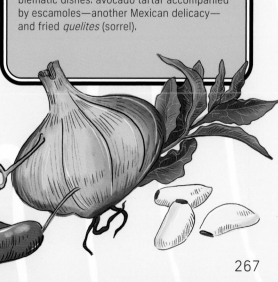

Avocado Tofu with and Nikkei Ponzu

Note: Nikkei cuisine is a distinct cuisine created by Japanese immigrants in Peru.

Ingredients
4 servings

Avocado Tofu
- 2 cups or 16 oz (460 ml) unsweetened soy milk
- 2 (460 g) avocados
- 1 .25 oz envelope powdered gelatin (3 gelatin sheets)
- ½ teaspoon (3 g) salt

Nikkei Ponzu**
- 3.4 oz (100 ml) soy sauce
- 1 tablespoon (15 ml) lime juice
- 2¾ tablespoon (5 g) cilantro
- 1 teaspoon (5 g) ajís (chili peppers)
- 1 teaspoon (5g) ginger, grated

Assembly
- 1.25 oz (35 g) avocado tofu (recipe below)
- .20 oz (6 g) salmon roe

Jorge Muñoz

Chef, Astrid & Gastón
Lima, Peru
@jorge_munoz_castro

Born in Trujillo, he moved from the Peruvian coast to the jungle as a child, until he migrated with his family to Europe in 2000. Through cooking, he constructed a bridge between Europe and his homeland for the nineteen years he worked in Barcelona. In 2019, he returned to Peru working for Astrid & Gastón, the leading professional Peruvian cooking school in the world. One of his biggest dreams was to return to his country, and he has done so as an international ambassador of gastronomy.

His story with this dish
This tofu was born in the Pakta restaurant in Barcelona, which means 'union' in Quechua. It is basically avocado combined with soy milk and gelatin. An easy recipe to make with an incredible texture because of the vegetable fat of the two products, one Japanese and the other Latin American. A fantastic combination of two cultures.

Preparation

Avocado tofu
1. Pour the soy milk into a pot and heat it to 150°F (60°C).
2. Remove it from the heat and add the gelatin. Mix well.
3. Peel the avocados and cut them into pieces.
4. Mix the avocado with the soy milk, salt, and process in a blender to make a homogeneous paste.
5. Pour the mixture into custard containers three eighths inch (1 cm) thick (or cubed ice cube trays).
6. Cover with plastic wrap and refrigerate until firm (6 hours or overnight).

Nikkei Ponzu
1. Mix all the ingredients and leave it to steep to let the flavors blend.
2. Strain the mixture and refrigerate.

Assembly
1. Serve the avocado tofu with the ponzu sauce and sea urchin on top.

Avocado Seed Pipián

Ingredients
3 servings

Pipián**
- 1 avocado seed
- 1 ¾ teaspoons (5 g) sesame seeds
- ¾ teaspoon (1 g) coriander seeds
- ½ teaspoon (1 g) black pepper
- ⅔ tablespoon (5 g) squash seeds
- 1 clove
- 1.75 oz (50 g) manzano
  (or other) tomatoes
- 2 teaspoons (5 g) serrano chili
- 5 teaspoons (10 g) poblano pepper
- 3 tablespoons (10 g) white onion
- 1 clove of garlic
- 5 tablespoons (10 g) avocado leaves*
- 1 ½ tablespoons (20 g) corn oil
  (or other neutral oil)
- ¾ cup (25 g) spinach
- ½ cup (10 g) cilantro
- ¼ cup (5 g) radish leaves
  (or other peppery green like arugula)
- 1 tablespoon sea salt
- 1 tablespoon (10 g) avocado pulp

Tree cabbage sauerkraut
3 servings

- 2 oz (50 g) tree cabbage***
- ½ teaspoon (3 g) sea salt

Kefir
- 1 cup (200 ml) whole milk
- ⅕ cup (50 g) kefir
- 2 tablespoons of avocado oil

Assembly
- ¾ cup (100 g) avocado
- ⅛ cup (25 g) fermented tree
  cabbage (sauerkraut)
- ¼ cup (50 g) avocado seed pipián
- ½ cup (40 g) kefir whey
- 1 tablespoon (15 g) avocado oil
- 1 tablespoon sea salt
- 1 g hoja santa (Mexican pepperleaf)
  powder (dehydrate and grind it).

*Tip: You can buy avocado leaves online.

**Note: Pipián is essentially a type of mole, made with blended greens and thickened with seeds or nuts (in this case, with avocado seed).

***Note: Tree cabbage is a type of hearty green with a long stalk and large, palm-like leaves. If you can't find tree cabbage, use regular sauerkraut.

Preparation

Tree cabbage sauerkraut

1. Clean the tree cabbage leaves, put them in a basin or plastic bowl and squeeze them with the sea salt. Let sit for half an hour and pack them tightly into a glass container, pressing down to avoid leaving any spaces between the leaves. Put a bag full of water on top to keep the cabbage submerged in the brine. Put in a cool, dry place, checking it every day for one or two weeks.

Pipián

1. Toast the avocado seeds and set aside.
2. In a frying pan, toast the sesame seeds, coriander seeds, black pepper, squash seeds, and clove. Set aside.
3. On a hot griddle, char the tomatoes, chilis, onion, garlic, and set aside.
4. Put the avocado leaves in 1 and a half quarts (1.5 l) of water to steep and set aside.
5. In a grinding bowl or mortar, grind the seeds, onion and garlic into a fine paste. Then grind the tomato, chili, toasted avocado seeds and the avocado leaves, and set aside.
6. In a deep cooking pot (like a Dutch oven), add oil and sauté the seed paste until the oils come out, then immediately add the tomato paste.

Continue cooking until the oils separate, let them reduce to thicken the sauce. Season to taste and set aside.

7. Put the spinach, cilantro, and radish leaves into a blender with the sea salt and blend.
8. Add leaf mixture to the pot with the avocado pulp. Stir to combine.

Avocado oil

1. You can buy avocado oil at most grocery stores. You can also make your own.
2. On an oven tray, spread out the pulp and put it in the oven at 194 °F (90 °C) for about an hour or until it turns black and loses half the moisture. Put the avocado paste into a cheesecloth and squeeze to get the oil. Set aside.

Kefir

1. Heat the milk to 77 °F (25 °C), put it in the glass container with the kefir. Leave it covered with a cheesecloth for 24 hours. Strain it and separate the solids from the whey.

Assembly

1. Place the sauerkraut in a ring, followed by the avocado and press it to make a steak or round shape. Set aside.
2. Heat the pipián over a low heat, set aside.
3. In another bowl, mix the kefir whey and the avocado oil.

4. To assemble, use a round plate, put the pipián in the middle and place the avocado-sauerkraut steak on top of it; sprinkle with powdered hoja santa and the whey-avocado dressing.

Xrysw Ruelas and Óscar Segundo

**Chefs, Restaurante Xokol
Guadalajara, Mexico
@xokol_**

This couple has set out to reconnect with local flavors and bring them to the table. They have worked in restaurants including La Leche, Hueso, and Café des Artistes, in Jalisco, until they opened Xokol together in a traditional barrio in Guadalajara, where the cornfield is the basis for their menus. Over the years, they have both been recognized as the best chefs in Latin America when they were crowned in the Latin American semifinal of the San Pellegrino Young Chef Academy and contender in the Grand Finale.

Their story with this dish
This recipe is part of the philosophy at Xokol, where food traceability and sustainability guide us. We want to raise awareness about the use of an ingredient in its entirety. We use the seeds, pulp, and leaves of avocados to make the pipián and the oil. We're Mexicans, we eat lots of avocado, but the idea is to have a much more intimate relationship with it. It is like baring it and seeing how we can use each part, which is why we developed this recipe.

Avocado Bonbon and Foie Gras with Chocolate

Ingredients
9 servings

Caramel ganache
- ⅞ cups (175 g) sugar
- 1 ¼ cup (300 g) cream
- ⅓ cup (25 g) glucose syrup (or corn syrup)
- 7 oz (200 g) milk chocolate, melted
- 4½ tablespoons (65 g) butter

Foie gras
- 7 oz (200 g) foie gras
- 2 tablespoons (30 g) port
- 3.5 oz (100 g) hazelnut praline
- 2 tablespoons (15 g) cacao butter
- 1 teaspoon (5 g) truffle
- ½ teaspoon (3 g) salt

Hass avocado purée
- 1 Hass avocado

White and Mycryo chocolate and coating
- 6.2 oz (175 g) white chocolate
- 2 ½ cups (250 g) Mycryo**

Assembly
- Caramelized chocolate ganache
- Toasted peanuts
- Salt flakes to taste

Note: Mycryo is a powdered cacao butter sold in specialized baking shops, or available online.

Joel Ornelas

Chef, Tintoque
Puerto Vallarta, Mexico
www.tintoque.com.mx

He is a chef from Puerto Vallarta who was trained in the United Kingdom, Spain, Thailand, Japan and in Mexico, with Grupo Pangea, of Monterrey. In 2016, he opened his concept restaurant: Tintoque, where he combines his innovative approach to cooking with his unique interpretation. He has been nominated and won awards, such as the competition "Young Talents Millesime Mexico." He has other projects in the works, one called El Puerco de Oro, a taco spot specializing in pork pancetta and he recently opened Barra y Leña, for seafood and wood grilling.

His story with this dish
The avocado is something that we all love. There are restaurants solely for avocados. Something as fatty as foie gras with creamy avocado is an interesting combination that completely departs from the ordinary. When people taste the bonbon, which I have as a starter in the tasting menu at my restaurant, they are surprised because bonbons are normally eaten as a dessert, like petit four, but we use it as a starter, like amuse-bouche.

Preparation

Caramel ganache
1. Melt the sugar into a soft caramel.
2. Boil the cream with the glucose syrup.
3. Combine these two mixtures when they are hot.
4. Pour in the chocolate, mixing with a wire whisk.
5. Add the butter, little by little, to produce a smooth mixture. Set aside.

Foie gras
1. Weigh all the ingredients in the Thermomix container and at speed 10, or in a conventional blender for 2 minutes, blend and set aside.

Hass avocado purée
1. Grind and pass through a fine sieve to incorporate it in layer in the mold.

White and Mycryo chocolate coating
1. Combine and melt both ingredients at 113 °F (45 °C).

Assembly
1. In a mold, put a base coating of white chocolate, refrigerate, and when it solidifies, add the caramelized chocolate ganache, the sweet foie gras mixture, the purée, and the toasted peanuts in layers.
2. Cover with more of the white chocolate coating and refrigerate.
3. Add a touch of salt on top as a decoration and to add texture.

Photo Credits

Chapter 1

- Avocado silhouettes, Trilce Ediciones, p. 2
- Avocado silhouette, Flickr, p. 3
- Avocado cutouts (Rawpixel and Ken Love and USDA National Agricultural Library, U.S. Department of Agriculture Watercolor Pomological Collection, Rare and Special Collections, Beltsville, MD 20705), pp. 4, 5, and 6
- Avocado drawing, Rawpixel, p. 7
- "Tlayuda stall," painting by Elena Climet, 2016, pp. 8 and 9
- Vendor arranging avocados in basket, photo by Alberto Leal, p. 10.
- Two fruit vendors, 1908, Archivo General de la Nación, Fondo: Secretaría de Instrucción Pública y Bella Artes, Serie: Propiedad Artística y literaria, PAL/4552, p. 12
- Avocado production advertising, from *Report of the First Semi-Annual Meeting of the California Avocado Association*, Los Angeles, October 25, 1915, n.p./Biodiversity Heritage Library, p. 14
- Young "Fuerte" avocado trees, from *Report of the First Semi-Annual Meeting of the California Avocado Association*, Los Angeles, May–October 1917, n.p./Biodiversity Heritage Library, p. 14.
- Trapp avocado packed in crates, from *Report of the First Semi-Annual Meeting of the California Avocado Association*, Los Angeles, May–October 1917, n.p./Biodiversity Heritage Library, p. 14
- Original McDonald avocado tree, from Willis Pope, *The Guatemala Avocado in Hawaii*, United States Department of Agriculture, Washington, D.C., Government Printing Office, 1924, n.p. /HathiTrust Digital Library, p. 14
- Truck to transport avocado trees, from *Report of the First Semi-Annual Meeting of the California Avocado Association*, Los Angeles, October 25, 1926, p. 16.
- *Acoyates* from: Samuel de Champlain, *Brief discours de choses plus remarquables que Samuel Champlain de Brouage á reconneues aux Indes Occidentalles*, France, n.p., 1602 © John Carter Brown Library, p. 18
- *Persea americana* © Copyright MEISE BOTANIC GARDEN, generated with Kakadu Software, p. 19.
- Plants and animals from Ecuador, including the guava, avocado, cherimoya, passion flower and fruit, llama, opossum, tapir, *Polylepis* tree, tufted airplant, from Antonio de Ulloa, *Relación histórica del viaje a Améica meridional*, Spain, Antonio Marín, 1748.
© John Carter Brown Library, pp. 20 and 21
- A prehistoric man defends his family from an attacking bear: the man's family huddle together in a cave, while mammoths, a tiger, a rhinoceros, and cattle roam in the landscape beyond, colored lithograph by J. F. Schreiber in *Der Mensch und die Thiere der Diluvialzeit in Mitteleuropa*, Germany, n.p., ca. 1800–1900, Wellcome Library, pp. 22 and 23
- Avocado fossil record in California, p. 24
- Prehistoric animal, mammoth. Evgenii–stock.adobe.com, p. 24
- Rock paintings found in cave of the musicians, Puebla. Photo: Luis R. Castañeda.
- Maize cave, photo: H. Ayuntamiento de Coxcatlán, Mexico, pp. 26 and 27

- Fossilized avocados from the Tehuacán Valley, D.R. © Agustín Uzarraga /Arqueología Mexicana / Raíces. SECRETARÍA DE CULTURA.-INAH.-MEX. "Reproducción autorizada por el Instituto Nacional de Antropología e Historia," por tratarse de bienes de la Nación Mexicana, p. 27
- Genital-shaped avocados, Pixabay, p. 28
- Codex Borgia, This plate shows a large image of Yayauhqui Tezcatlipoca, "Dark Smoking Mirror," accompanied by two female deities, Wikimedia, p. 29
- Mauricio Antón, Ice Age Fauna, 2008 © 2008 Public Library of Science, p. 31
- Graphic details of urban art, *Sensacional de diseño mexicano*, Trilce Ediciones, pp. 30 and 31
- Igloos, FreePik, p. 30
- Gloved hand, FreePik, p. 30
- Stela from the ruins of Copan, from: Frederick Catherwood, *Views of Ancient Monuments in Central America*, Chiapas and Yucatan, London, F. Catherwood, 1844, p. 32
- Young woman with Guatemalan variety avocado from: *Report of the First Semi-Annual Meeting of the California Avocado Association*, Los Angeles, October 25, 1915, p. 109/Biodiversity Heritage Library, p. 33
- Drawing by Biajojo, glyph of the fourteenth month of the Maya calendar, based on John Montgomery, *Dictionary of Maya Hieroglyphs*, June 20, 2015, Wikimedia, p. 34
- Map of the Yucatán Peninsula, from: Frederick Catherwood, *Views of Ancient Monuments in Central America, Chiapas and Yucatan*, London, F. Catherwood, 1844/ HathiTrust Digital Library, p. 34
- Stucco portrait of K'inich Janaab Pakal I (A.D. 603–683), ruler of Palenque, Museo National de Antropología. LA SECRETARÍA DE CULTURA.-INAH.-MEX. "Reproducción autorizada por el Instituto Nacional de Antropología e Historia," por tratarse de bienes de la Nación Mexicana, p. 34
- Ruins of Palenque, from: Frederick Catherwood, *Views of Ancient Monuments in Central America, Chiapas and Yucatan*, London, F. Catherwood, 1844/HathiTrust Digital Library, p. 35
- Graves goods of the ruler Pakal, reproduction, Museo Nacional de Antropología, SECRETARÍA DE CULTURA.-INAH.-MEX. "Reproducción autorizada por el Instituto Nacional de Antropología e Historia," por tratarse de bienes de la Nación Mexicana, p. 35
- Detail of a page from the Codex Mendoza, an Aztec codex created shortly after the conquest. This page lists some of the victories, Wikimedia, p. 36
- A page from the Matrícula de los tributos, one of the so-called Mexica codices, made between 1520 and 1530 on amate paper, probably from a Mexica original and copied years after the conquest. It was painted by Mexica scribes, who used the ancient pictorial format, Biblioteca Nacional de Antropología e Historia. SECRETARÍA DE CULTURA.-INAH.-MEX. "Reproducción autorizada por el Instituto Nacional de Antropología e Historia," por tratarse de bienes de la Nación Mexicana, p. 37
- Supe Valley, Adobe Stock Images, p. 38
- Palta Indian, sculpture in Catacocha, photo: ©Diario LA HORA Ecuador, Quipus Media QuipusEC S.A.S. Todos los derechos reservados 2022, p. 38
- Monument to the Avocado in Catacocha, photo: ©Diario LA HORA Ecuador, Quipus Media QuipusEC S.A.S. Todos los derechos reservados 2022, p. 39
- Vessel in the shape of a totora reed raft with two rowers, A.D. 300, Moche culture, Peru, photo: Sailko / Wikimedia, p. 40

- Mural of America in Tlaxcala, photo: Déborah Holtz, p. 41
- Carmen Miranda, Album, p. 42
- Bag with avocados, Shutterstock, p. 42
- Avocado fields, Shutterstock, p. 43
- Representation of avocado tree from Fray Bernardino de Sahagún, *Historia general de las cosas de Nueva España*, vol. 3, Book XI, folio 113r/Biblioteca Medicea Laurenziana, p. 44
- Christopher Columbus's first voyage, 1893. © Courtesy of Prints & Photographs Division, Library of Congress, p. 45
- Cover of Francisco Hernández, *Nova plantarum, animalium et mineralium Mexicanorum historia*, Rome, n.p., 1649. © John Carter Brown Library, p. 46
- Text on the avocado tree, from Francisco Hernández, *Nova plantarum, animalium et mineralium Mexicanorum historia*, Rome, n.p., 1649. © John Carter Brown Library, p. 46
- Ritual ceremony of New World natives, from Claude-Augustin Duflos, *Historia de los reyes incas del Perú*, Amsterdam, Jean Frederic Bernard, 1737 © John Carter Brown Library, p. 47
- Speech glyph, Trilce Ediciones, p. 47
- Scissors, Rawpixel, p. 47
- "Después de haber entrado los españoles en Tzintzuntzan, acudían indios con comidas para los soldados," Archivo General de la Nación, Mapas, Planos e Ilustraciones no. 205, p. 48
- Altarpiece of San Pascual Bailón, 16th century (saint of cooks), Coll. Museo José Luis Bello y González, Puebla, p. 48
- Moctezuma's table of food, Casa de México in Madrid, p. 49
- William Krome with his parents and family in the town of Islamorada, ca. 1907, Keys History & Discovery Center, Jerry Wilkinson Collection, p. 50
- "Alligator pears" hanging from branch located at 607 Ashe Street - Key West, Florida. 20th century. State Archives of Florida, Florida Memory. <https://www.floridamemory.com/items/show/101884>, accessed 7 April 2022.
- William Krome, ca. 1909, State Archives of Florida, p. 51
- Sign SW 296 St., Avocado Dr., Trilce Ediciones, p. 51
- First international transcontinental shipment of avocados by air from Los Angeles, CA to Toronto for the Canadian National Exhibition, California, USA, 1927, photo: Jack S. Shepherd, vía <Avocadosource.com>, pp. 52 and 53
- Image of: Rudolph Hass and wife Elizabeth Hass in front of the Mother Hass Tree. Courtesy of the La Habra Heights Historical Committee, p. 54
- Hass Mother Tree Commemoration. Photo Credit: La Habra Review. P. 55.
- Image of: Historical Marker of the Mother Hass Tree permanently mounted bronze plaque supplied by the California Avocado Society and California Historical Society. GinaRose Kimball, Hass Avocado Historian. P. 55.
- Field in California, Rancho Resplandor, p. 56
- Margarito Veyna 1954, Alexa's great-grandfather, taken in Orange County Nursery, p. 56
- "My grandmother, Esther Veyna, my mother, Elaine Bannatyne, my uncles, Richard and Robert Veyna," in Orange County Nursery around 1950, p. 56
- Gonzalo Veyna, Bryce's father and Alexa's grandfather, 1954, p. 56

- Cut avocados, Ken Love and Pixabay, p. 56
- Recipe illustrations, Rawpixel, p. 58
- Menorah, Madeleine–stock.adobe.com, p. 59
- Michael Katz, photo: Judith Harpaz, p. 59
- Cut avocados, Ken Love, p. 59
- The Great Wave off Kanagawa, by Katsushika Hokusai, Creazilla, pp. 60 and 61
- Fish, *Sensacional de diseño mexicano*, Trilce Ediciones, pp. 60 and 61
- Chinese merchant, from: El Reino de China con los países vecinos de Siam y Bengala, map published in Leiden, 1707 © John Carter Brown Library, p. 63
- Model of the port of Manila, Museo de Historia de Manila, p. 63
- Hidekazu Tojo, Japanese-Canadian chef at his restaurant called Tojo in Vancouver, British Columbia, Leila Kwok, p. 64
- California Sushi Roll, Adobe Stock Images, p. 64
- Godzilla-Avocado, photo: Fernando Islas, Retoque: Eduardo González, p. 65
- Ignaz Sebastian Klauber, Death of James Cook during a Battle in Hawaii, editor Abraham Honkoop, publisher Johannes Allart, The Hague, Amsterdam, 1803, Rijksmuseum, p. 66
- Hawaiian avocados, Ken Love, p. 66
- Palm trees, Rawpixel, p. 66
- Francisco de Paula Marín Grassi, illustration by Juan Carlos Mena, p. 67
- Wilson Popenoe from: *Report of the First Semi-Annual Meeting of the California Avocado Association*, Los Angeles, October 25, 1915, p. 107/Biodiversity Heritage Library, p. 67
- Plant explorer David Fairchild in Ceylon preparing to drink coconut milk in 1926, Research Gate, p. 67
- Crates of harvested avocados, photos: Luis Enrique Granados, p. 68
- Sky, Rawpixel, p. 68
- Details of urban art, *Sensacional de diseño mexicano*, Trilce Ediciones, p. 70
- Logotype of Avocados from Mexico Always Good, Avocados from Mexico, p. 70
- Avocado with sombrero, illustration: Juan Carlos Mena, p. 70
- Chef Alex Quintana, from Quintana Bistro, photo: Mónica Molina, p. 71
- Avocado harvest in Tancítaro, photo: Luis Enrique Granados, pp. 72 and 73
- Sign at entrance to Uruapan, Trilce Ediciones, pp. 74 and 75
- Tancítaro, monument to the avocado, photo: Luis Enrique Granados, p. 74
- Guinness Record for the Largest Guacamole in the World, photo: EFE Agency, p. 75
- Urani avocado popsicles, Urani.mx, p. 76
- Mural in Gratissima restaurant and artisanal avocado beer, Gratissima.mx, p. 77
- Pitcher with avocado water, photo: Sweet Life, p. 78
- Avocado harvest in Tancítaro, photo: Luis Enrique Granados, p. 78
- Crates with avocados, photo: Luis Enrique Granados, pp. 79 and 80
- Avocado packing plant, photo: Luis Enrique Granados, pp. 81, 82 and 83
- Organic avocado plantation in the mountains, Adobe Stock Images, p. 84
- Women selling fruit and corn under a covered stand in Guanajuato, 1908, Archivo General de la Nación, Fondo: Secretaría de Instrucción Pública y Bellas Artes. Serie: Propiedad Artística y Literaria. PAL/4556, Archivo General de la Nación, p. 86
- Street stand in Mérida, Shutterstock, p. 87
- Addi María Ay Che, finalist in the "Flavor of the Nation" competition, Dirección de Culturas Populares, Indígenas y Urbanas, p. 88

Bibliography

Chapter 1
A Star Is Born
- Bergh, B. O. (1992). "The Origin, Nature and Genetic Improvement of Avocado," California Avocado Society 1992 Yearbook 76: 61–75, accessed November 2021 at http://www.avocadosource.com/cas_yearbooks/cas_76_1992/cas_1992_pg_061.pdf.
- Fedick, S. L. (1995). "Indigenous Agriculture in the Americas," Journal of Archeological Research 3:257–303.
- Galindo-Tovar, M. E., and A. M. Arzate Fernández. (2010). "Consideraciones sobre el origen y primera dispersión del aguacate (Persea americana, Lauraceae)," Cuadernos de Biodiversidad, accessed November 2021 at http://hdl.handle.net/10045/15292.
- Goebel, T., M. Waters, and D. O'Rourke. (2008). "The Late Pleistocene Dispersal of Modern Humans in the Americas," Science 319:1497–1502, accessed November 2021 at https://www.science.org/doi/abs/10.1126/science.1153569.
- MacNeish, R. S. (1964). "Ancient Mesoamerican Civilization," Science 143:531–537, accessed November 2021 at https://www.science.org/doi/10.1126/science.143.3606.531.
- Messer, E. (2003). "Plantas alimenticias zapotecas: Transformación de dos culturas," in Conquista y comida. Consecuencias del encuentro de dos mundos, Janet Long (ed.), pp. 312–337, Mexico City: Universidad Nacional Autónoma de México.
- Smith, C. J. (1966). "Archeological evidence for Selection in Avocado," Economic Botany 20:169–175.
——. (1969). "Additional Notes on Pre-conquest Avocados in Mexico," Economic Botany 23:135–140.

Around the World
- Bernal Romero, Guillermo (2012). "Historia dinástica de Palenque: la era de K'inich Janahb' Pakal," (615683 D.C.) Revista Digital Universitaria 13, no 12.
- Colunga, P., and D. Zizumbo (2004). "Domestication of Plants in Maya Lowlands," Economic Botany 58 (Supplement): S101-S110, accessed November 2021 at https://www.researchgate.net/profile/Patricia-Colunga-Garciamarin/publication/225601394_Domestication_of_Plants_in_Maya_Lowlands/links/0f317537ce823ec9af000000/Domestication-of-Plants-in-Maya-Lowlands.pdf.
- Gama Campillo, Lilia M. (1994). "Studies on the Systematic and Ethnobotany of the Subgenus Persea," Ph.D. dissertation, University of California, Riverside.
- Gama, L. M., and A. Gomez-P. (1992). "An Ethnoecological Approach for the Study of Persea: A Case Study in the Maya Area," Proceedings of Second World Avocado Congress: 11–17.
- Ruz Lhuillier, Alberto. (1962). "Exploraciones arqueológicas en Palenque: 1957," Anales del INAH, época 6, tomo 14, pp. 35–90.

——. (1973). El Templo de las Inscripciones: Palenque. Mexico City: Instituto Nacional de Antropología e Historia.
——. (1991). Costumbres funerarias de los antiguos mayas. Mexico City: IIF-CEM.UNAM.

From the Palta (Avocado), to the Palate
- Cieza de León, Pedro. (1553), Crónica del Perú, Antwerp.
- Cobo, Bernabé. (1653). Historias del Nuevo Mundo, E. Rasco, Seville (1890–1895).
- Garcilaso de la Vega, I. (1609). Comentarios Reales de los Incas, Lisbon.
- Lenz, R. (1912). Elementos indios del castellano en Chile, Coni Hnos., Buenos Aires.
- Pickersgill, B. (2007). "Domestication of Plants in the Americas: Insights from Mendelian and Molecular Genetics," Annals of Botany 100: 925–940.
- Uhle, Max. (2014). Las ruinas de Moche, Pontificia Universidad Católica del Perú, Lima.
- Wolters, B. (1999). "Dispersion and Ethnobotany of the Cacao Tree and Other Amerindian Crop Plants," Angewandte Botanik 73: 128–137.

The Green American Dream
- Bergh, B. (1992). "The Origin, Nature and Genetic Improvement of the Avocado, California," Avocado Society Yearbook 76:61–75.
- Campbell, C. W. (1979). "Characteristics of Florida Avocado Cultivars," Homestead Agricultural Research and Educational Center Research Report (University of Florida, Experimental Station Reports) SB79-5.
- Fairchild, D. (1945). "Personal Recollections of George B. Cellon, Horticultural Pioneer of South Florida," Proceedings of the Florida State Horticultural Society 58:205–209.
- Froehling, H. (1881). Therapeutic Gazette, 401.
- Knight, R. J., Jr., and C. W. Campbell. (1999). "Ecological Adaptation and the Evolution of Modern Avocado Cultivars," Revista Chapingo, Serie Horticultura (Universidad Autónoma de Chapingo) vol. 5, pp. 49–54.
- Monroy, Samara. "Los beneficios de comer hojas de aguacate." El Universal, November 29, 2021, at https://www.eluniversal.com.mx/menu/beneficios-que-aportan-la-hojas-de-aguacate.
- Wolfe, H. S., L. R. Toy, and A. L. Stahl (G. D. Ruehle, revised). (1949). Avocado Production in Florida, Agricultural Extension Service, University of Florida, Bulletin (Gainesville, Fl) 141, p. 124.

Green Beauty
- "6 usos cosméticos que le puedes dar al aguacate," Mejor con Salud, accessed November 2021 at: https://mejorconsalud.as.com/6-usos-cosmeticos-que-le-puedes-dar-alaguacate/.
- Palacios, Vanessa. "Descubre qué puede hacer el aguacate por tus uñas y pestañas," El Universal, November 19, 2021, accessed November 2021 at https://www.eluniversal.com.mx/de-ultima/los-beneficios-del-aguacate-para-tus-unas-y-pestanas.
- "Propiedades y beneficios del aguacate para la piel," Caña Nature, January 4, 2021

at: https://www.cnature.es/blog/salud/propiedades-beneficios-aguacate-para-la-piel/.

Keep Them Green!
- "Australia: Tecnología que evita el oscurecimiento de las paltas," Informaciones Agronómicas accessed November 2021 at: https://agronoticias2012.blogspot.com/2016/06/australia-tecnologia-que-evita-el.html.
- "¿Qué es la liofilización?," accessed November 2021 at https://avodehy.com/.
- Thomson, Julie, "We tried 3 methods of preventing avocados from browning. Here's the sad truth," Huffington Post, October 1, 2012, accessed November 2021 at: https://www.huffpost.com/entry/keeping-avocados-from-turning-brown_n_1196633.

Genuine or Imitation
- "El extraño aguacate sin semilla creado para evitar la dolorosa 'mano de aguacate'," BBC, December 18, 2017, accessed November 2021 at: https://www.bbc.com/mundo/noticias-42396228.
- López, Eva. "¿El aguacate es malo para los perros?," ExpertoAnimal, accessed November 2021 at: https://www.expertoanimal.com/el-aguacate-es-malo-para-los-perros-22748.html.
- Saiz, Yaiza. "'Aguacate light', el último gran invento de una empresa de Madrid," La Vanguardia, September 27, 2017, accessed November 2021 at https://www.lavanguardia.com/comer/materia-prima/20170927/431594061525/aguacate-light-menos-grasa.html.

Much More than Pulp
- "Balám Bartolomé," Fundación Casa Wabi accessed at: https://casawabi.org/balam-bartolom.
- "Bioplástico con cáscara de aguacate para conservación de fresa," Plastics Technology Mexico, accessed November 2021 at: https://www.pt-mexico.com/noticias/post/desarrollan-bioplstico-con-cscara-de-aguacate-para-conservaci%C3%B3n-de-fresa.
- "Esta tendencia de Instagram es lo más perturbador o satisfactorio que verás hoy," Buzzfeed, accessed at: https://www.buzzfeed.com/mx/javieraceves/thai-carving-omg.
- "Estos productos con aguacate te sorprenderán," Deléitese, accessed November 2021 at: http://www.deleitese.co/estos-productos-con-aguacate-te-sorprenderan-1280.
- "Natural Dye: The Chipotle Goods," Chipotle Goods, accessed at: https://chipotlegoods.com/collections/chipotle-goods/natural-dye.
- Sánchez Fermín, Sheila. "La moda de los productos de aguacate: desde cervezas hasta plásticos," Expansión, June 8, 2018,

accessed November 2021 at: https://expansion.mx/empresas/2018/06/08/la-moda-de-los-productos-de-aguacate-desde-cervezas-hasta-plasticos.
- "Usan desechos de plátano y aguacate para acelerar el crecimiento de plantas," Agriculturers, Red de Especialistas en Agricultura, August 19, 2014, accessed November 2021 at: https://agriculturers.com/usan-desechos-de-platano-y-aguacate-para-acelerar-el-crecimiento-de-plantas/.

Sow Your Own Avocado Seeds
- "5 beneficios de la hoja del aguacate," Hola Doctor, July 30, 2015, accessed: https://holadoctor.com/es/hierbas-a-z/aguacate-hojas-remedios-caseros.
- "Aprende a cultivar aguacate en una maceta y olvídate de ir al mercado," Bienestar 180, accessed at: https://www.salud180.com/salud-dia-a-dia/como-cultivar-aguacate-en-casa.
- "Cómo eliminar la cochinilla algodonosa," unCOMO, accessed at: https://www.mundodeportivo.com/uncomo/hogar/articulo/como-eliminar-la-cochinilla-algodonosa-49822.html.
- Juste, Irene. "Cómo hacer pesticida con tabaco," unCOMO, accessed at: https://www.mundodeportivo.com/uncomo/hogar/articulocomo-hacer-pesticida-con-tabaco-44213.html.
- Ruiz, Mariana. "Aprende a hacer un insecticida de aguacate para tus plantas," AD, September 22, 2021, accessed at: https://www.admagazine.com/sustentabilidad/insecticida-de-aguacate-para-las-plantas-20210922-9046-articulos.
- Ruiz, Laura, "Cómo hacer im fungicida casero," unCOMO, accessed at: https://www.mundodeportivo.com/uncomo/hogar/articulo/como-hacer-un-fungicida-casero-44278.html.

Chapter 3
A Century of Fever
- "Avo-Condo, el primer hotel con forma de aguacate," Travel and Leisure, accessed at: https://travelandleisure.mx/destinos/2019/07/22/avo-condo-es-el-primer-hotel-en-forma-de-aguacate/.
- Peñas, Esther. "La 'gourmetización' de las ciudades," Ethic, February 11, 2019, accessed at: https://ethic.es/2019/02/gentrificacion-alimentaria-gourmetizacion-ciudades/.
- Uribe Llamas, Jorge Pedro, "Gentrificación gastronómica en la Ciudad de México," HojaSanta, accessed at: https://revistahojasanta.com/salimos/2018/5/6/gentrificacin-gastronmica-en-la-ciudad-de-mxico.

An Internet Idol
- Infante, Mamen, "¿Qué le pasa a Instagram con el aguacate?," Harper's Bazaar July 21, 2015, accessed at: https://www.harpersbazaar.com/es/belleza/dieta-ejercicios-adelgazar-belleza/g189491/quele-pasa-a-instagram-con-el-aguacate/.
- "Bagel de aguacate de oro de 18 kilates de un artista alemán está a la venta en Art Miami por 2,9 millones de dólares," Local 10, accessed at: https://www.local10.com/espanol/2021/12/03/bagel-de-aguacate-de-oro-de-18-quilates-de-un-artista-aleman-esta-a-laventa-en-art-miami-por-29-millonesde-dolares/#:~:text=%E2%80%93%20Tim%20Bengel%20utiliz%C3%B3%20un%20esc%C3%A1ner,atenci-C3%B3n%20del%20cantante%20Joe%20Jonas.
- "De Gwyneth Paltrow al palacio real: Meghan introduce la moda del aguacate en la corte," Vanity Fair, January 21, 2019, accessed at: https://www.revistavanityfair.es/realeza/articulos/de-gwyneth-paltrow-a-palacio-meghan-introduce-la-moda-del-aguacate-en-la-corte/35881.
- "Artista multipremiado transforma aguacates en obras de arte," El Heraldo de San Luis Potosí, July 12, 2021, accessed at: https://elheraldoslp.com.mx/2021/07/12/artista-multipremiado-transforma-aguacates-en-obras-de-arte/.
- "Artista japonés crea preciosos patrones esculpidos a mano en frutas y verduras," ArchDaily, accessed at: https://www.archdaily.mx/mx/892535/artista-japones-crea-preciosos-patrones-esculpidos-a-mano-en-frutas-y-verduras.
- "Patrones intrincados tallados a mano en frutas y verduras por Takehiro Kishimoto," Cultura Inquieta, accessed at: https://culturainquieta.com/es/arte/escultura/item/16560-patrones-intrincados-tallados-a-mano-en-frutas-y-verduras-por-takehiro-kishimoto.html.

Alligator Pear Lovers
- "Aleida Núñez recomienda a sus fans consumir aguacate en vez de operarse," TvNotas, October 20, 2021, accessed at: https://www.tvnotas.com.mx/noticias-espectaculos-mexico/aleida-nunez-recomienda-sus-fans-consumir-aguacate-en-vez-de-operarse.
- Ayuso, Miguel, "Al habla con Xavier Equihua, Mr. Aguacate: 'Somos el Kim Kardashian del mundo de la fruta, no hay otro producto así'," Directo al Paladar, accessed at: https://www.directoalpaladar.com/actualidad-1/al-habla-mr-aguacate-somos-kim-kardashian-mundo-fruta-no-hay-otro-producto-asi.
- "Salma Hayek acaba de lanzar una línea de batidos que se doblan como mascarillas," Fashiontabs, accessed at: https://es.fashiontabs.com/id1369-salma-hayek-juice-generation-smoothies-face-masks.

Guacamole Touchdown!
- "Brocomole, la nueva moda del 'guacamole' sostenible y económico," December 1, 2020, La Vanguardia, accessed at: https://www.lavanguardia.com/comer/tendencias/20201201/6062173/brocomole-guacamole-sostenible-economico.html.
- Melara, Josselin, "Brocomole: aprende a hacer guacamole con brócoli para botanear," Cocina Fácil, accessed at: https://www.cocinafacil.com.mx/recetas-de-comida/receta/como-hacer-guacamole-con-brocoli-brocomole/.
- Nadal, Paco, "Guacamole, una historia de mitología . . . ¡y erotismo!," For Travel Lovers, accessed at: https://www.fortravelovers.com/es/guacamole-una-historia-de-mitologia-y-erotismo.
- "El origen de la receta del guacamole nos remite a Quetzalcóatl y el erotismo," Más de Méx, July 7, 2016, accessed at: https://masdemx.com/2016/07/la-receta-del-guacamole-que-quetzalcoatl-brindo-a-su-pueblo/.
- Pérez, Marlene, "Beyoncé comparte su receta para preparar guacamole a su propio estilo," Show!, accessed at: https://www.show.news/music/Beyonce-te-ensena-a-preparar-guacamole-a-su-propio-estilo-20200806-0018.html.
- Recker, Bree, "El guacamole: de dónde viene y cómo se hace," The Gourmet Journal, accessed at: https://www.thegourmetjournal.com/afondo/el-guacamole-de-donde-viene-ycomo-se-hace/.
- Reyes Castro, Nayeli, "¿Guacamole sin aguacate? Estos son los alimentos que usan para sustituirlo," El Financiero, November 8, 2021, accessed at: https://www.elfinanciero.com.mx/food-and-drink/2021/11/08/guacamole-sin-aguacate-estos-son-los-alimentos-que-usan-para-sustituirlo/.
- Silverio, Fernanda, "Así puedes preparar un falso guacamole sin aguacate," Gastrolab, accessed at: https://www.gastrolabweb.com/recetas/2021/1/25/asi-puedes-preparar-un-falso-guacamole-sin-aguacate-6011.html.